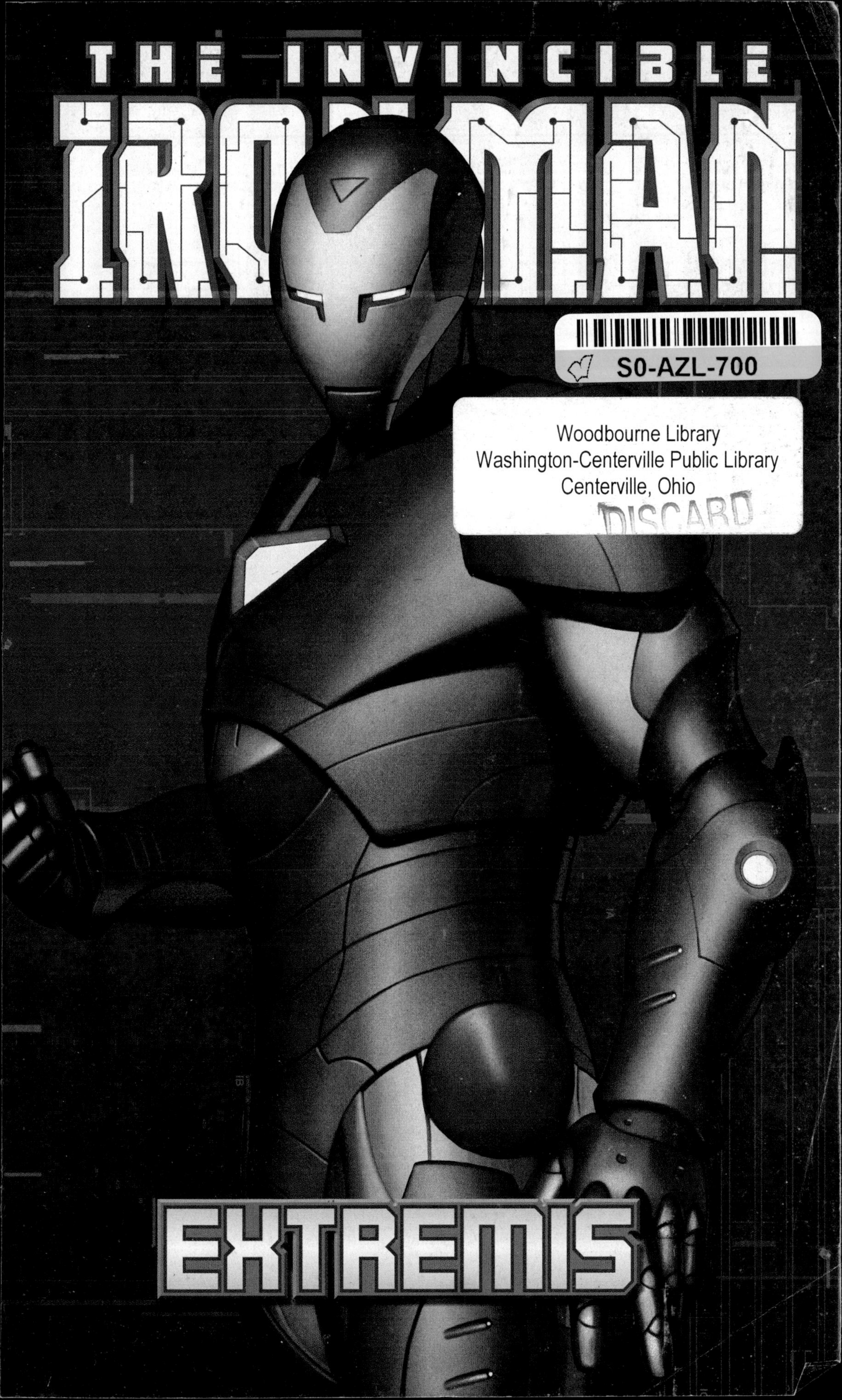
THE INVINCIBLE
IRON MAN
EXTREMIS

THE INVINCIBLE IRON MAN

EXTREMIS

WRITER: Warren Ellis
ART: Adi Granov

LETTERS: Virtual Calligraphy's Randy Gentile
ASSISTANT EDITORS: Molly Lazer, Aubrey Sitterson,
Stephanie Moore & Nicole Boose
ASSOCIATE EDITOR: Andy Schmidt
EDITOR: Tom Brevoort

COLLECTION EDITOR: Jennifer Grünwald
ASSISTANT EDITOR: Michael Short
ASSOCIATE EDITOR: Mark D. Beazley
SENIOR EDITOR, SPECIAL PROJECTS: Jeff Youngquist
SENIOR VICE PRESIDENT OF SALES: David Gabriel
PRODUCTION: Jerry Kalinowski
BOOK DESIGNER: Patrick McGrath
VICE PRESIDENT OF CREATIVE: Tom Marvelli

EDITOR IN CHIEF: Joe Quesada
PUBISHER: Dan Buckley

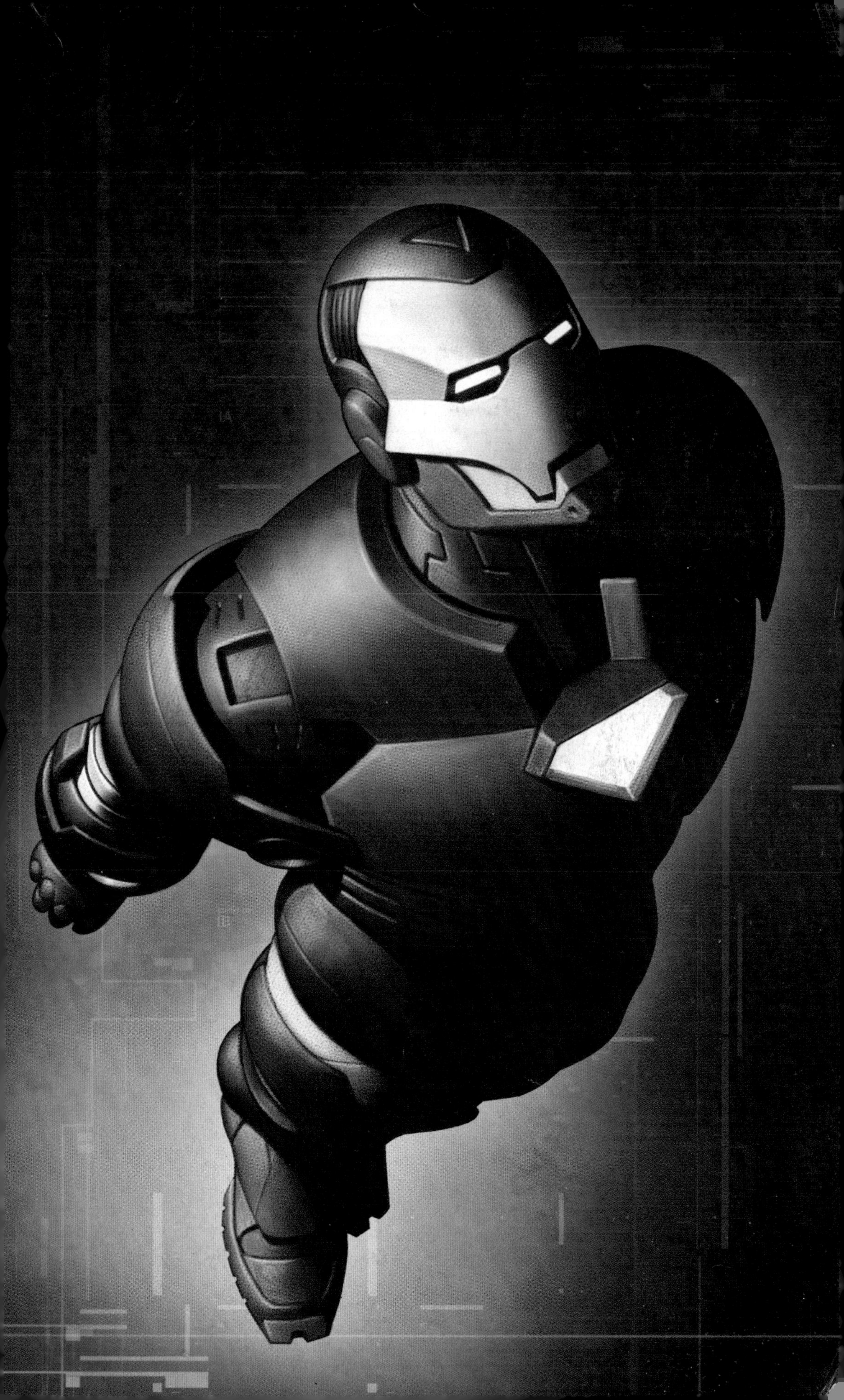

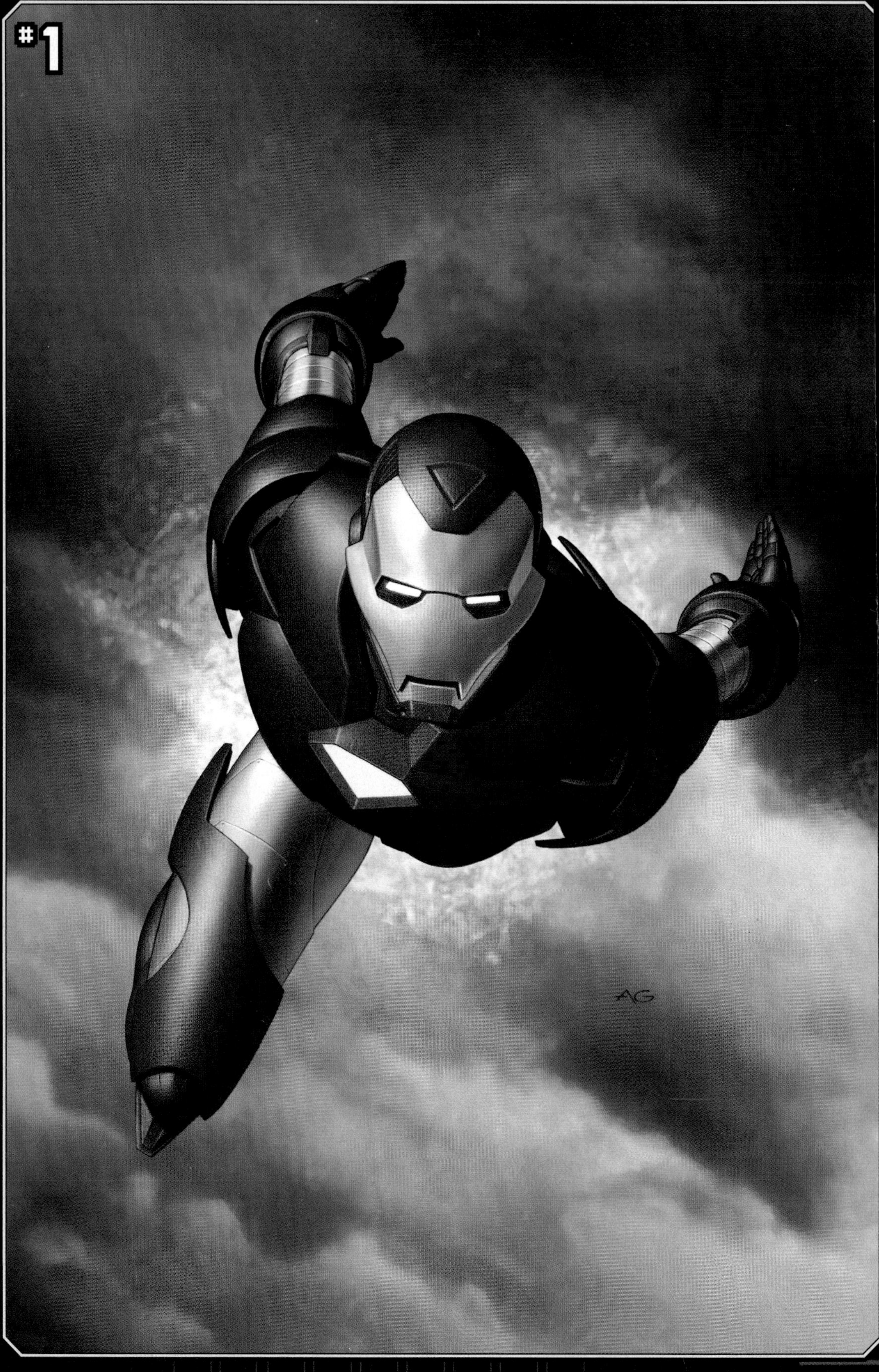
#1
AG

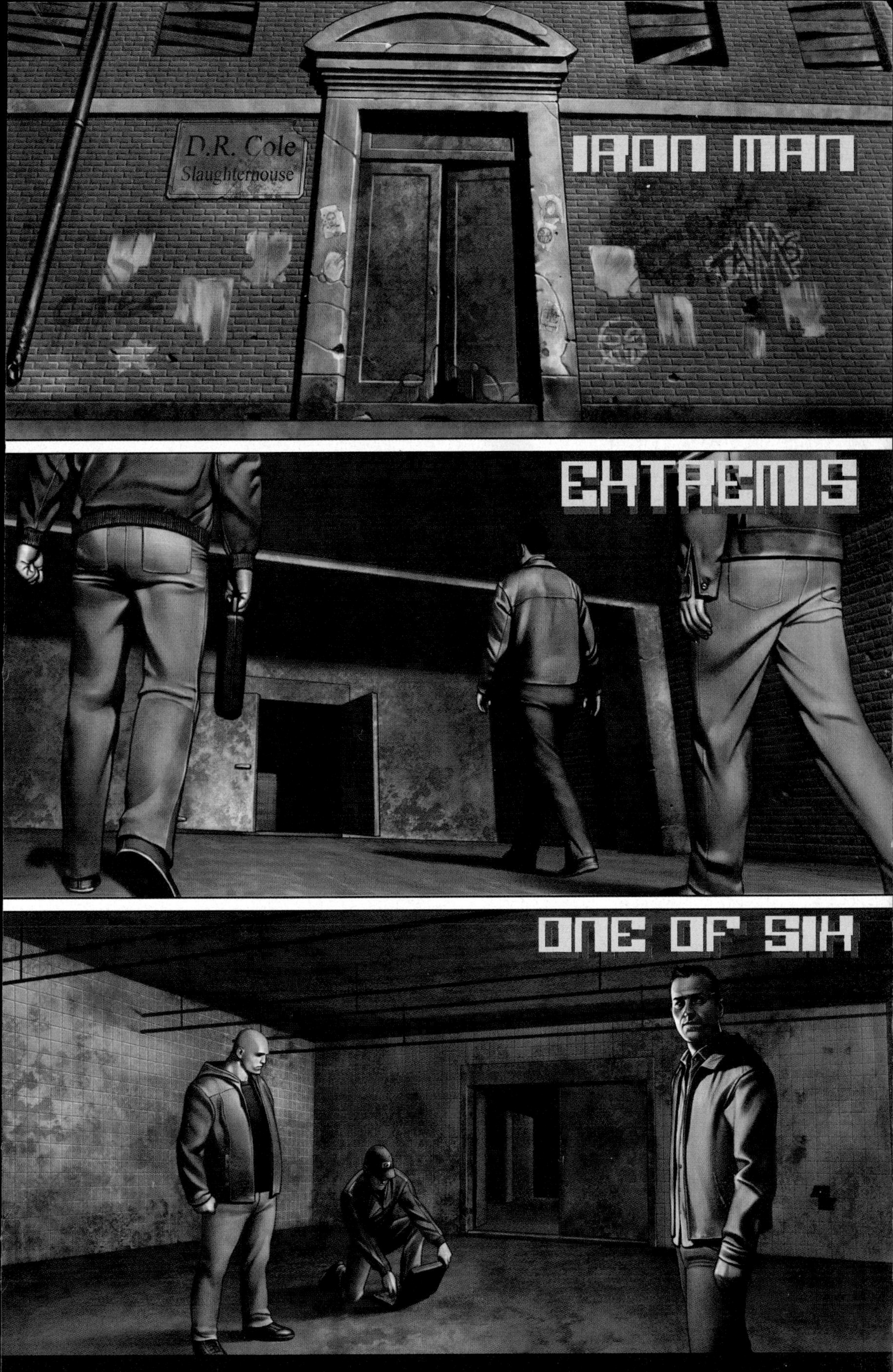
D.R. Cole
Slaughterhouse
IRON MAN
EXTREMIS
ONE OF SIX

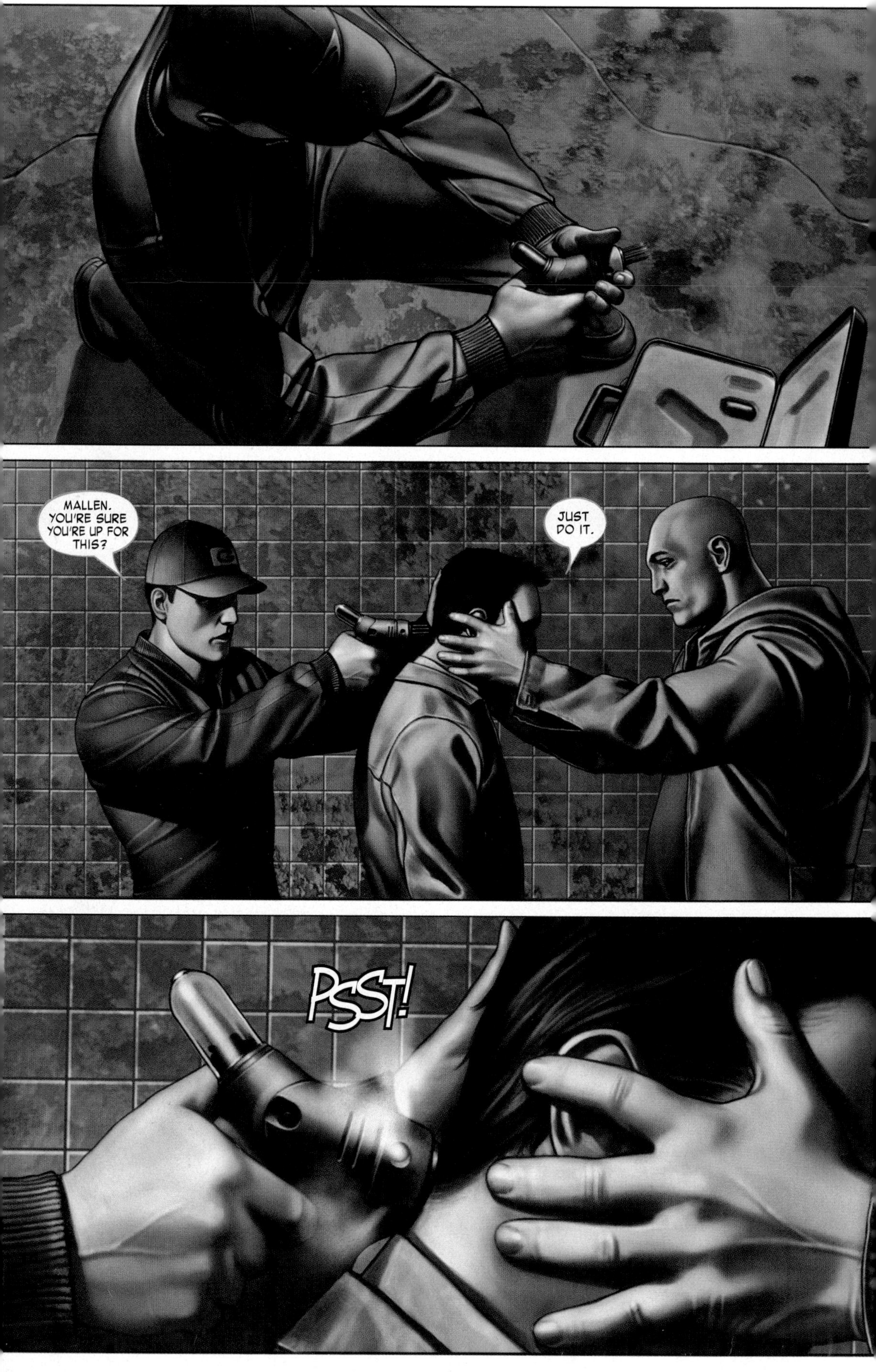
MALLEN. YOU'RE SURE YOU'RE UP FOR THIS?
JUST DO IT.
PSST!

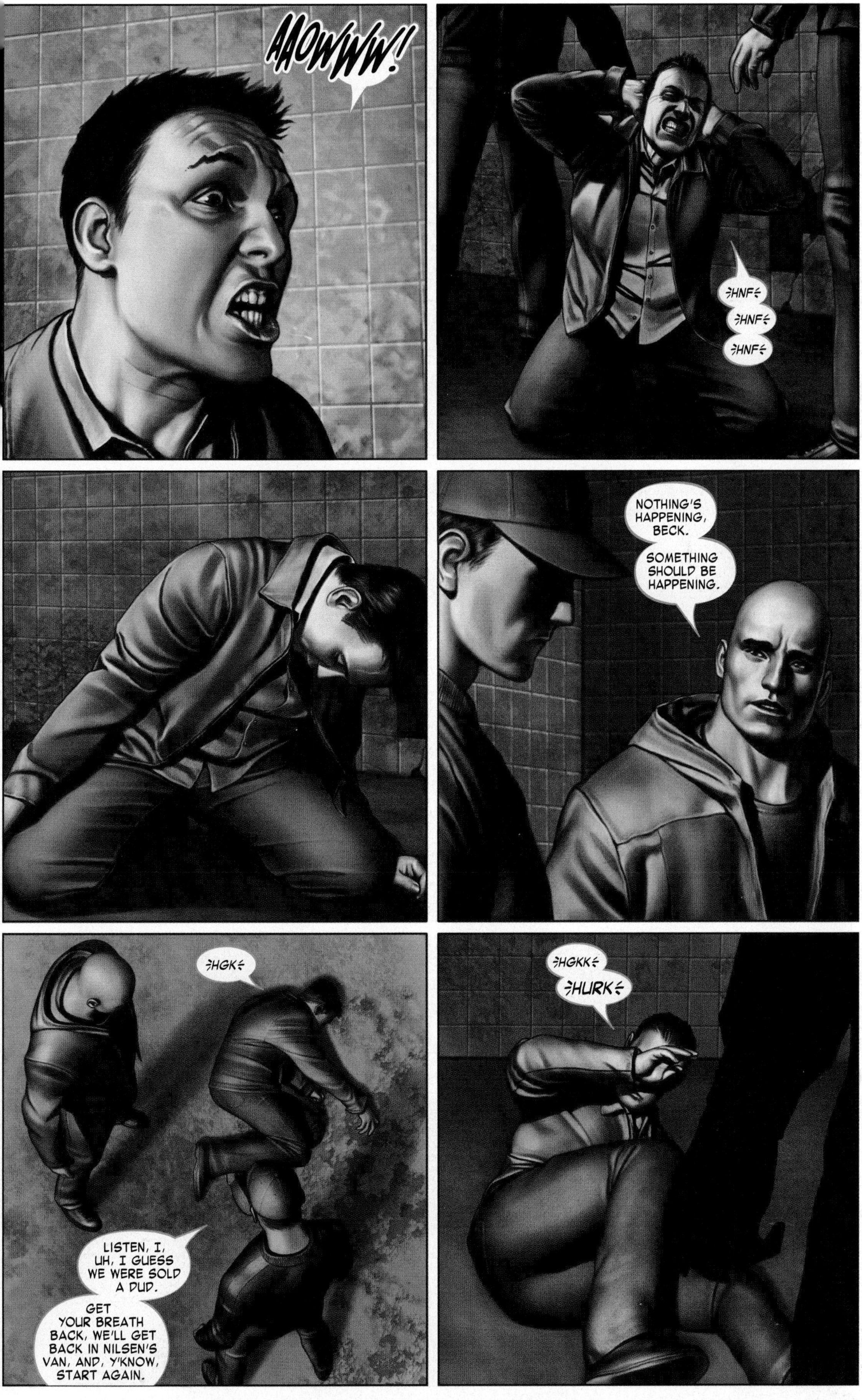
AAOWWW!
HNF
HNF
HNF
NOTHING'S HAPPENING, BECK.
SOMETHING SHOULD BE HAPPENING.
HGK
LISTEN, I, UH, I GUESS WE WERE SOLD A DUD.
GET YOUR BREATH BACK, WE'LL GET BACK IN NILSEN'S VAN, AND, Y'KNOW, START AGAIN.
HGKK
HURK

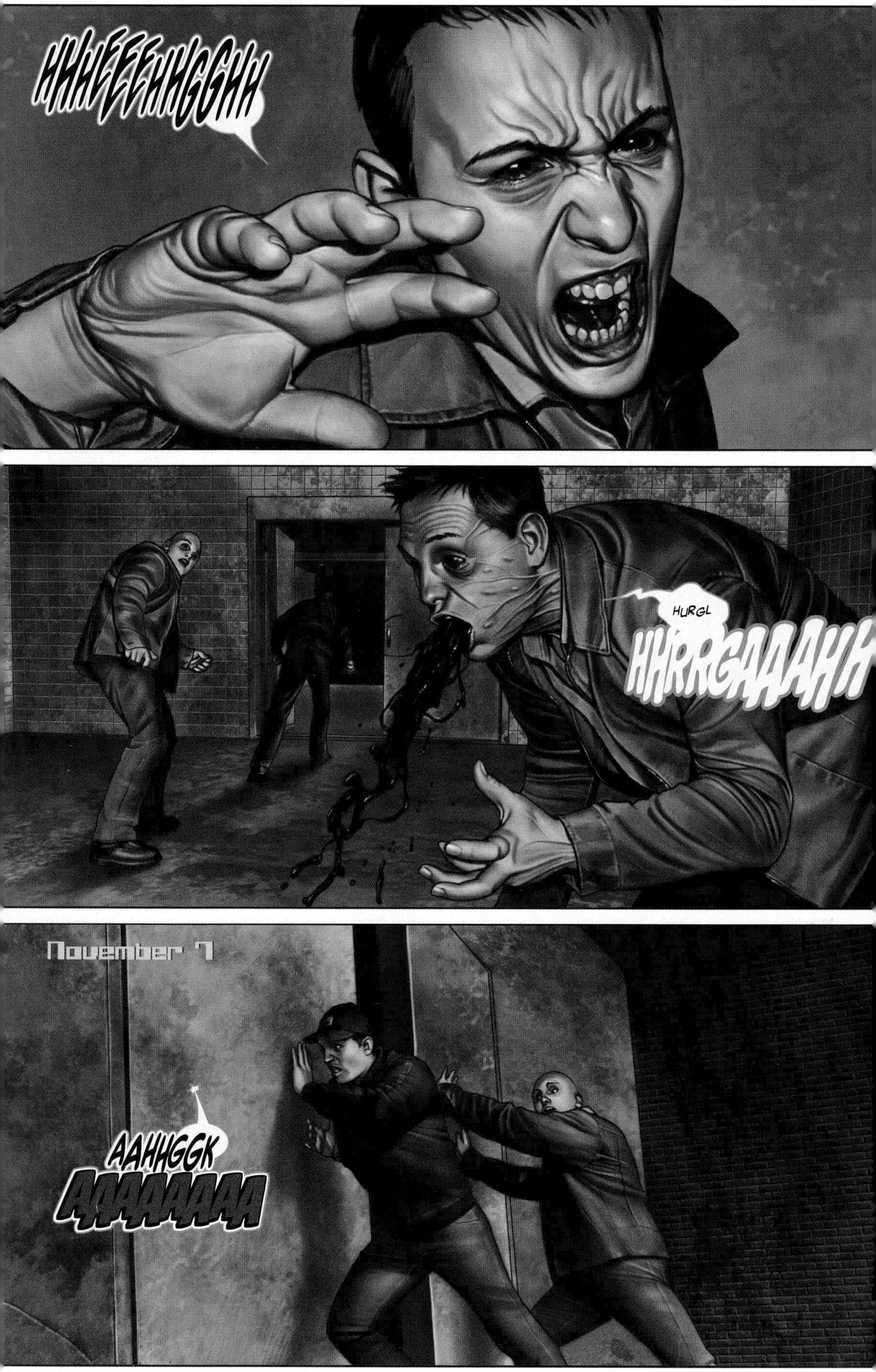
HHHEEEHHGGHH
HURGL
HHRRGAAAHH
November 7
AAHHGGK
AAAAAAA

BZZT!
BZZT!

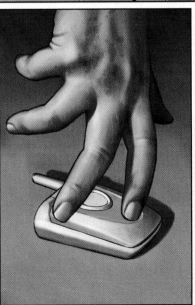

YEAH.

MR.
STARK?

YEAH.

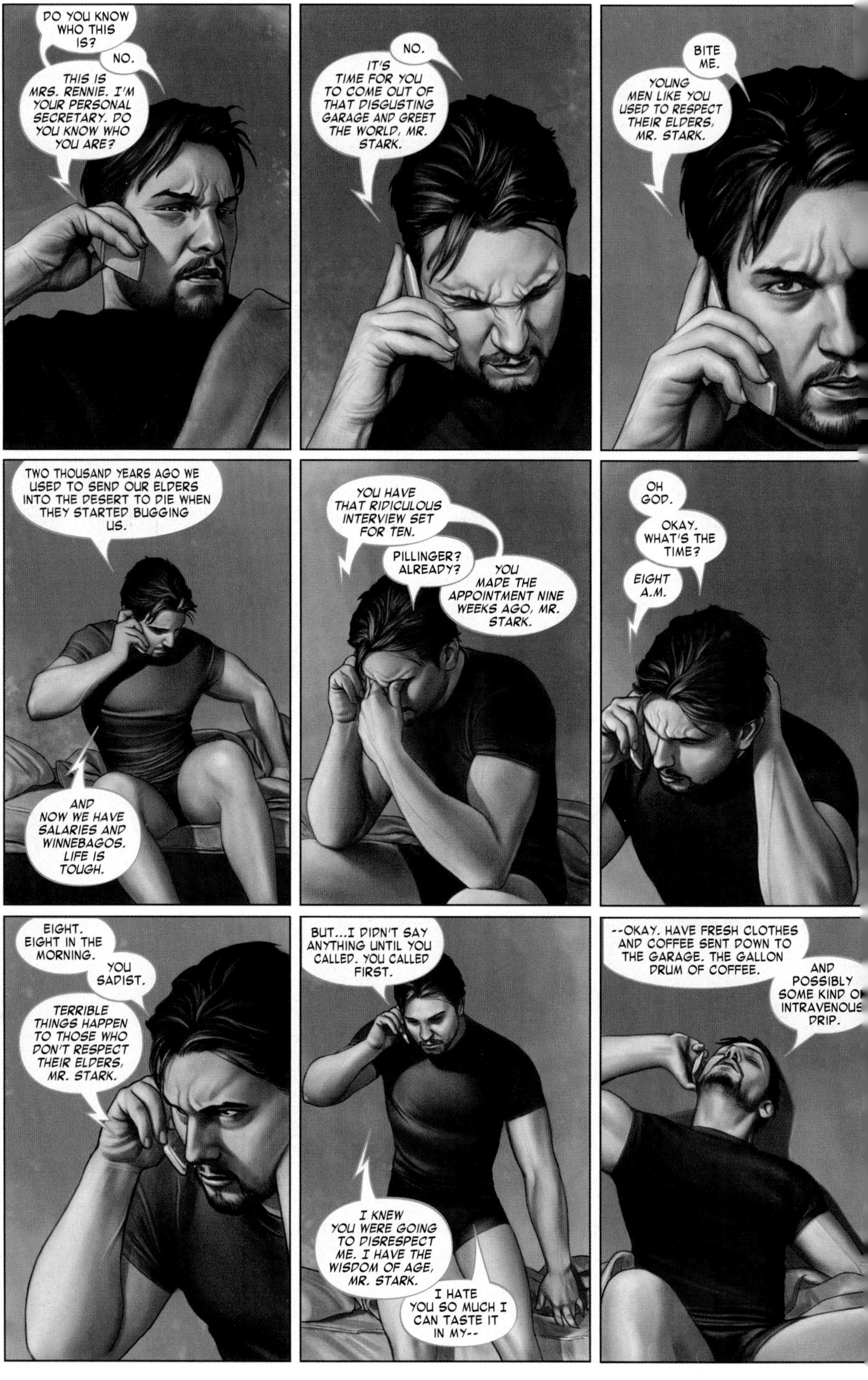
DO YOU KNOW WHO THIS IS?
NO.
THIS IS MRS. RENNIE. I'M YOUR PERSONAL SECRETARY. DO YOU KNOW WHO YOU ARE?
NO.
IT'S TIME FOR YOU TO COME OUT OF THAT DISGUSTING GARAGE AND GREET THE WORLD, MR. STARK.
BITE ME.
YOUNG MEN LIKE YOU USED TO RESPECT THEIR ELDERS, MR. STARK.
TWO THOUSAND YEARS AGO WE USED TO SEND OUR ELDERS INTO THE DESERT TO DIE WHEN THEY STARTED BUGGING US.
AND NOW WE HAVE SALARIES AND WINNEBAGOS. LIFE IS TOUGH.
YOU HAVE THAT RIDICULOUS INTERVIEW SET FOR TEN.
PILLINGER? ALREADY?
YOU MADE THE APPOINTMENT NINE WEEKS AGO, MR. STARK.
OH GOD.
OKAY. WHAT'S THE TIME?
EIGHT A.M.
EIGHT. EIGHT IN THE MORNING.
YOU SADIST.
TERRIBLE THINGS HAPPEN TO THOSE WHO DON'T RESPECT THEIR ELDERS, MR. STARK.
BUT...I DIDN'T SAY ANYTHING UNTIL YOU CALLED. YOU CALLED FIRST.
I KNEW YOU WERE GOING TO DISRESPECT ME. I HAVE THE WISDOM OF AGE, MR. STARK.
I HATE YOU SO MUCH I CAN TASTE IT IN MY--
--OKAY. HAVE FRESH CLOTHES AND COFFEE SENT DOWN TO THE GARAGE. THE GALLON DRUM OF COFFEE.
AND POSSIBLY SOME KIND OF INTRAVENOUS DRIP.

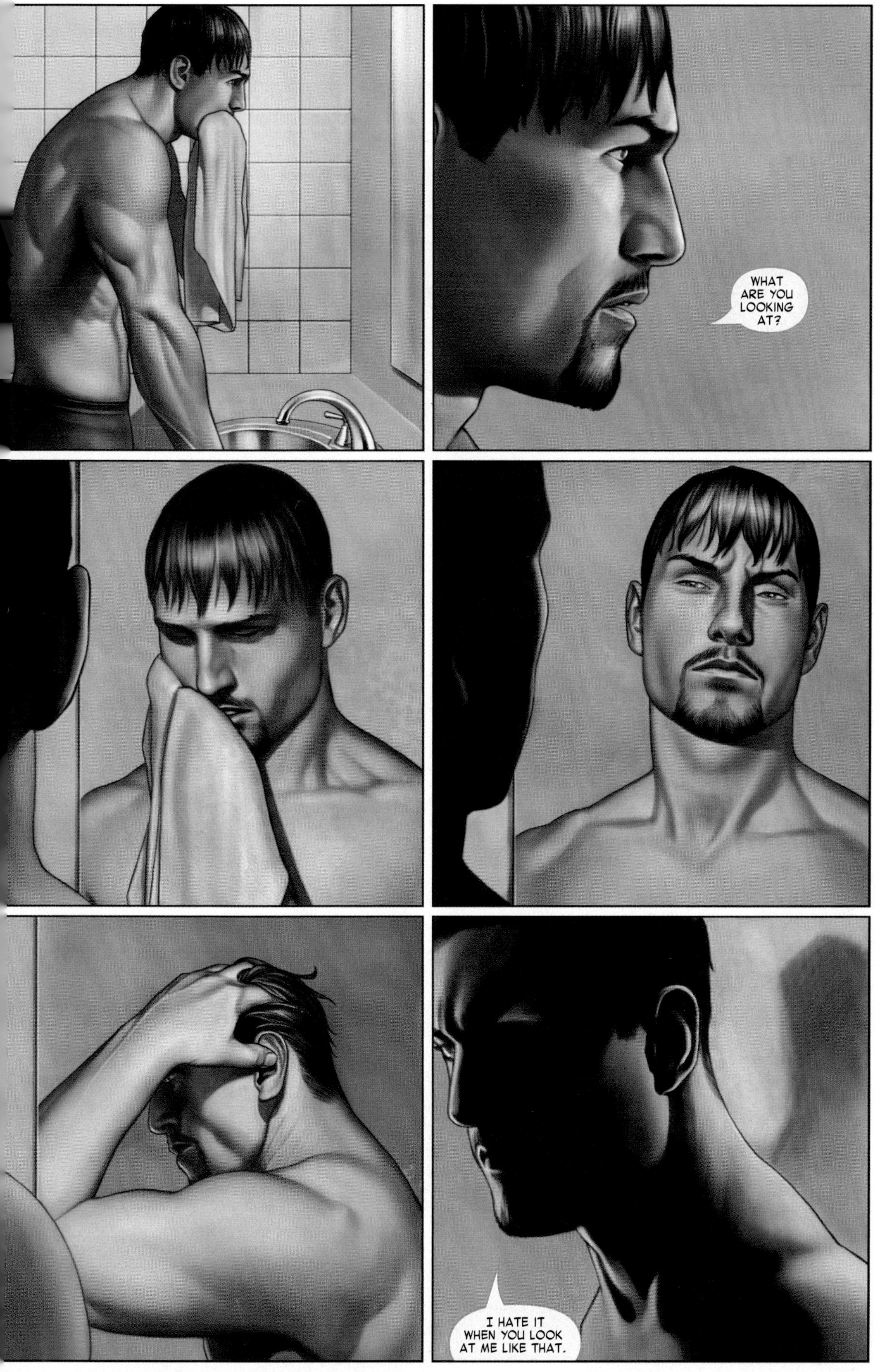
WHAT ARE YOU LOOKING AT?
I HATE IT WHEN YOU LOOK AT ME LIKE THAT.

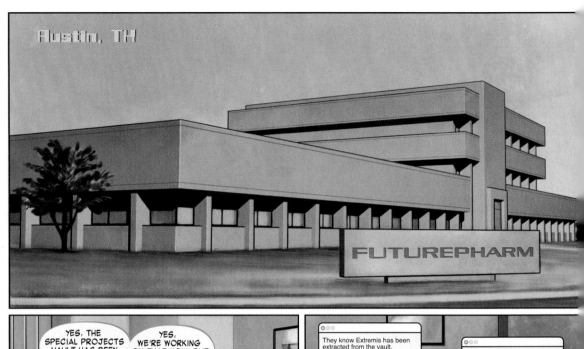

Austin, TH

YES, THE SPECIAL PROJECTS VAULT HAS BEEN COMPROMISED.

YES, WE'RE WORKING ON THAT NOW, BUT I HAVE TO REFER YOU TO GENERAL FISHER--

--NO, DR. KILLIAN IS GUIDING THE EFFORT FROM THIS END.

Dr ALDRICH KILLIAN

They know Extremis has been extracted from the vault.
It's chaos, outside my blessed door.

This place is so badly organized: no one seems to be qualified to know what has been stolen or what to do about it.

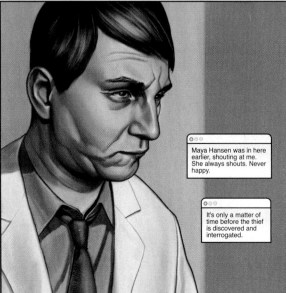

Maya Hansen was in here earlier, shouting at me. She always shouts. Never happy.

It's only a matter of time before the thief is discovered and interrogated.

I won't get through an interrogation.

I know that I've loosed something terrible. Knowing that it had to be done: it doesn't ease the burden.

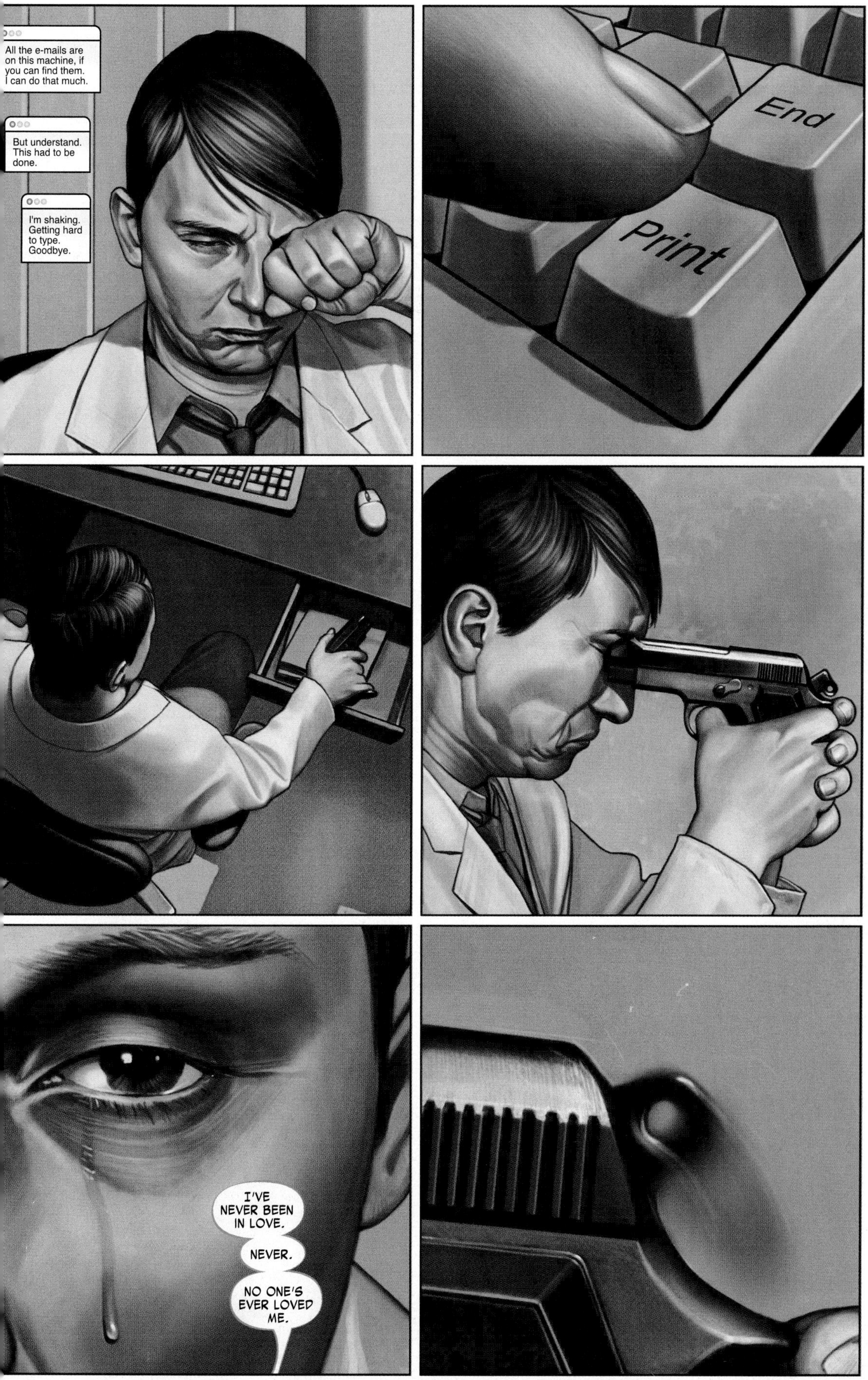

All the e-mails are on this machine, if you can find them. I can do that much.
But understand. This had to be done.
I'm shaking. Getting hard to type. Goodbye.
End
Print
I'VE NEVER BEEN IN LOVE.
NEVER.
NO ONE'S EVER LOVED ME.

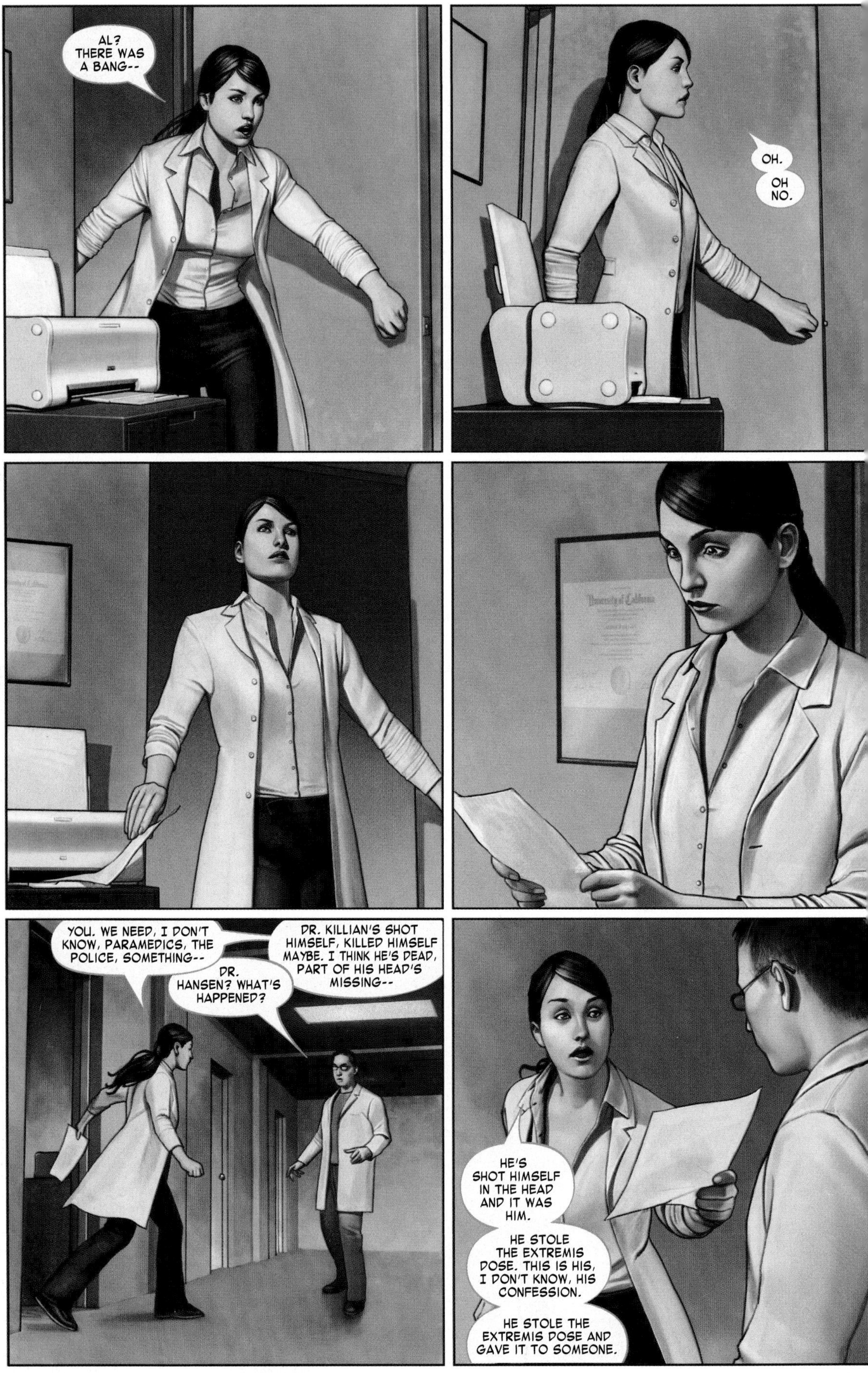
AL? THERE WAS A BANG--
OH.
OH NO.
YOU. WE NEED, I DON'T KNOW, PARAMEDICS, THE POLICE, SOMETHING--
DR. HANSEN? WHAT'S HAPPENED?
DR. KILLIAN'S SHOT HIMSELF, KILLED HIMSELF MAYBE. I THINK HE'S DEAD, PART OF HIS HEAD'S MISSING--
HE'S SHOT HIMSELF IN THE HEAD AND IT WAS HIM.
HE STOLE THE EXTREMIS DOSE. THIS IS HIS, I DON'T KNOW, HIS CONFESSION.
HE STOLE THE EXTREMIS DOSE AND GAVE IT TO SOMEONE.

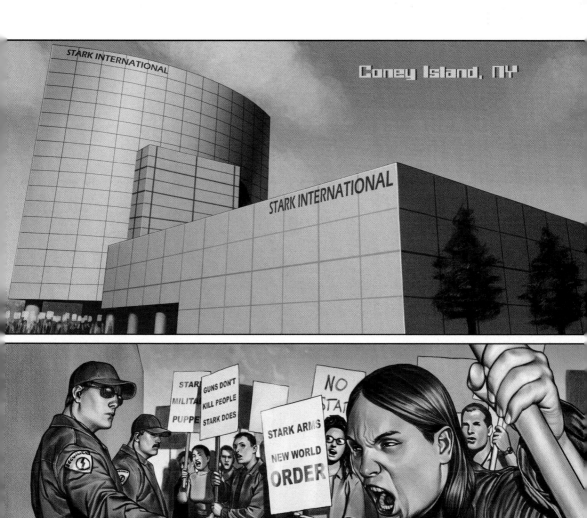

STARK INTERNATIONAL

STARK INTERNATIONAL

STARK
MILITA
PUPPE

GUNS DON'T
KILL PEOPLE
STARK DOES

STARK ARMS

NEW WORLD

ORDER

NO
STA

"MY DAD USED TO TELL ME CONEY ISLAND WAS THE MOST FABULOUS PLACE IN THE WORLD."

THE AMUSEMENTS. THE FANTASTIC CONSTRUCTIONS.

PEOPLE BELIEVED THEY HAD TO BE LIVING IN THE FUTURE, TO BE ABLE TO VISIT A PLACE LIKE CONEY ISLAND.

AND AT NIGHT THEY WOULDN'T GO HOME. THEY'D SLEEP ON THE BEACH, SO THEY COULD WAKE UP IN THIS FUTURE PLACE.

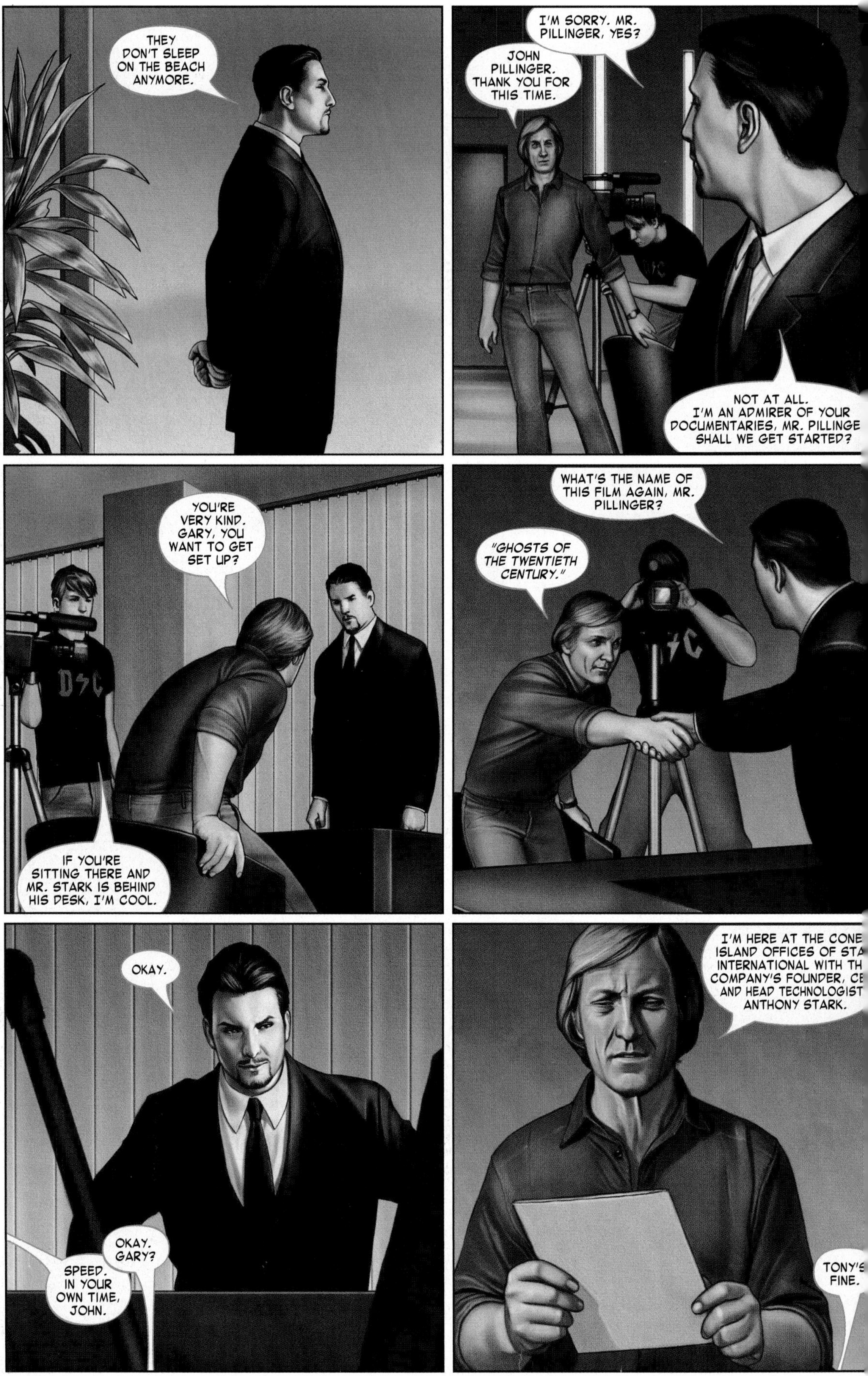
THEY DON'T SLEEP ON THE BEACH ANYMORE.
I'M SORRY. MR. PILLINGER, YES?
JOHN PILLINGER. THANK YOU FOR THIS TIME.
NOT AT ALL. I'M AN ADMIRER OF YOUR DOCUMENTARIES, MR. PILLINGE SHALL WE GET STARTED?
YOU'RE VERY KIND. GARY, YOU WANT TO GET SET UP?
IF YOU'RE SITTING THERE AND MR. STARK IS BEHIND HIS DESK, I'M COOL.
WHAT'S THE NAME OF THIS FILM AGAIN, MR. PILLINGER?
"GHOSTS OF THE TWENTIETH CENTURY."
OKAY.
OKAY. GARY?
SPEED. IN YOUR OWN TIME, JOHN.
I'M HERE AT THE CONE ISLAND OFFICES OF STA INTERNATIONAL WITH TH COMPANY'S FOUNDER, CE AND HEAD TECHNOLOGIST ANTHONY STARK.
TONY'S FINE.

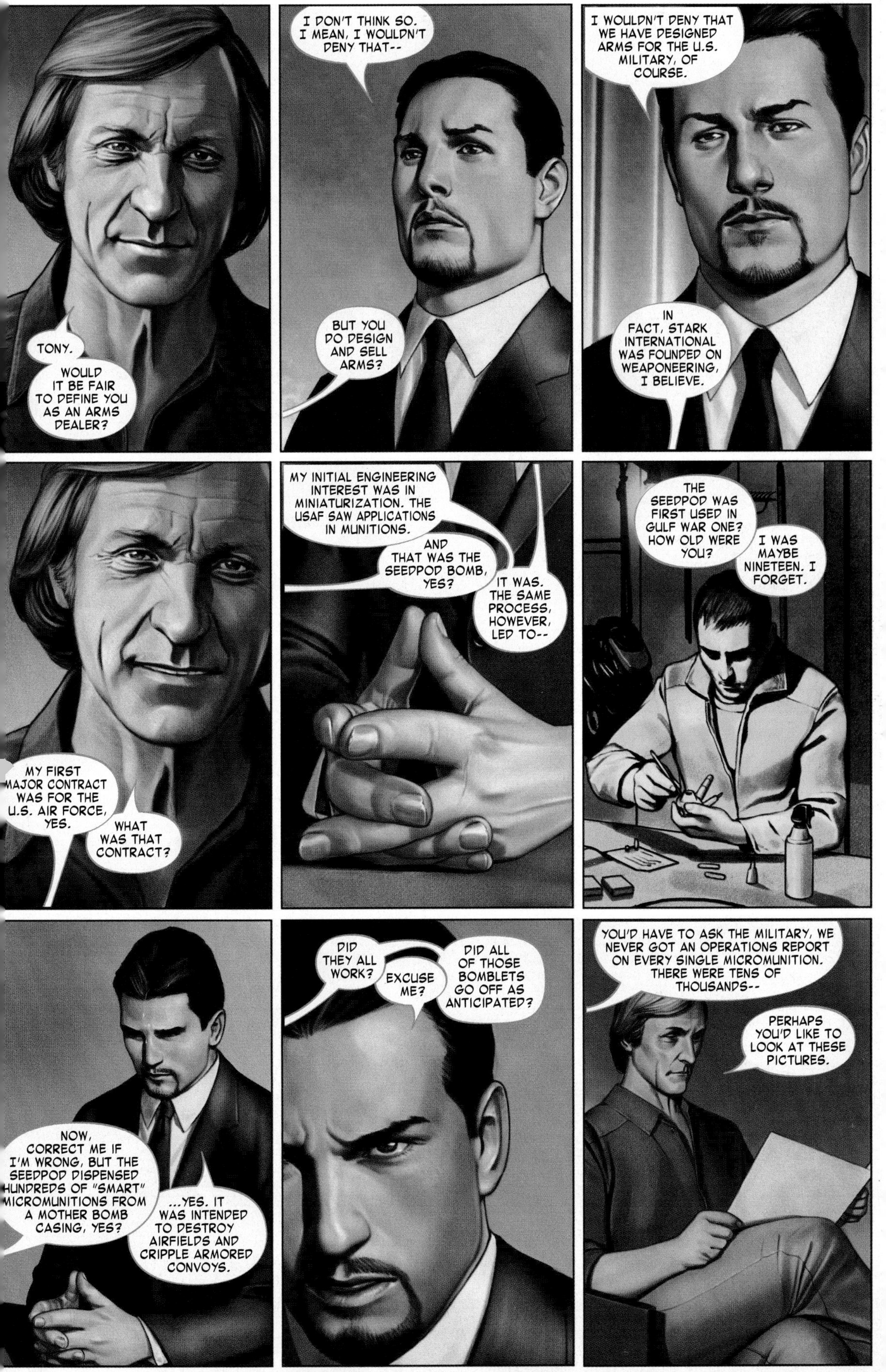
TONY.
WOULD IT BE FAIR TO DEFINE YOU AS AN ARMS DEALER?
I DON'T THINK SO. I MEAN, I WOULDN'T DENY THAT--
BUT YOU DO DESIGN AND SELL ARMS?
I WOULDN'T DENY THAT WE HAVE DESIGNED ARMS FOR THE U.S. MILITARY, OF COURSE.
IN FACT, STARK INTERNATIONAL WAS FOUNDED ON WEAPONEERING, I BELIEVE.
MY FIRST MAJOR CONTRACT WAS FOR THE U.S. AIR FORCE, YES.
WHAT WAS THAT CONTRACT?
MY INITIAL ENGINEERING INTEREST WAS IN MINIATURIZATION. THE USAF SAW APPLICATIONS IN MUNITIONS.
AND THAT WAS THE SEEDPOD BOMB, YES?
IT WAS. THE SAME PROCESS, HOWEVER, LED TO--
THE SEEDPOD WAS FIRST USED IN GULF WAR ONE? HOW OLD WERE YOU?
I WAS MAYBE NINETEEN. I FORGET.
NOW, CORRECT ME IF I'M WRONG, BUT THE SEEDPOD DISPENSED HUNDREDS OF "SMART" MICROMUNITIONS FROM A MOTHER BOMB CASING, YES?
...YES. IT WAS INTENDED TO DESTROY AIRFIELDS AND CRIPPLE ARMORED CONVOYS.
DID THEY ALL WORK?
EXCUSE ME?
DID ALL OF THOSE BOMBLETS GO OFF AS ANTICIPATED?
YOU'D HAVE TO ASK THE MILITARY, WE NEVER GOT AN OPERATIONS REPORT ON EVERY SINGLE MICROMUNITION. THERE WERE TENS OF THOUSANDS--
PERHAPS YOU'D LIKE TO LOOK AT THESE PICTURES.

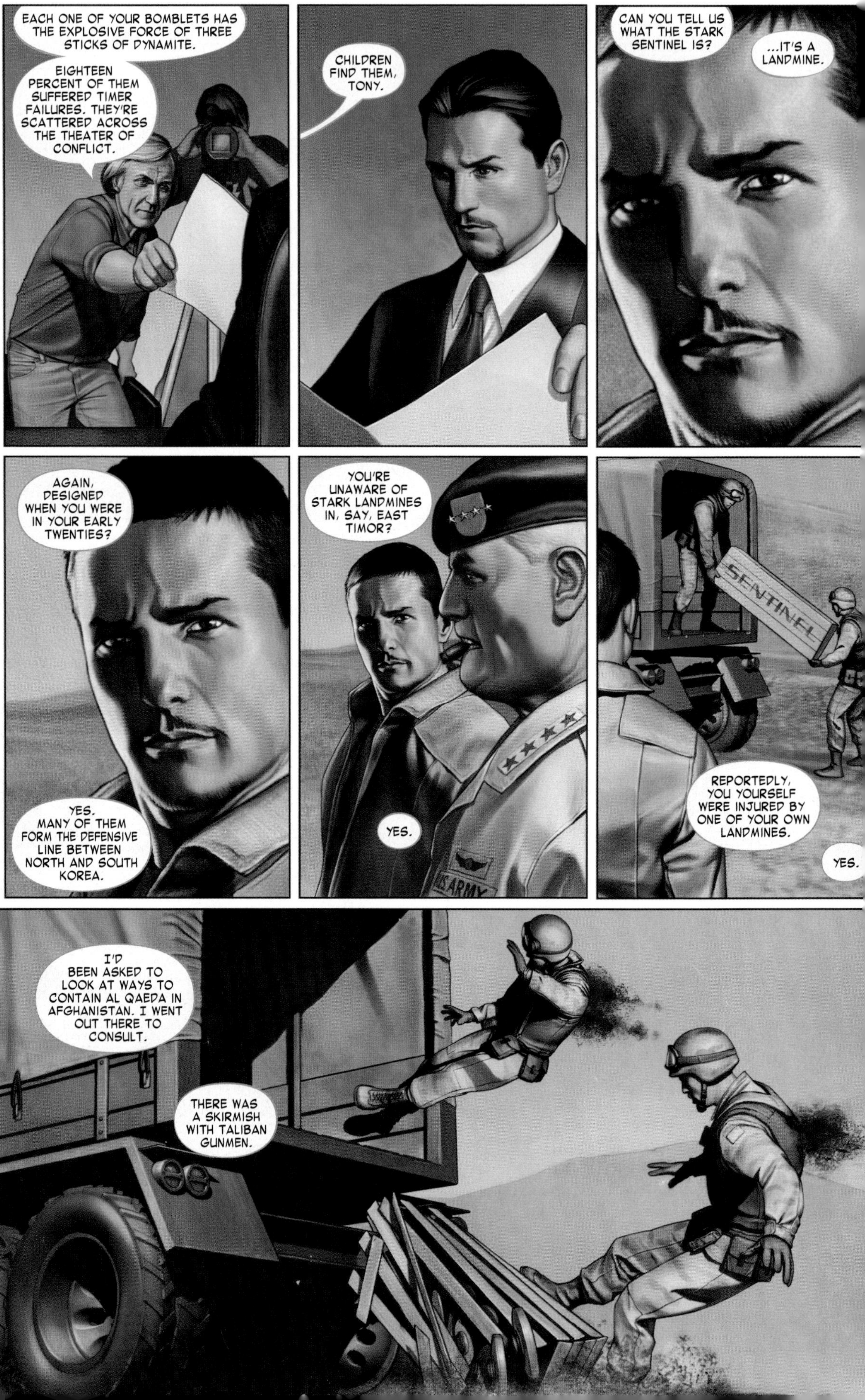
EACH ONE OF YOUR BOMBLETS HAS THE EXPLOSIVE FORCE OF THREE STICKS OF DYNAMITE.
EIGHTEEN PERCENT OF THEM SUFFERED TIMER FAILURES. THEY'RE SCATTERED ACROSS THE THEATER OF CONFLICT.
CHILDREN FIND THEM, TONY.
CAN YOU TELL US WHAT THE STARK SENTINEL IS?
...IT'S A LANDMINE.
AGAIN, DESIGNED WHEN YOU WERE IN YOUR EARLY TWENTIES?
YES. MANY OF THEM FORM THE DEFENSIVE LINE BETWEEN NORTH AND SOUTH KOREA.
YOU'RE UNAWARE OF STARK LANDMINES IN, SAY, EAST TIMOR?
YES.
US ARMY
SENTINEL
REPORTEDLY, YOU YOURSELF WERE INJURED BY ONE OF YOUR OWN LANDMINES.
YES.
I'D BEEN ASKED TO LOOK AT WAYS TO CONTAIN AL QAEDA IN AFGHANISTAN. I WENT OUT THERE TO CONSULT.
THERE WAS A SKIRMISH WITH TALIBAN GUNMEN.

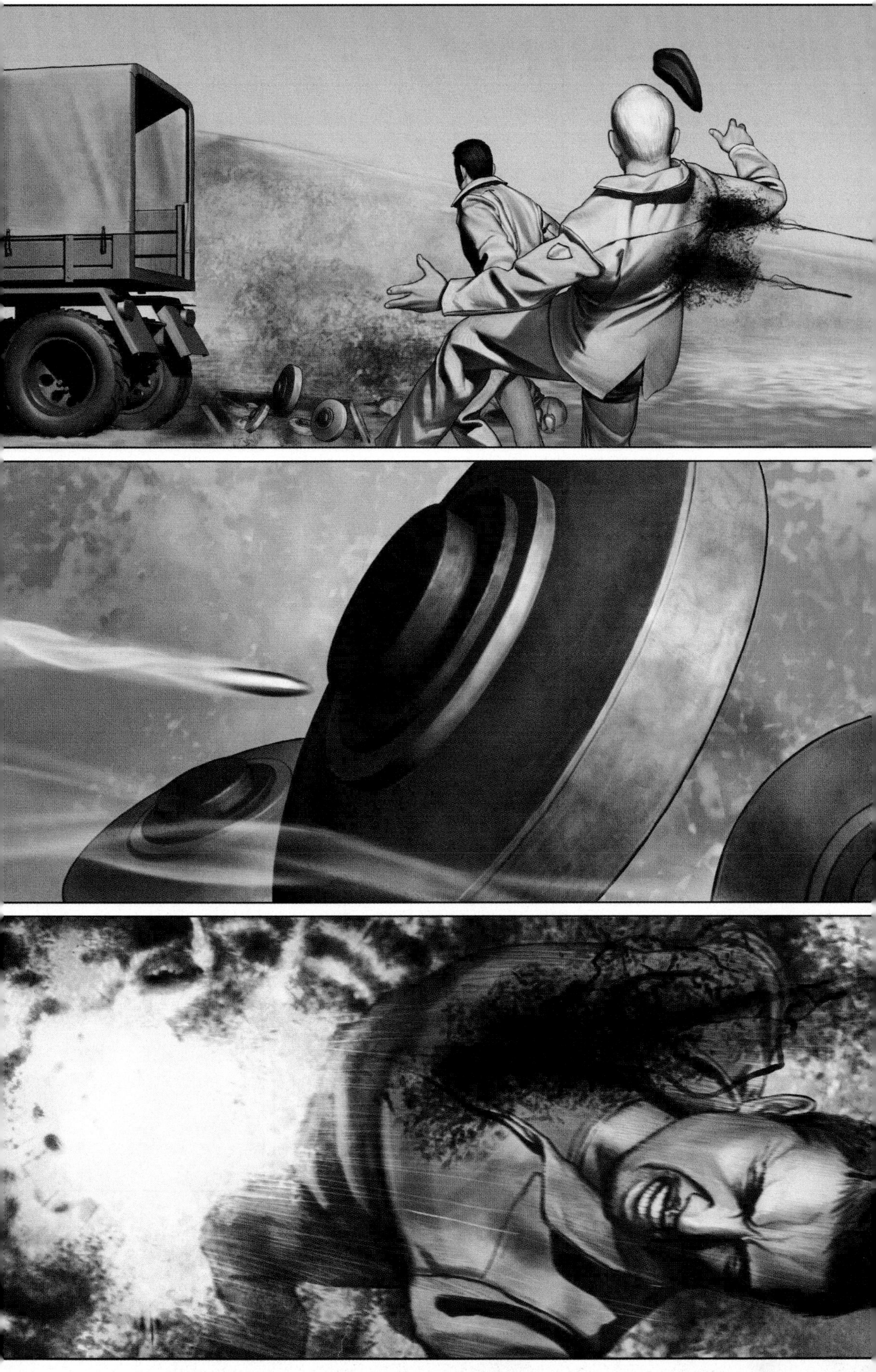

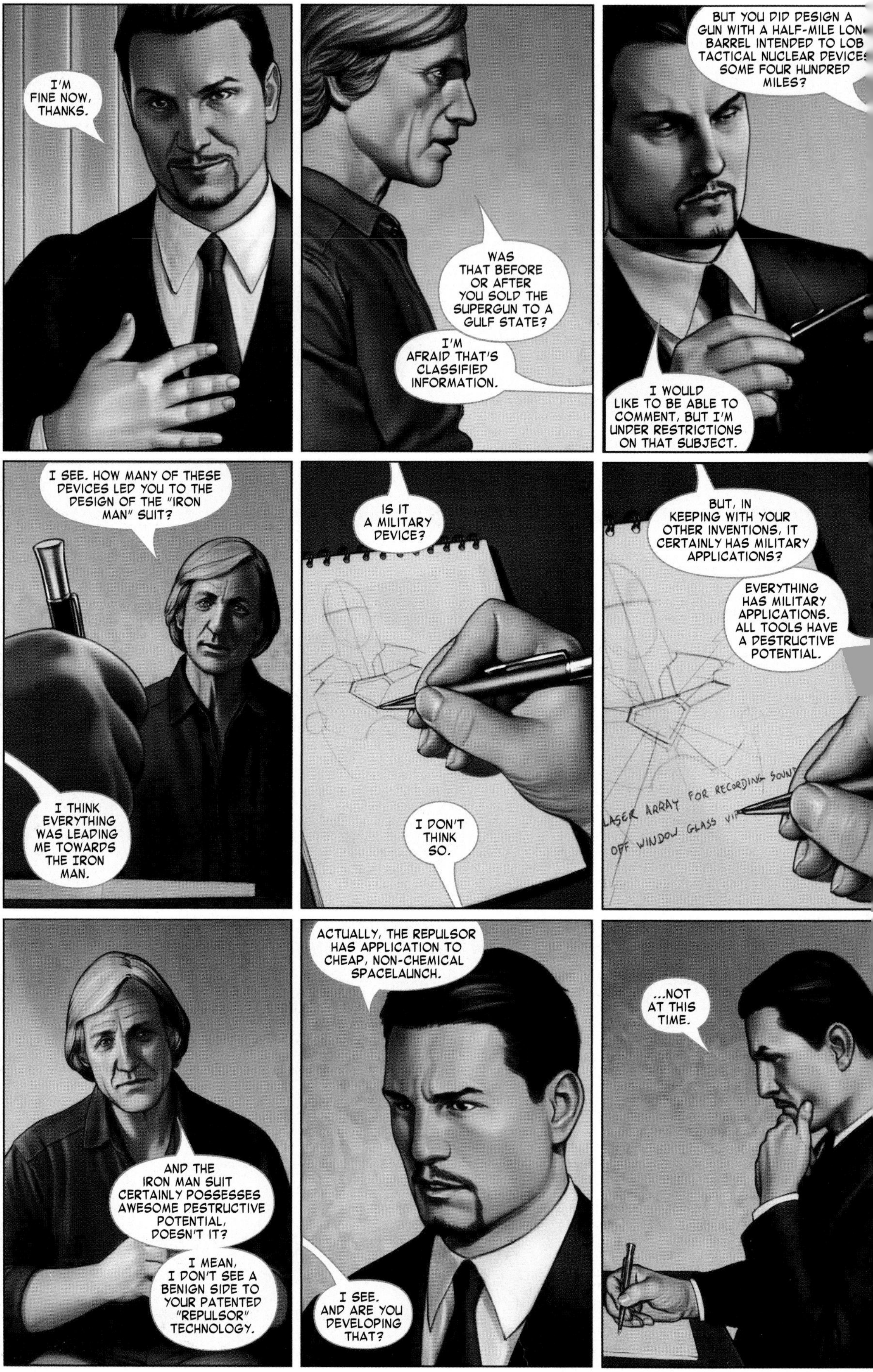
I'M FINE NOW, THANKS.
WAS THAT BEFORE OR AFTER YOU SOLD THE SUPERGUN TO A GULF STATE?
I'M AFRAID THAT'S CLASSIFIED INFORMATION.
BUT YOU DID DESIGN A GUN WITH A HALF-MILE LONG BARREL INTENDED TO LOB TACTICAL NUCLEAR DEVICES SOME FOUR HUNDRED MILES?
I WOULD LIKE TO BE ABLE TO COMMENT, BUT I'M UNDER RESTRICTIONS ON THAT SUBJECT.
I SEE. HOW MANY OF THESE DEVICES LED YOU TO THE DESIGN OF THE "IRON MAN" SUIT?
I THINK EVERYTHING WAS LEADING ME TOWARDS THE IRON MAN.
IS IT A MILITARY DEVICE?
I DON'T THINK SO.
BUT, IN KEEPING WITH YOUR OTHER INVENTIONS, IT CERTAINLY HAS MILITARY APPLICATIONS?
EVERYTHING HAS MILITARY APPLICATIONS. ALL TOOLS HAVE A DESTRUCTIVE POTENTIAL.
LASER ARRAY FOR RECORDING SOUND
OFF WINDOW GLASS VI
AND THE IRON MAN SUIT CERTAINLY POSSESSES AWESOME DESTRUCTIVE POTENTIAL, DOESN'T IT?
I MEAN, I DON'T SEE A BENIGN SIDE TO YOUR PATENTED "REPULSOR" TECHNOLOGY.
ACTUALLY, THE REPULSOR HAS APPLICATION TO CHEAP, NON-CHEMICAL SPACELAUNCH.
I SEE. AND ARE YOU DEVELOPING THAT?
...NOT AT THIS TIME.

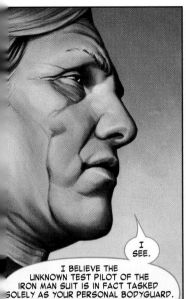

I BELIEVE THE UNKNOWN TEST PILOT OF THE IRON MAN SUIT IS IN FACT TASKED SOLELY AS YOUR PERSONAL BODYGUARD.

I SEE.

THAT'S A LITTLE DISINGENUOUS OF YOU, JOHN.

YOU'RE WELL AWARE THAT I DONATE IRON MAN'S SERVICES TO SPECIAL RESPONSE GROUPS LIKE THE AVENGERS ALL THE TIME.

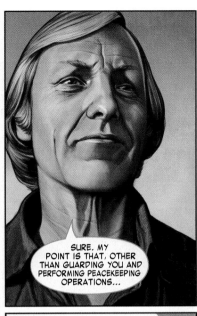

SURE. MY POINT IS THAT, OTHER THAN GUARDING YOU AND PERFORMING PEACEKEEPING OPERATIONS...

...WELL, THE IRON MAN SUIT ISN'T USED FOR ANYTHING ELSE. THEREFORE, REALLY, IT'S JUST A DEFENSE INDUSTRY APPLICATION, RIGHT?

ALL TECHNOLOGIES HAVE THAT KIND OF APPLICATION.

MY POINT--AND I DON'T WANT TO TALK OVER YOU, JOHN, BUT YOU'VE RUN ME OVER WHENEVER I'VE TRIED TO EXPAND ON AN ANSWER--

--MY POINT, JOHN, IS THAT STARK MICROELECTRONIC BREAKTHROUGHS HAVE ALL LED TO USEFUL SOCIAL TECHNOLOGIES THROUGH THAT INITIAL MILITARY FUNDING.

NO, I DIDN'T FIRST THINK TO MYSELF THAT TAKING MICROCHIPS DOWN TO THE NANOMETER LIMIT WOULD BE GOOD FOR BOMBS.

AND THE MONEY FROM SEEDPOD WAS DRIVEN INTO MEDICAL BIOMETRIC IMPLANTS, CARDIAC REPLACEMENT MEDICINE AND INTERNAL ANALGESIC PUMPS.

AM I AN ARMS DEALER? NO. DID I START OUT AS A WEAPONS DESIGNER? YES. DO I INTEND TO DIE AS ONE? NO.

DO YOU THINK THEY HAVE YOUR PAINKILLING DRUG PUMPS IN IRAQ?

DO YOU THINK AN AFGHAN KID WITH HIS ARMS BLOWN OFF BY A LANDMINE IS REMOTELY IMPRESSED BY AN IRON MAN SUIT?

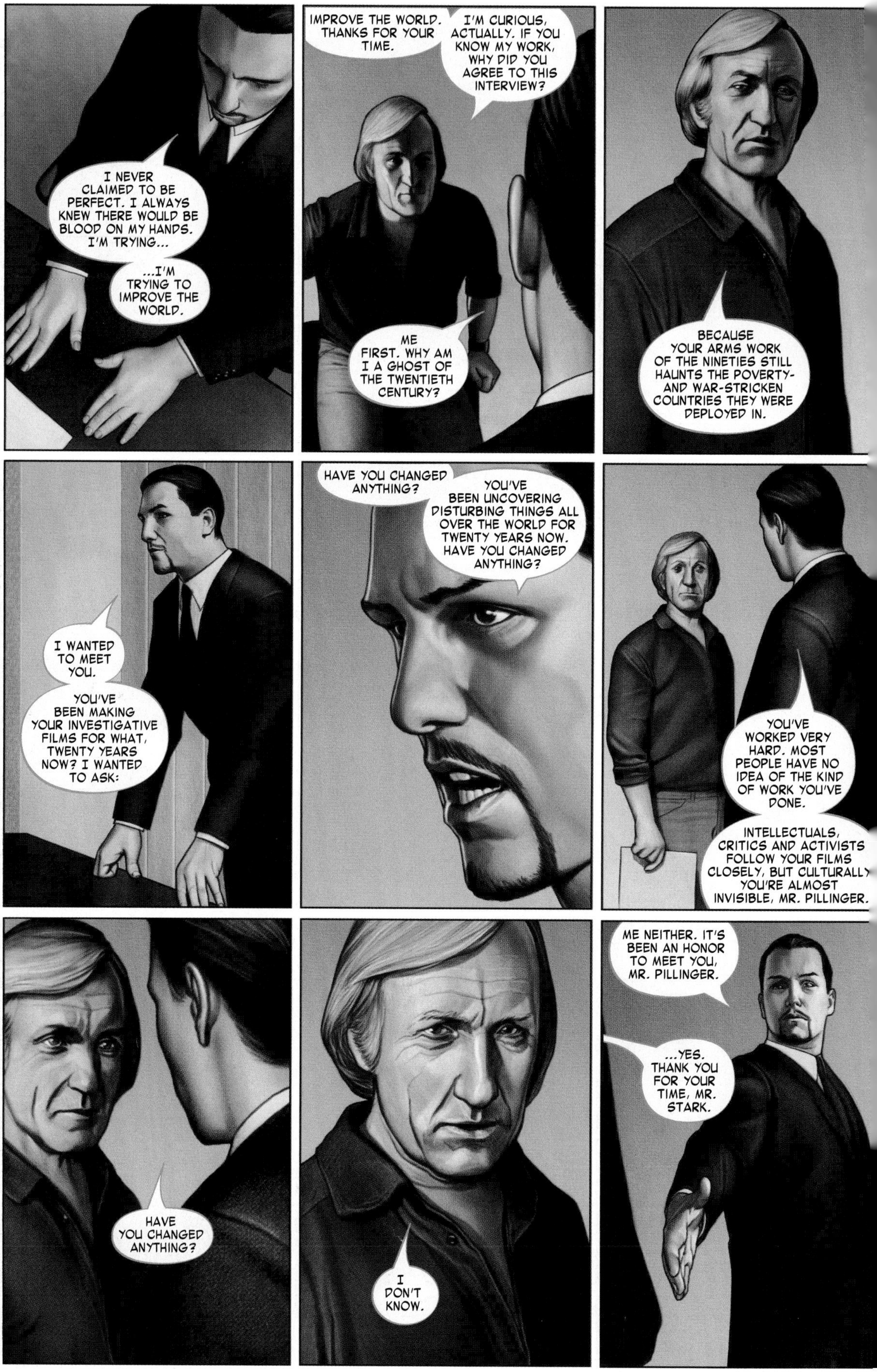
I NEVER CLAIMED TO BE PERFECT. I ALWAYS KNEW THERE WOULD BE BLOOD ON MY HANDS. I'M TRYING...
...I'M TRYING TO IMPROVE THE WORLD.
IMPROVE THE WORLD. THANKS FOR YOUR TIME.
I'M CURIOUS, ACTUALLY. IF YOU KNOW MY WORK, WHY DID YOU AGREE TO THIS INTERVIEW?
ME FIRST. WHY AM I A GHOST OF THE TWENTIETH CENTURY?
BECAUSE YOUR ARMS WORK OF THE NINETIES STILL HAUNTS THE POVERTY- AND WAR-STRICKEN COUNTRIES THEY WERE DEPLOYED IN.
I WANTED TO MEET YOU.
YOU'VE BEEN MAKING YOUR INVESTIGATIVE FILMS FOR WHAT, TWENTY YEARS NOW? I WANTED TO ASK:
HAVE YOU CHANGED ANYTHING?
YOU'VE BEEN UNCOVERING DISTURBING THINGS ALL OVER THE WORLD FOR TWENTY YEARS NOW. HAVE YOU CHANGED ANYTHING?
YOU'VE WORKED VERY HARD. MOST PEOPLE HAVE NO IDEA OF THE KIND OF WORK YOU'VE DONE.
INTELLECTUALS, CRITICS AND ACTIVISTS FOLLOW YOUR FILMS CLOSELY, BUT CULTURALLY YOU'RE ALMOST INVISIBLE, MR. PILLINGER.
HAVE YOU CHANGED ANYTHING?
I DON'T KNOW.
ME NEITHER. IT'S BEEN AN HONOR TO MEET YOU, MR. PILLINGER.
...YES. THANK YOU FOR YOUR TIME, MR. STARK.

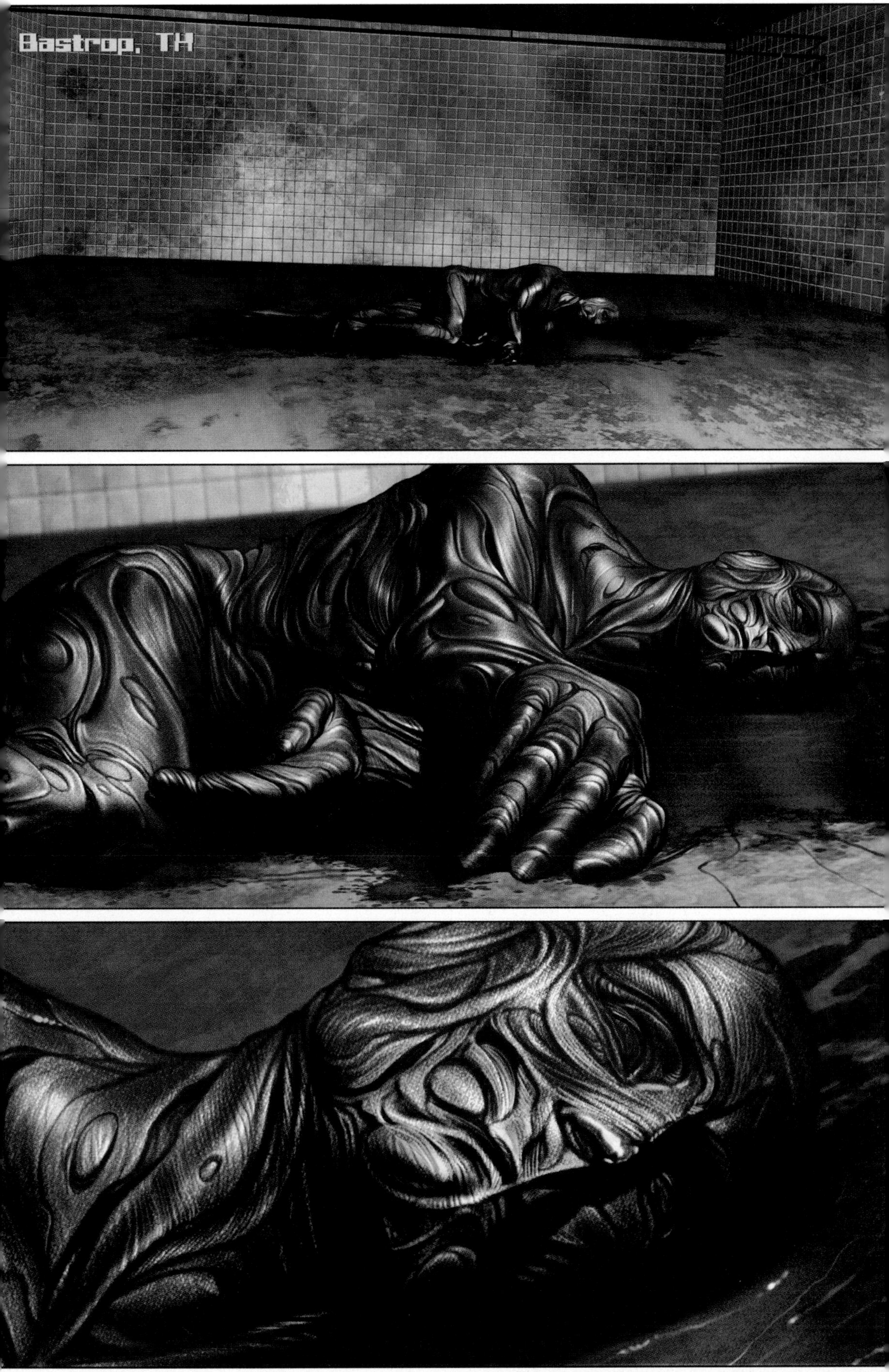
Bastrop, TX

MR. STARK, SINCE YOU'VE REJOINED THE LIVING, I'VE SCHEDULED A SENIOR STAFF MEETING FOR--

CANCEL IT. I'M GOING BACK DOWN TO THE GARAGE.

--NO, GEOFF, WE'LL TALK ABOUT THE INTERVIEW LATER.

I'M WELL AWARE THAT BILL STEPPED DOWN AS CEO OF MICROSOFT AND TOOK A "CHIEF TECHNOLOGIST" TITLE--

--ALL RIGHT. SENIOR STAFF AT FOUR. BUT NOW I NEED TO BE IN THE GARAGE.

STARK VOICELOG: RECORD: DATESTAMP.

JOHN PILLINGER SAYS THE IRON MAN SUIT IS A MILITARY APPLICATION.

I TOLD HIM HE WAS WRONG. I'M TRYING TO DECIDE IF I WAS LYING.

I'VE NEVER SOLD ANY ELEMENT OF THE IRON MAN TO THE MILITARY.

IT'S USED FOR EXTRAORDINARY RESCUE AND RESPONSE SITUATIONS.

IRON MAN SAVES LIVES.

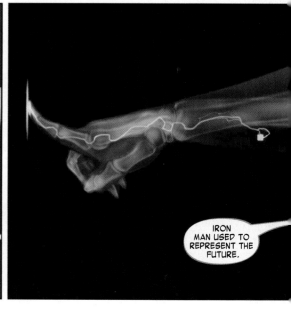

IRON MAN USED TO REPRESENT THE FUTURE.

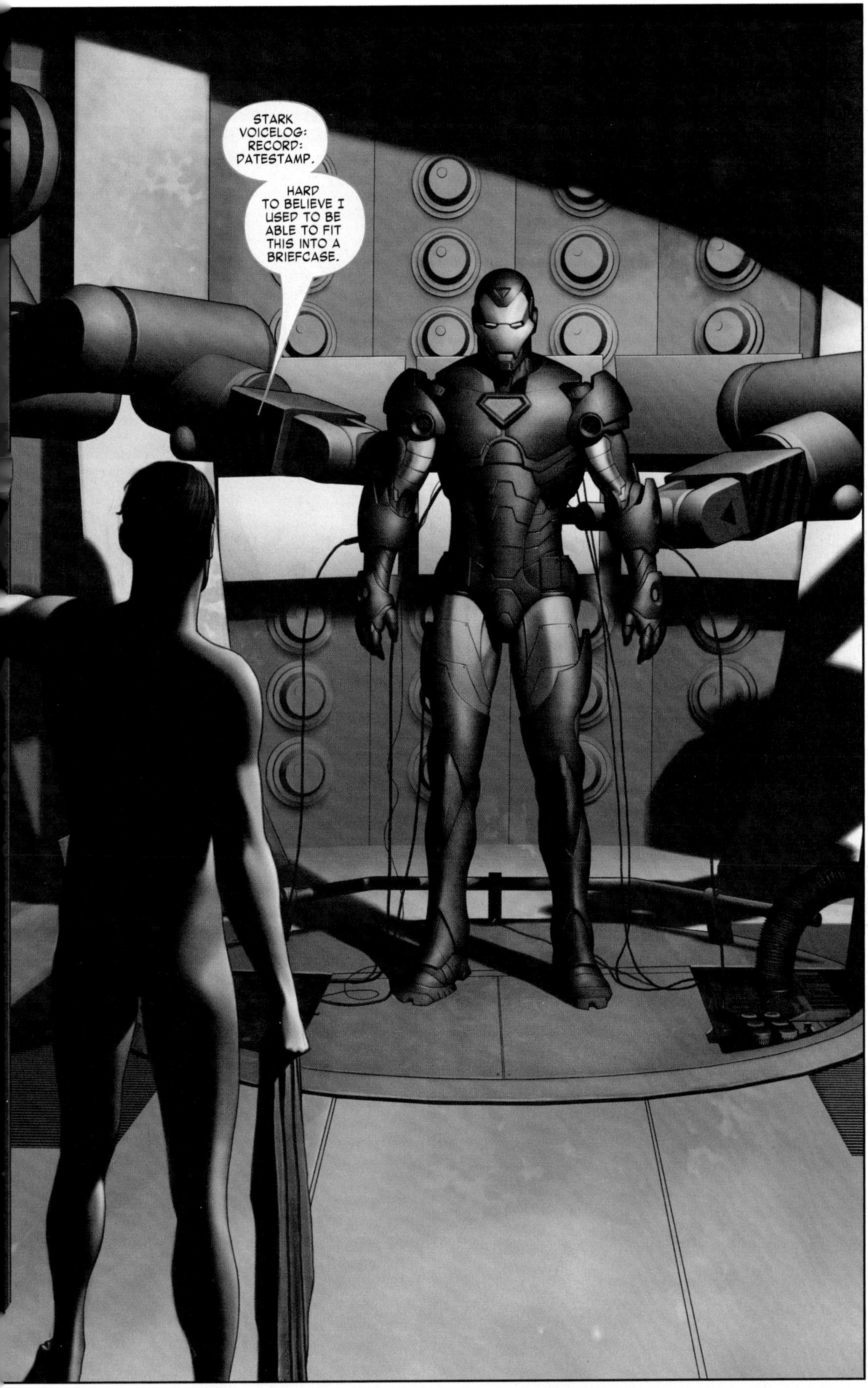
STARK VOICELOG: RECORD: DATESTAMP.
HARD TO BELIEVE I USED TO BE ABLE TO FIT THIS INTO A BRIEFCASE.

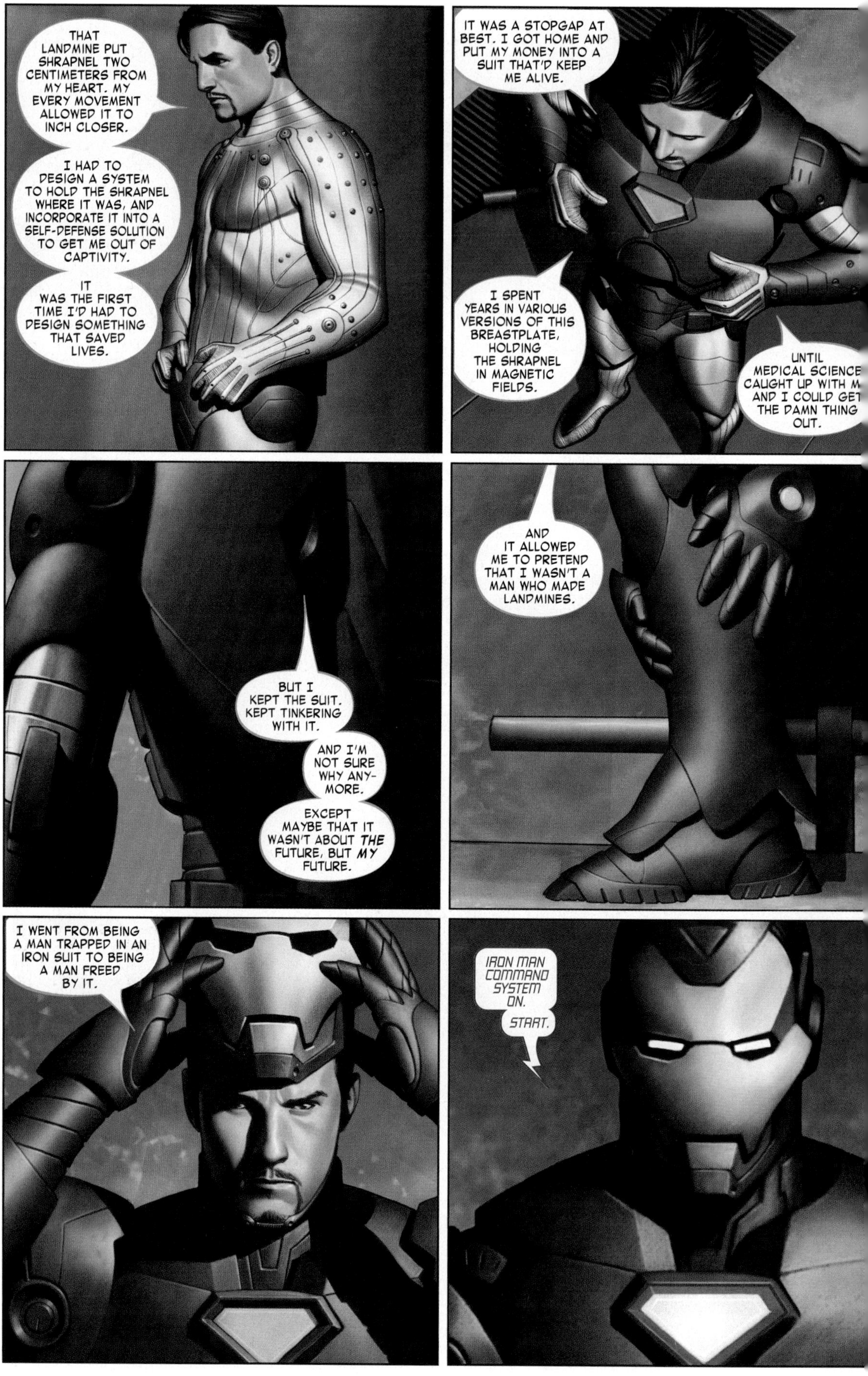
THAT LANDMINE PUT SHRAPNEL TWO CENTIMETERS FROM MY HEART. MY EVERY MOVEMENT ALLOWED IT TO INCH CLOSER.
I HAD TO DESIGN A SYSTEM TO HOLD THE SHRAPNEL WHERE IT WAS, AND INCORPORATE IT INTO A SELF-DEFENSE SOLUTION TO GET ME OUT OF CAPTIVITY.
IT WAS THE FIRST TIME I'D HAD TO DESIGN SOMETHING THAT SAVED LIVES.
IT WAS A STOPGAP AT BEST. I GOT HOME AND PUT MY MONEY INTO A SUIT THAT'D KEEP ME ALIVE.
I SPENT YEARS IN VARIOUS VERSIONS OF THIS BREASTPLATE, HOLDING THE SHRAPNEL IN MAGNETIC FIELDS.
UNTIL MEDICAL SCIENCE CAUGHT UP WITH M AND I COULD GET THE DAMN THING OUT.
BUT I KEPT THE SUIT. KEPT TINKERING WITH IT.
AND I'M NOT SURE WHY ANY-MORE.
EXCEPT MAYBE THAT IT WASN'T ABOUT *THE* FUTURE, BUT *MY* FUTURE.
AND IT ALLOWED ME TO PRETEND THAT I WASN'T A MAN WHO MADE LANDMINES.
I WENT FROM BEING A MAN TRAPPED IN AN IRON SUIT TO BEING A MAN FREED BY IT.
IRON MAN COMMAND SYSTEM ON.
START.

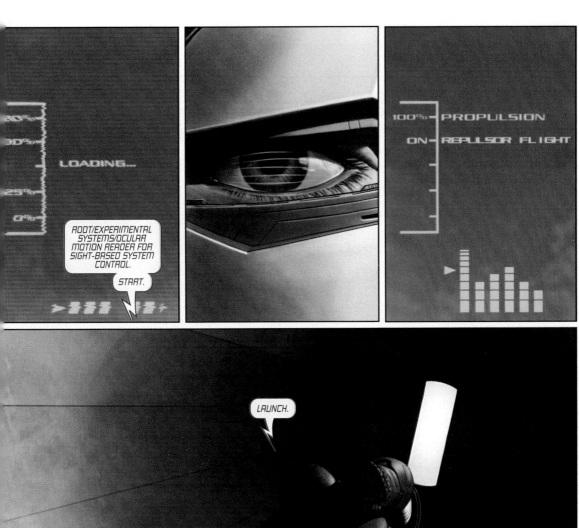

LOADING...

ROOT/EXPERIMENTAL SYSTEMS/OCULAR MOTION READER FOR SIGHT-BASED SYSTEM CONTROL.

START.

100% — PROPULSION
ON — REPULSOR FLIGHT

LAUNCH.

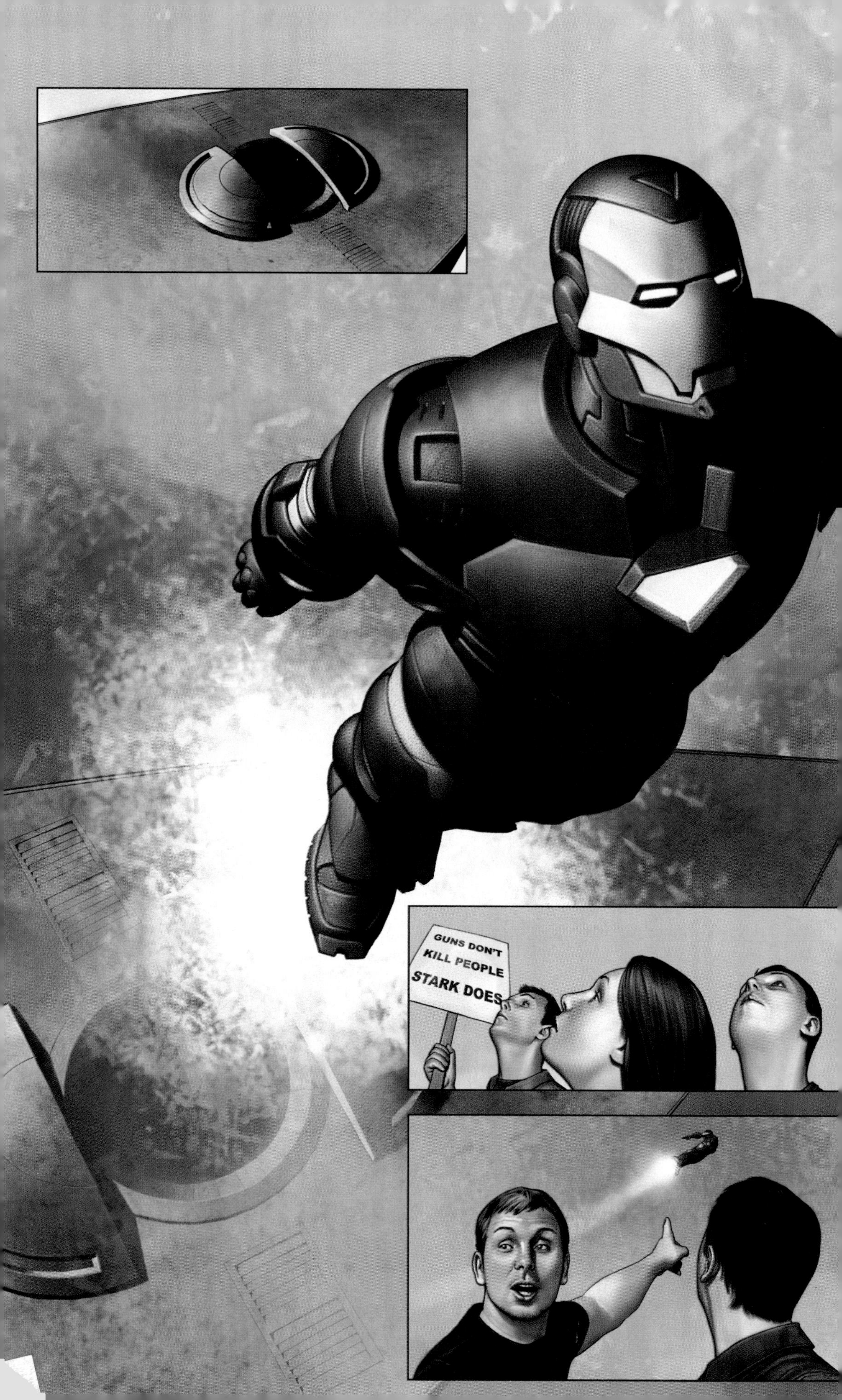
GUNS DON'T
KILL PEOPLE
STARK DOES

IRON MAN.

NEVER SAW HIM BEFORE.

IRON MAN'S COOL.

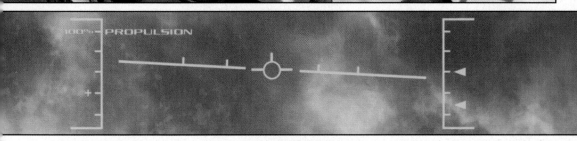

100% PROPULSION

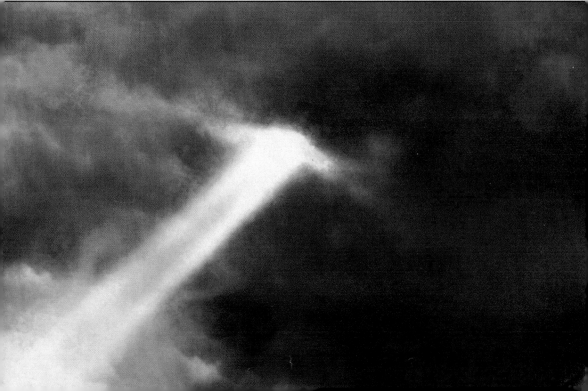

HAHAHAHAHA

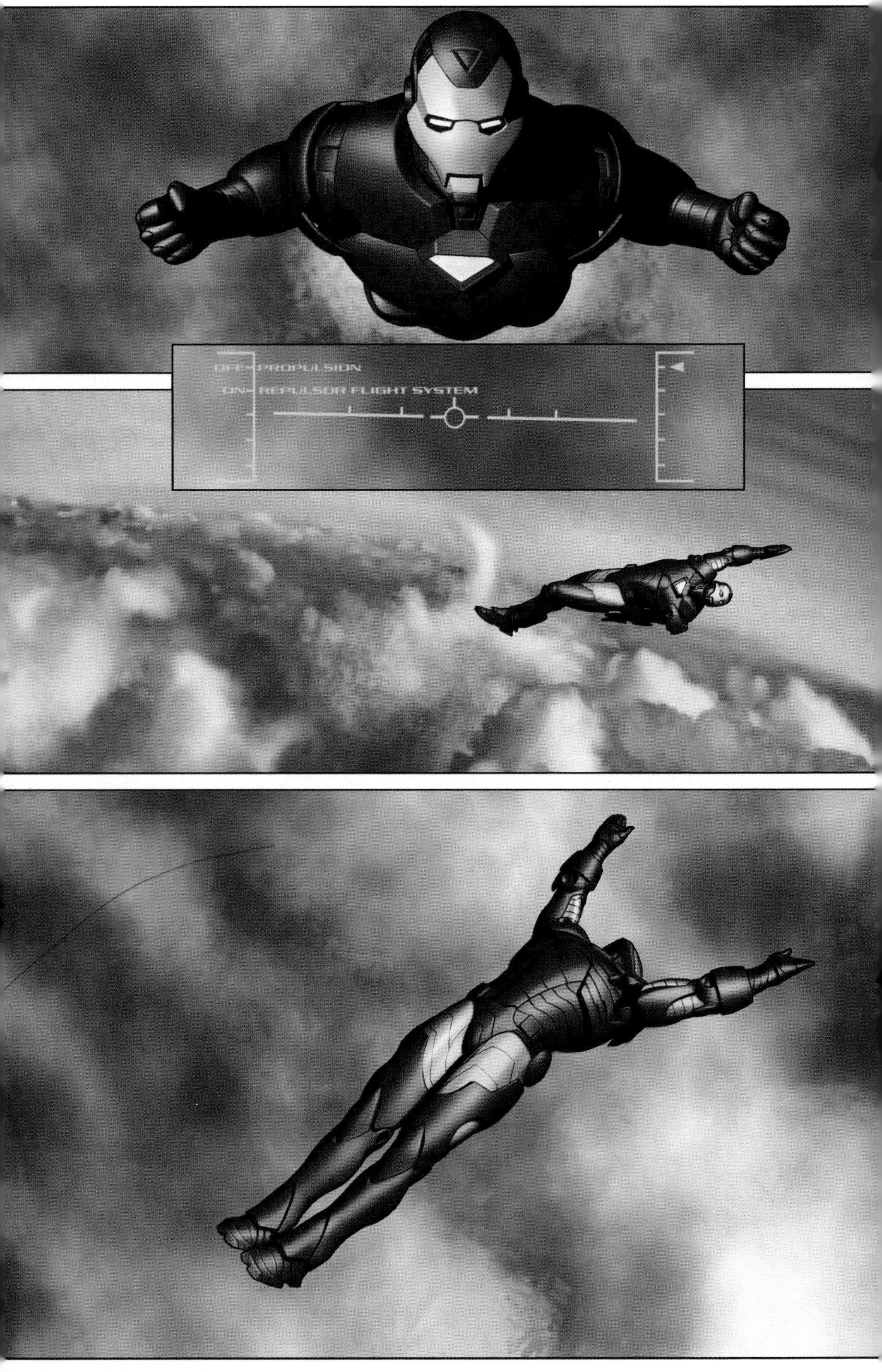
OFF- PROPULSION
ON- REPULSOR FLIGHT SYSTEM

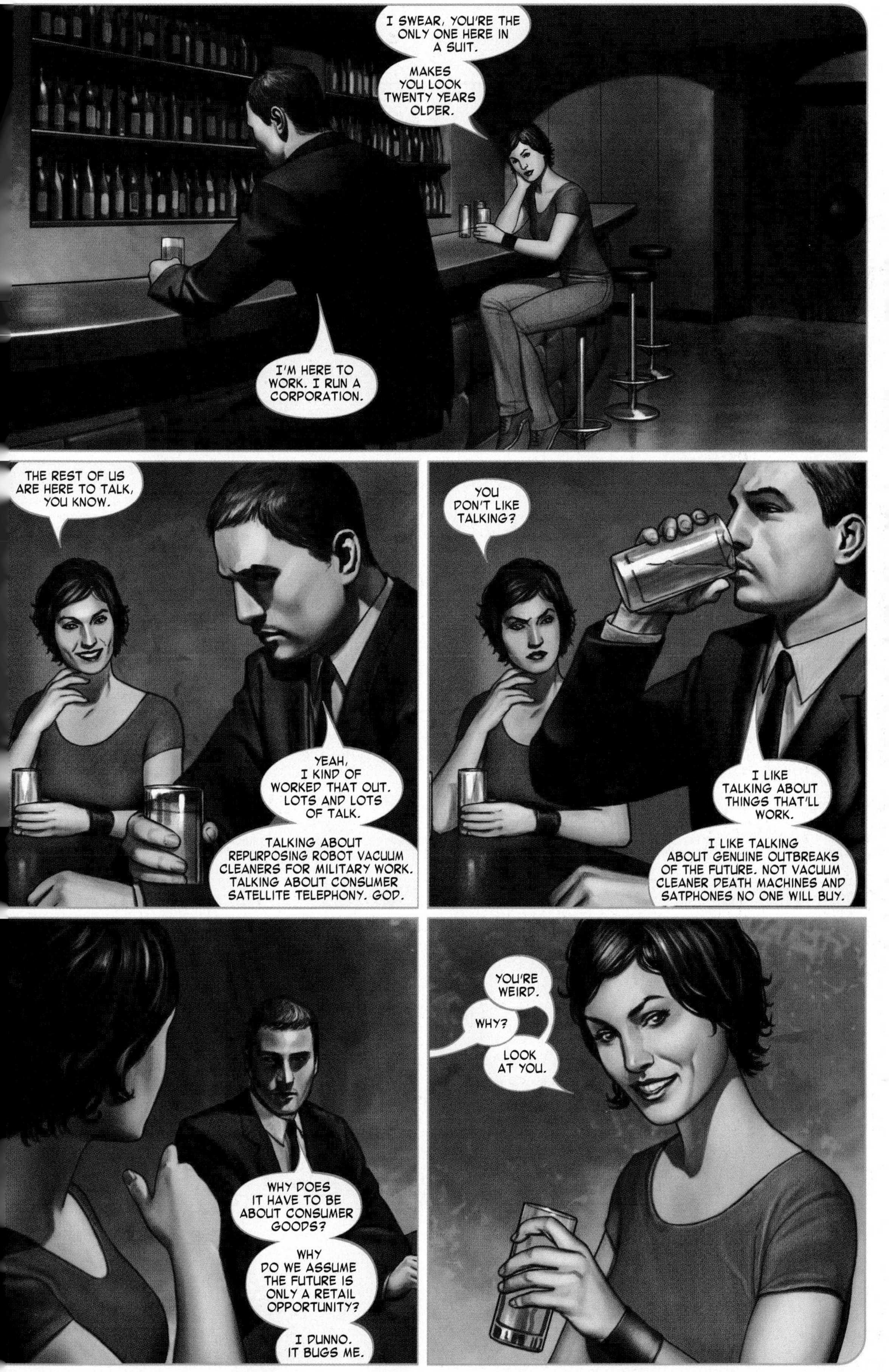
I SWEAR, YOU'RE THE ONLY ONE HERE IN A SUIT.
MAKES YOU LOOK TWENTY YEARS OLDER.
I'M HERE TO WORK. I RUN A CORPORATION.
THE REST OF US ARE HERE TO TALK, YOU KNOW.
YEAH, I KIND OF WORKED THAT OUT. LOTS AND LOTS OF TALK.
TALKING ABOUT REPURPOSING ROBOT VACUUM CLEANERS FOR MILITARY WORK. TALKING ABOUT CONSUMER SATELLITE TELEPHONY. GOD.
YOU DON'T LIKE TALKING?
I LIKE TALKING ABOUT THINGS THAT'LL WORK.
I LIKE TALKING ABOUT GENUINE OUTBREAKS OF THE FUTURE. NOT VACUUM CLEANER DEATH MACHINES AND SATPHONES NO ONE WILL BUY.
WHY DOES IT HAVE TO BE ABOUT CONSUMER GOODS?
WHY DO WE ASSUME THE FUTURE IS ONLY A RETAIL OPPORTUNITY?
I DUNNO. IT BUGS ME.
YOU'RE WEIRD.
WHY?
LOOK AT YOU.

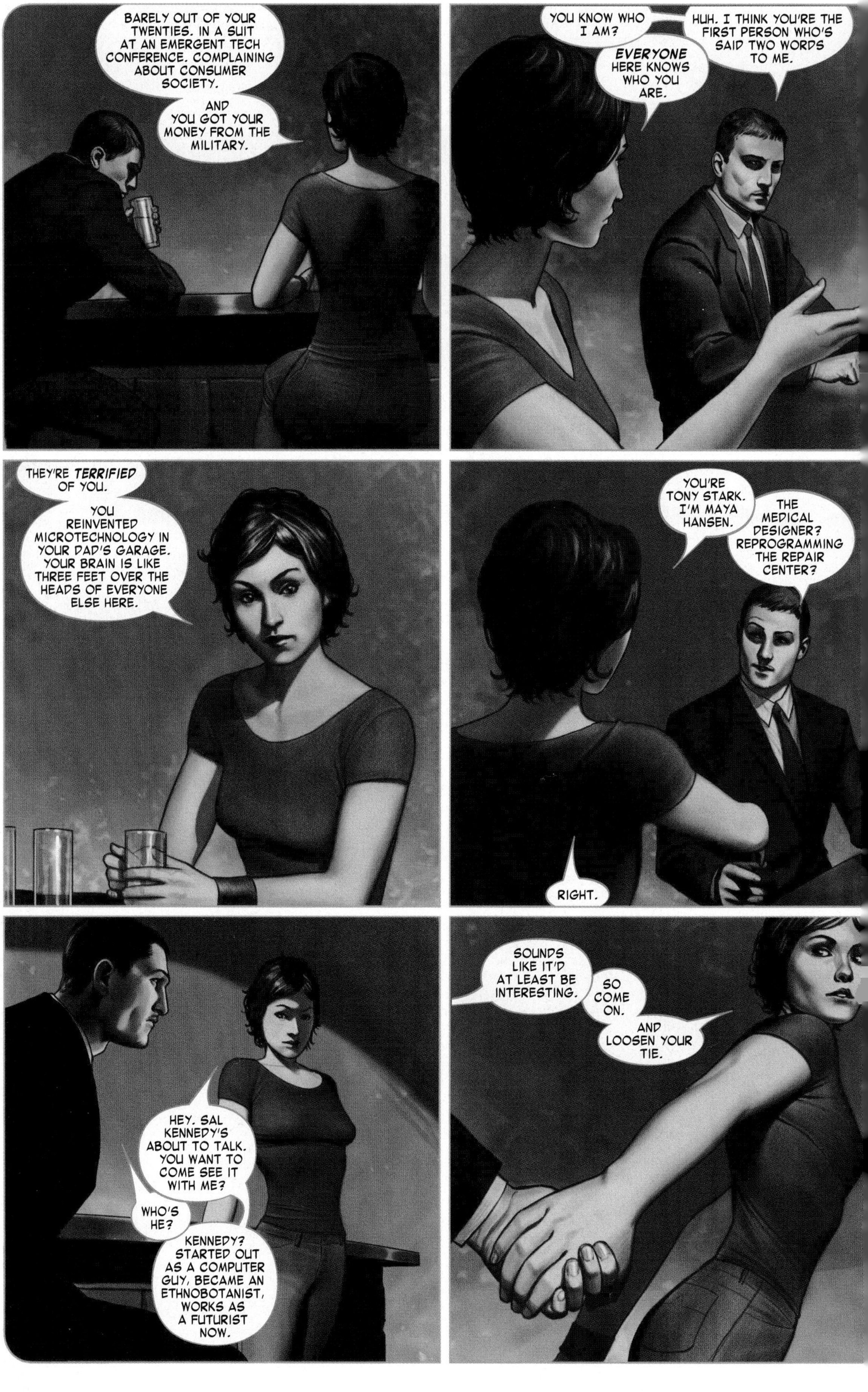
BARELY OUT OF YOUR TWENTIES. IN A SUIT AT AN EMERGENT TECH CONFERENCE. COMPLAINING ABOUT CONSUMER SOCIETY.
AND YOU GOT YOUR MONEY FROM THE MILITARY.
YOU KNOW WHO I AM?
EVERYONE HERE KNOWS WHO YOU ARE.
HUH. I THINK YOU'RE THE FIRST PERSON WHO'S SAID TWO WORDS TO ME.
THEY'RE TERRIFIED OF YOU.
YOU REINVENTED MICROTECHNOLOGY IN YOUR DAD'S GARAGE. YOUR BRAIN IS LIKE THREE FEET OVER THE HEADS OF EVERYONE ELSE HERE.
YOU'RE TONY STARK. I'M MAYA HANSEN.
THE MEDICAL DESIGNER? REPROGRAMMING THE REPAIR CENTER?
RIGHT.
HEY. SAL KENNEDY'S ABOUT TO TALK. YOU WANT TO COME SEE IT WITH ME?
WHO'S HE?
KENNEDY? STARTED OUT AS A COMPUTER GUY, BECAME AN ETHNOBOTANIST, WORKS AS A FUTURIST NOW.
SOUNDS LIKE IT'D AT LEAST BE INTERESTING.
SO COME ON.
AND LOOSEN YOUR TIE.

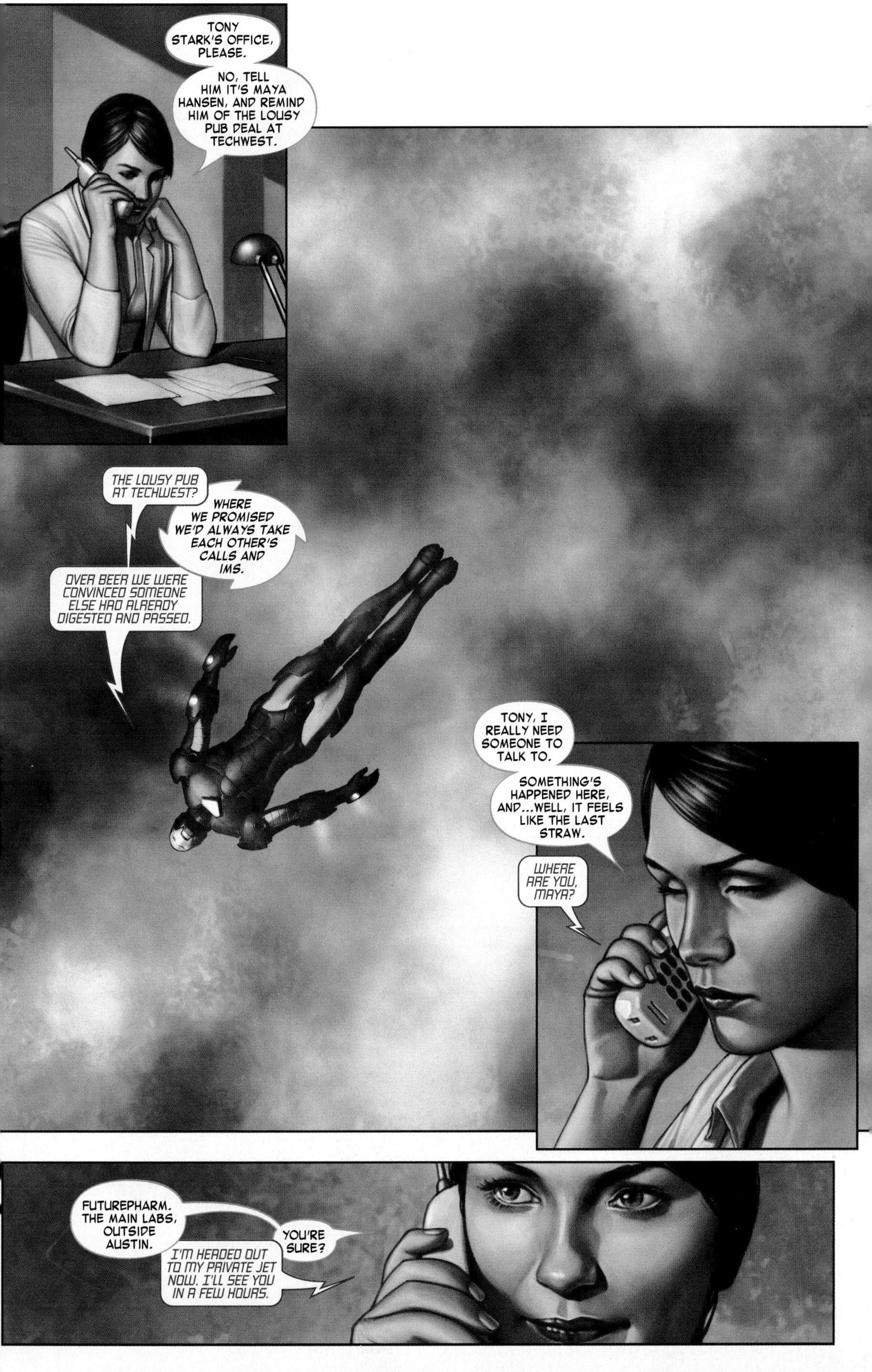
TONY STARK'S OFFICE, PLEASE.
NO, TELL HIM IT'S MAYA HANSEN, AND REMIND HIM OF THE LOUSY PUB DEAL AT TECHWEST.
THE LOUSY PUB AT TECHWEST?
WHERE WE PROMISED WE'D ALWAYS TAKE EACH OTHER'S CALLS AND IMS.
OVER BEER WE WERE CONVINCED SOMEONE ELSE HAD ALREADY DIGESTED AND PASSED.
TONY, I REALLY NEED SOMEONE TO TALK TO.
SOMETHING'S HAPPENED HERE, AND...WELL, IT FEELS LIKE THE LAST STRAW.
WHERE ARE YOU, MAYA?
FUTUREPHARM. THE MAIN LABS, OUTSIDE AUSTIN.
YOU'RE SURE?
I'M HEADED OUT TO MY PRIVATE JET NOW. I'LL SEE YOU IN A FEW HOURS.

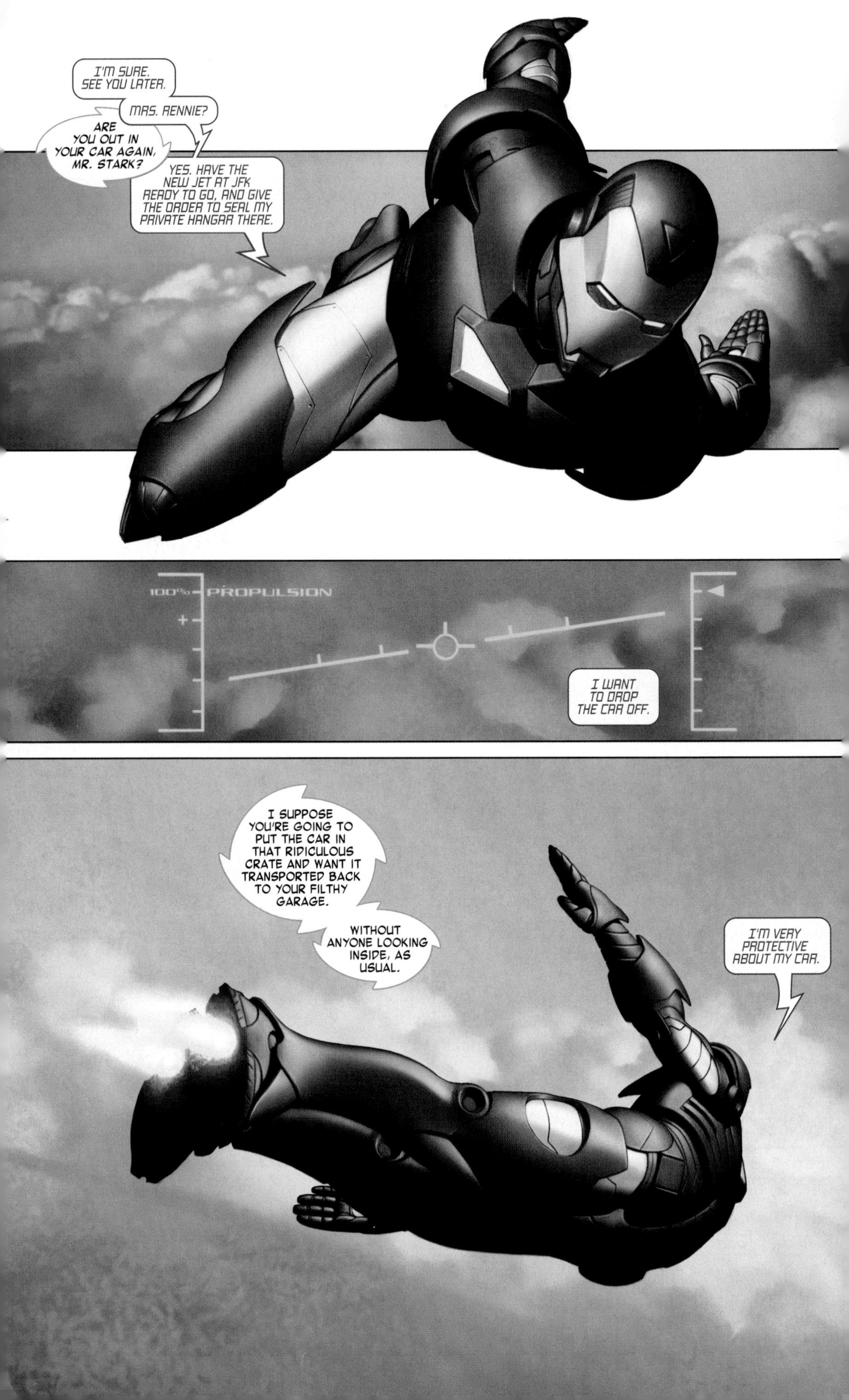
I'M SURE. SEE YOU LATER.
MRS. RENNIE?
ARE YOU OUT IN YOUR CAR AGAIN, MR. STARK?
YES. HAVE THE NEW JET AT JFK READY TO GO, AND GIVE THE ORDER TO SEAL MY PRIVATE HANGAR THERE.
100% PROPULSION
I WANT TO DROP THE CAR OFF.
I SUPPOSE YOU'RE GOING TO PUT THE CAR IN THAT RIDICULOUS CRATE AND WANT IT TRANSPORTED BACK TO YOUR FILTHY GARAGE.
WITHOUT ANYONE LOOKING INSIDE, AS USUAL.
I'M VERY PROTECTIVE ABOUT MY CAR.

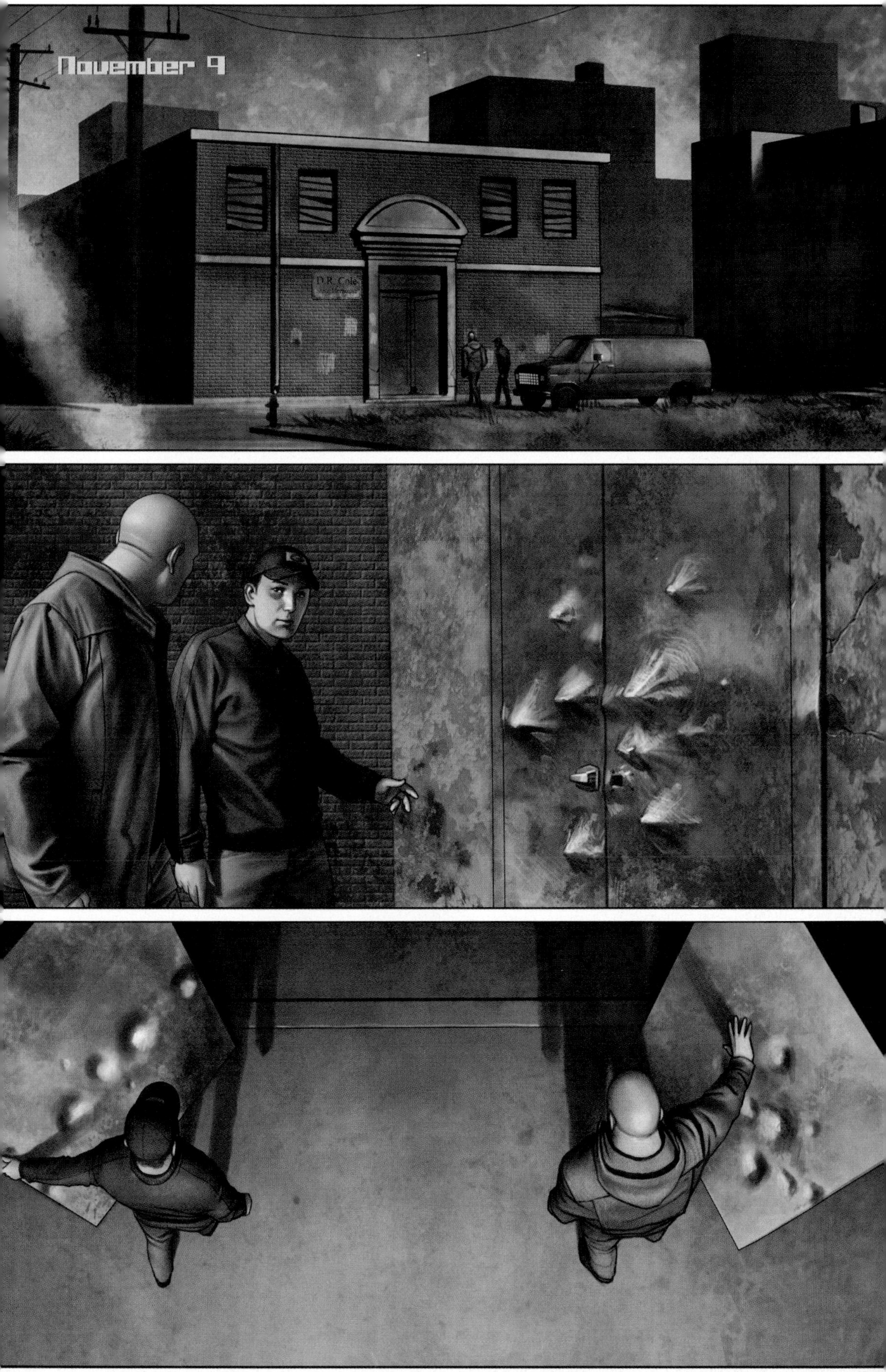
November 9
D.R. Cole

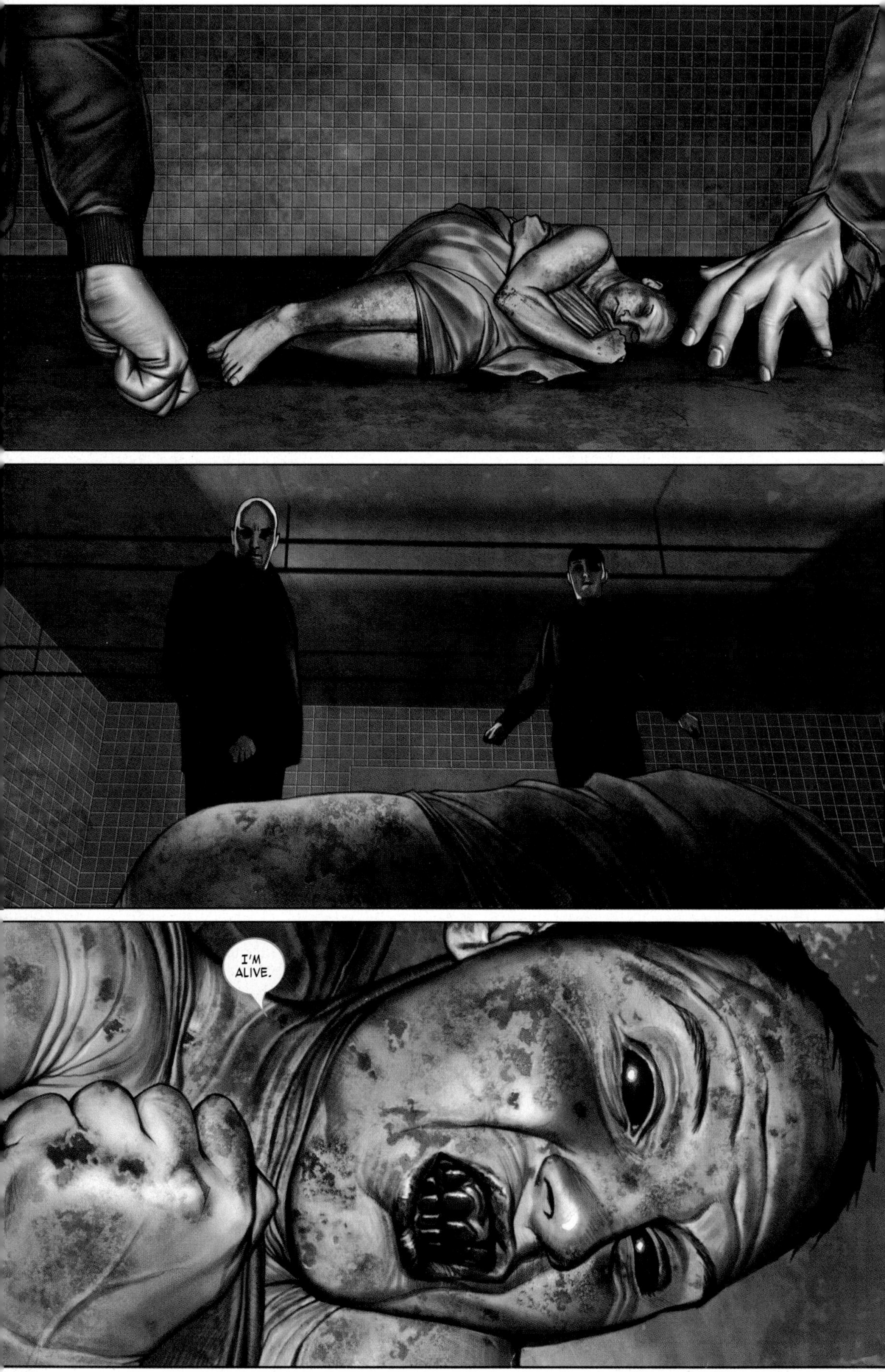
I'M ALIVE.

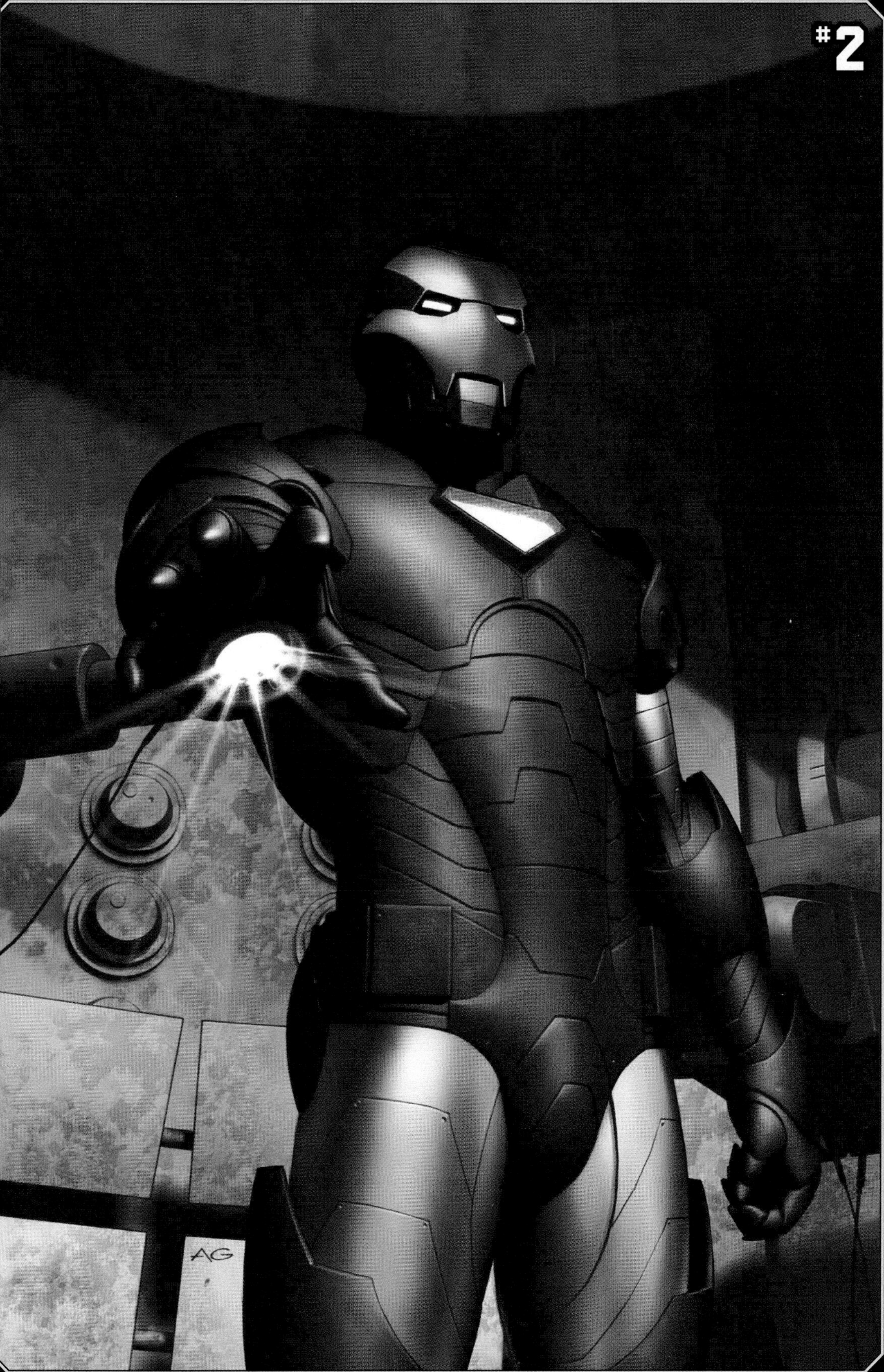
#2
AG

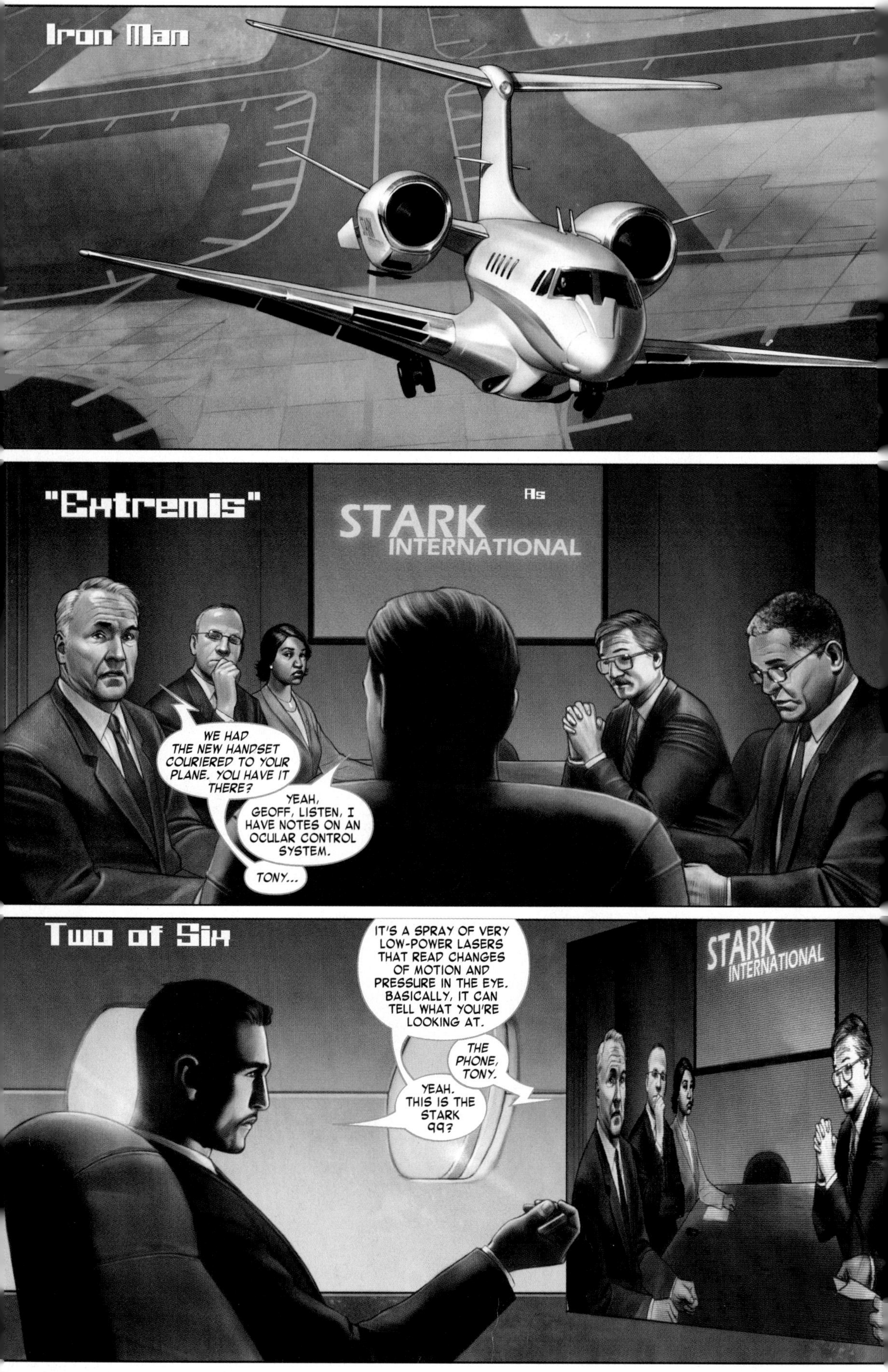
Iron Man
"Extremis"
As
STARK
INTERNATIONAL
WE HAD THE NEW HANDSET COURIERED TO YOUR PLANE. YOU HAVE IT THERE?
YEAH, GEOFF, LISTEN, I HAVE NOTES ON AN OCULAR CONTROL SYSTEM.
TONY...
Two of Six
IT'S A SPRAY OF VERY LOW-POWER LASERS THAT READ CHANGES OF MOTION AND PRESSURE IN THE EYE. BASICALLY, IT CAN TELL WHAT YOU'RE LOOKING AT.
THE PHONE, TONY.
YEAH. THIS IS THE STARK 99?
STARK
INTERNATIONAL

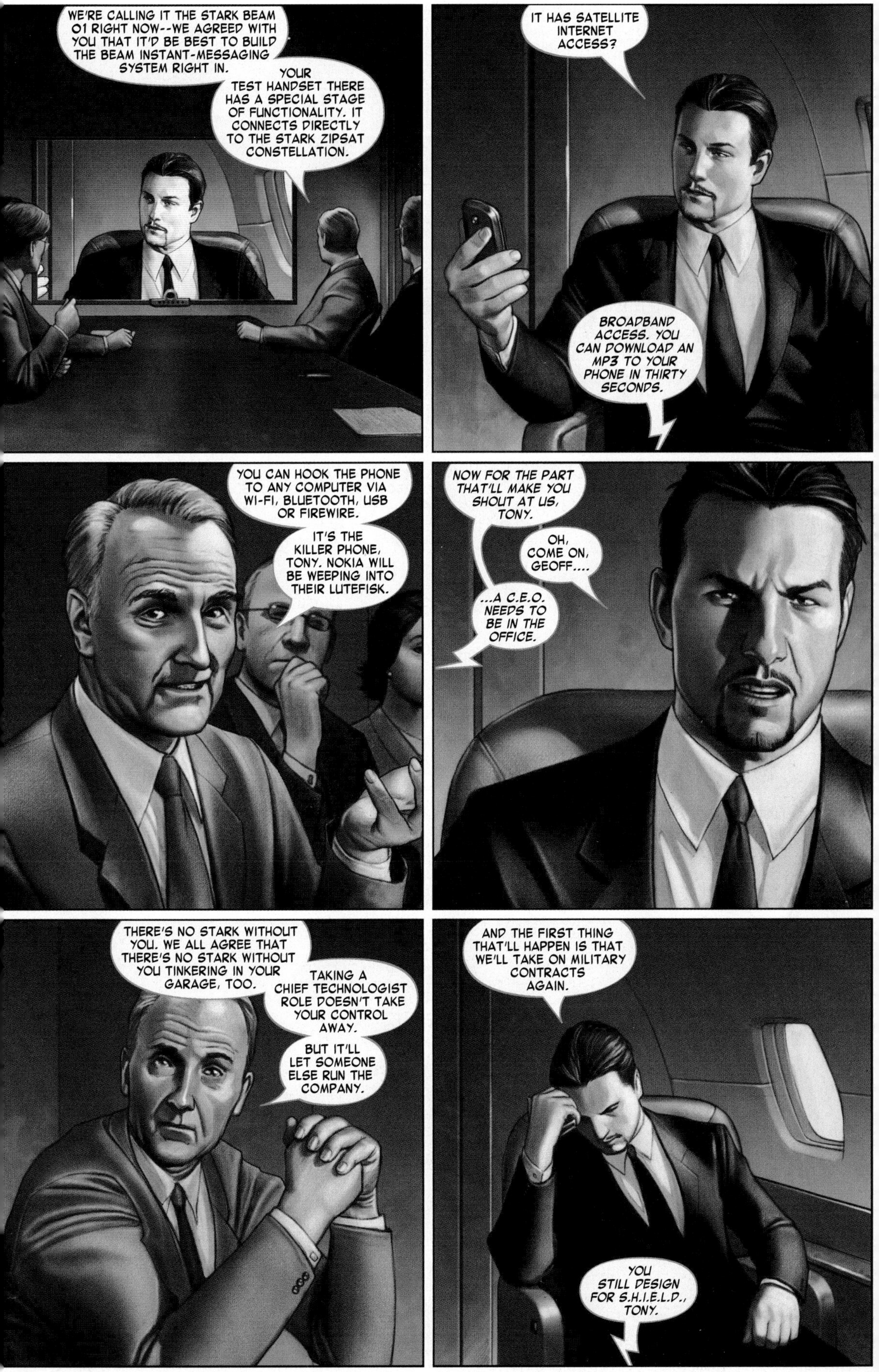
WE'RE CALLING IT THE STARK BEAM 01 RIGHT NOW--WE AGREED WITH YOU THAT IT'D BE BEST TO BUILD THE BEAM INSTANT-MESSAGING SYSTEM RIGHT IN.
YOUR TEST HANDSET THERE HAS A SPECIAL STAGE OF FUNCTIONALITY. IT CONNECTS DIRECTLY TO THE STARK ZIPSAT CONSTELLATION.
IT HAS SATELLITE INTERNET ACCESS?
BROADBAND ACCESS. YOU CAN DOWNLOAD AN MP3 TO YOUR PHONE IN THIRTY SECONDS.
YOU CAN HOOK THE PHONE TO ANY COMPUTER VIA WI-FI, BLUETOOTH, USB OR FIREWIRE.
IT'S THE KILLER PHONE, TONY. NOKIA WILL BE WEEPING INTO THEIR LUTEFISK.
NOW FOR THE PART THAT'LL MAKE YOU SHOUT AT US, TONY.
OH, COME ON, GEOFF....
...A C.E.O. NEEDS TO BE IN THE OFFICE.
THERE'S NO STARK WITHOUT YOU. WE ALL AGREE THAT THERE'S NO STARK WITHOUT YOU TINKERING IN YOUR GARAGE, TOO.
TAKING A CHIEF TECHNOLOGIST ROLE DOESN'T TAKE YOUR CONTROL AWAY.
BUT IT'LL LET SOMEONE ELSE RUN THE COMPANY.
AND THE FIRST THING THAT'LL HAPPEN IS THAT WE'LL TAKE ON MILITARY CONTRACTS AGAIN.
YOU STILL DESIGN FOR S.H.I.E.L.D., TONY.

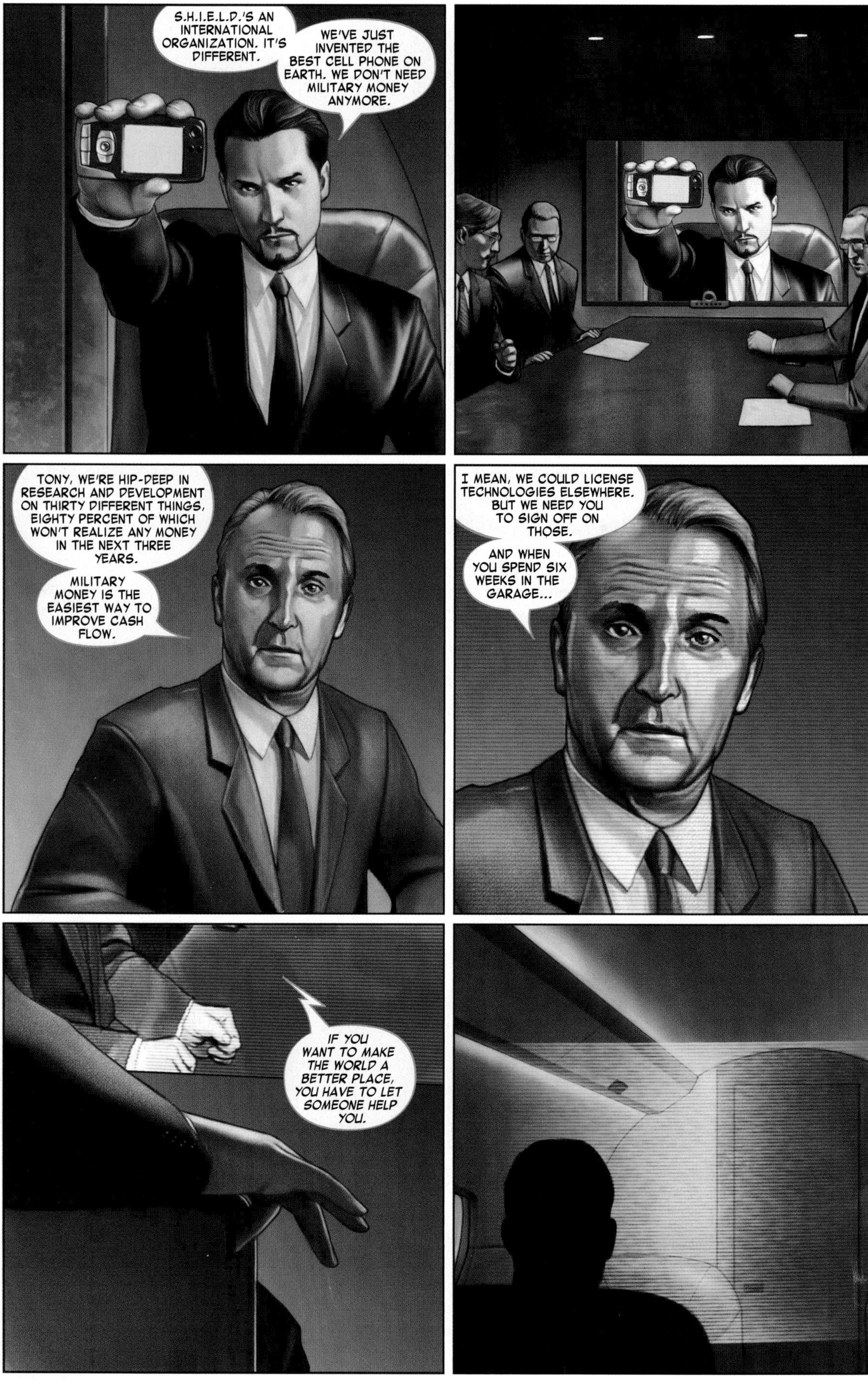
S.H.I.E.L.D.'S AN INTERNATIONAL ORGANIZATION. IT'S DIFFERENT.
WE'VE JUST INVENTED THE BEST CELL PHONE ON EARTH. WE DON'T NEED MILITARY MONEY ANYMORE.
TONY, WE'RE HIP-DEEP IN RESEARCH AND DEVELOPMENT ON THIRTY DIFFERENT THINGS, EIGHTY PERCENT OF WHICH WON'T REALIZE ANY MONEY IN THE NEXT THREE YEARS.
MILITARY MONEY IS THE EASIEST WAY TO IMPROVE CASH FLOW.
I MEAN, WE COULD LICENSE TECHNOLOGIES ELSEWHERE. BUT WE NEED YOU TO SIGN OFF ON THOSE.
AND WHEN YOU SPEND SIX WEEKS IN THE GARAGE...
IF YOU WANT TO MAKE THE WORLD A BETTER PLACE, YOU HAVE TO LET SOMEONE HELP YOU.

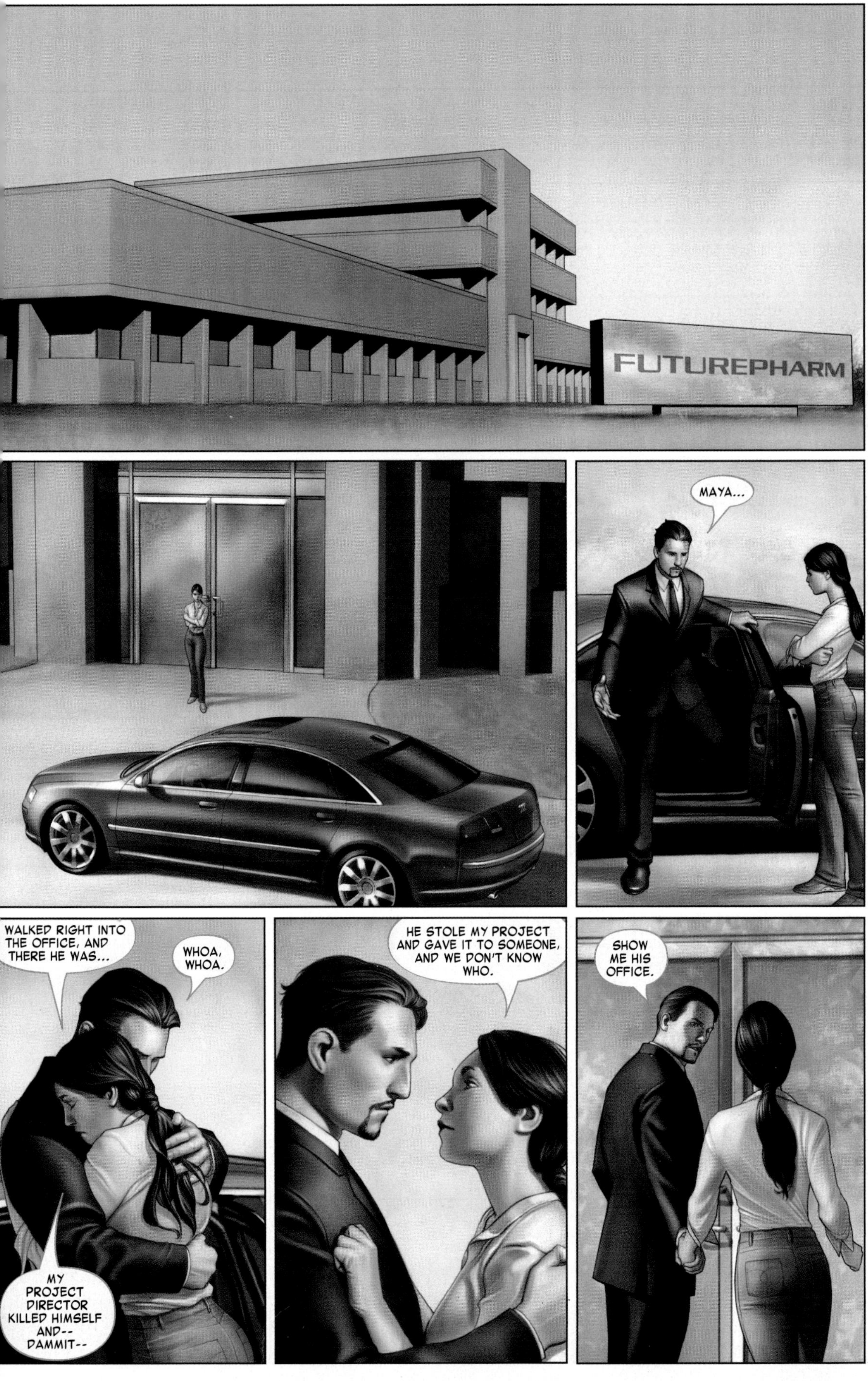
FUTUREPHARM
MAYA...
WALKED RIGHT INTO THE OFFICE, AND THERE HE WAS...
WHOA, WHOA.
MY PROJECT DIRECTOR KILLED HIMSELF AND-- DAMMIT--
HE STOLE MY PROJECT AND GAVE IT TO SOMEONE, AND WE DON'T KNOW WHO.
SHOW ME HIS OFFICE.

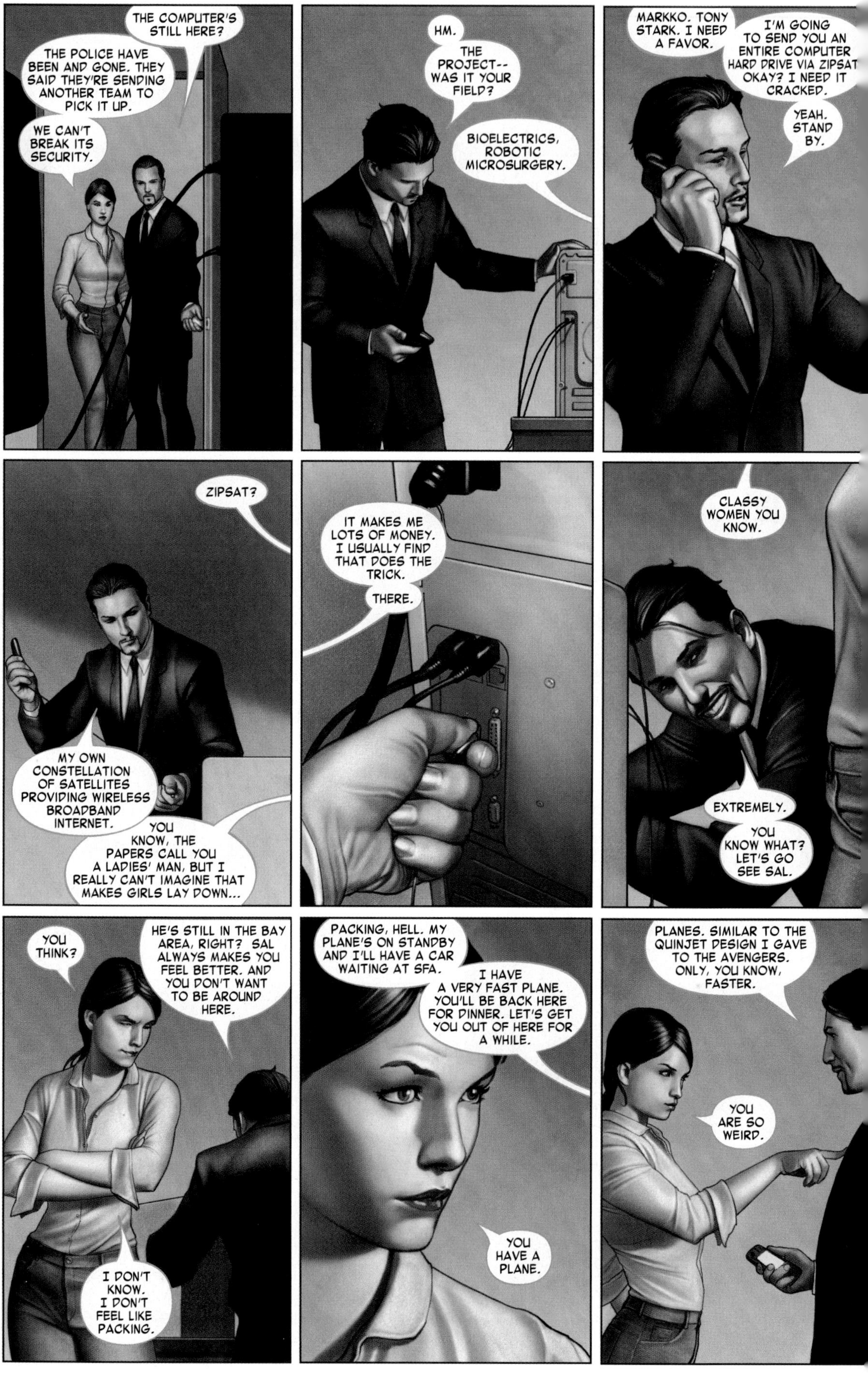
THE COMPUTER'S STILL HERE?
THE POLICE HAVE BEEN AND GONE. THEY SAID THEY'RE SENDING ANOTHER TEAM TO PICK IT UP.
WE CAN'T BREAK ITS SECURITY.
HM.
THE PROJECT-- WAS IT YOUR FIELD?
BIOELECTRICS, ROBOTIC MICROSURGERY.
MARKKO. TONY STARK. I NEED A FAVOR.
I'M GOING TO SEND YOU AN ENTIRE COMPUTER HARD DRIVE VIA ZIPSAT OKAY? I NEED IT CRACKED.
YEAH. STAND BY.
ZIPSAT?
MY OWN CONSTELLATION OF SATELLITES PROVIDING WIRELESS BROADBAND INTERNET.
YOU KNOW, THE PAPERS CALL YOU A LADIES' MAN, BUT I REALLY CAN'T IMAGINE THAT MAKES GIRLS LAY DOWN...
IT MAKES ME LOTS OF MONEY. I USUALLY FIND THAT DOES THE TRICK.
THERE.
CLASSY WOMEN YOU KNOW.
EXTREMELY.
YOU KNOW WHAT? LET'S GO SEE SAL.
YOU THINK?
HE'S STILL IN THE BAY AREA, RIGHT? SAL ALWAYS MAKES YOU FEEL BETTER. AND YOU DON'T WANT TO BE AROUND HERE.
I DON'T KNOW. I DON'T FEEL LIKE PACKING.
PACKING, HELL. MY PLANE'S ON STANDBY AND I'LL HAVE A CAR WAITING AT SFA.
I HAVE A VERY FAST PLANE. YOU'LL BE BACK HERE FOR DINNER. LET'S GET YOU OUT OF HERE FOR A WHILE.
YOU HAVE A PLANE.
PLANES. SIMILAR TO THE QUINJET DESIGN I GAVE TO THE AVENGERS. ONLY, YOU KNOW, FASTER.
YOU ARE SO WEIRD.

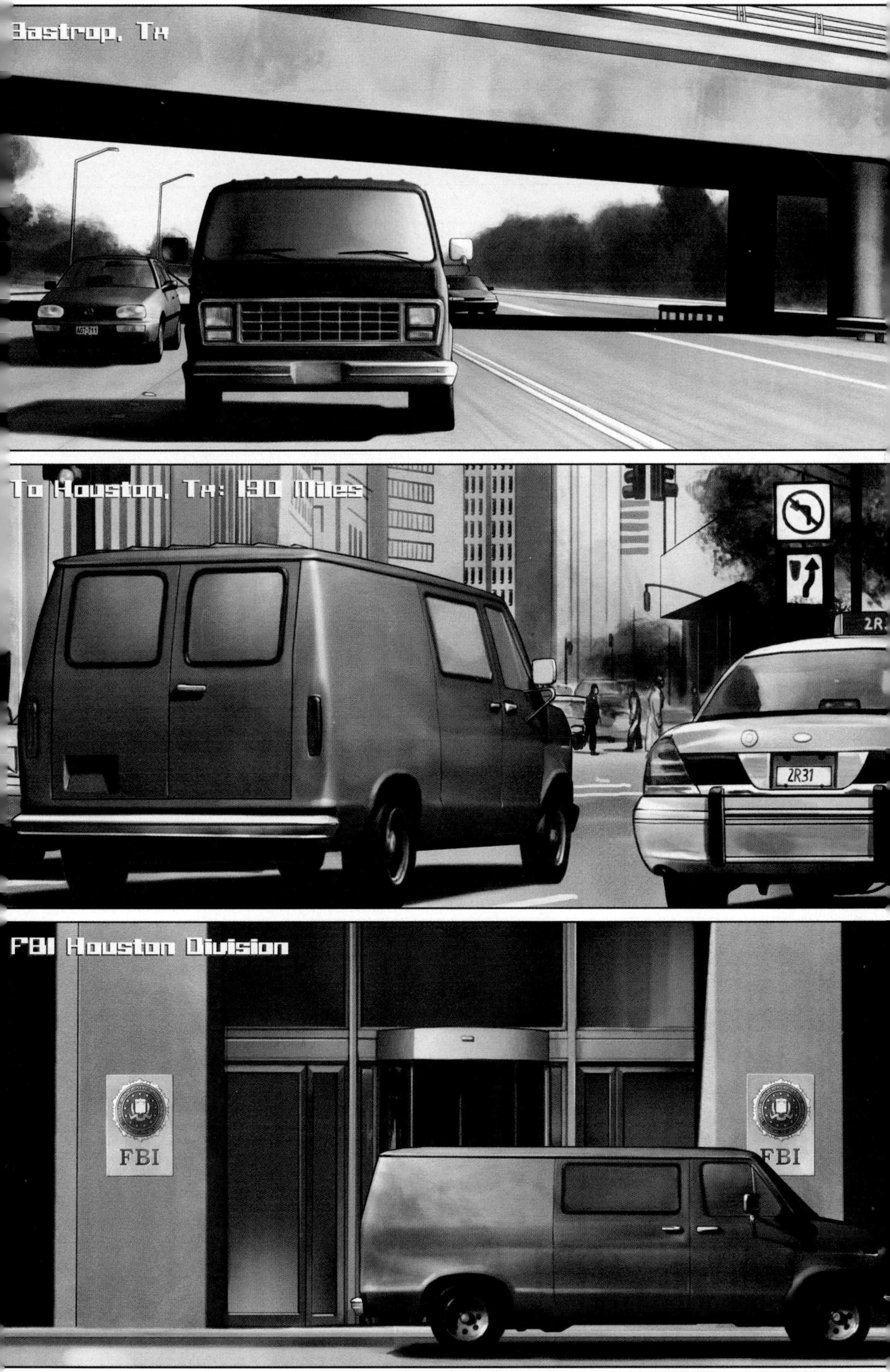
Bastrop, Tx
To Houston, Tx: 190 Miles
2R31
FBI Houston Division
FBI
FBI

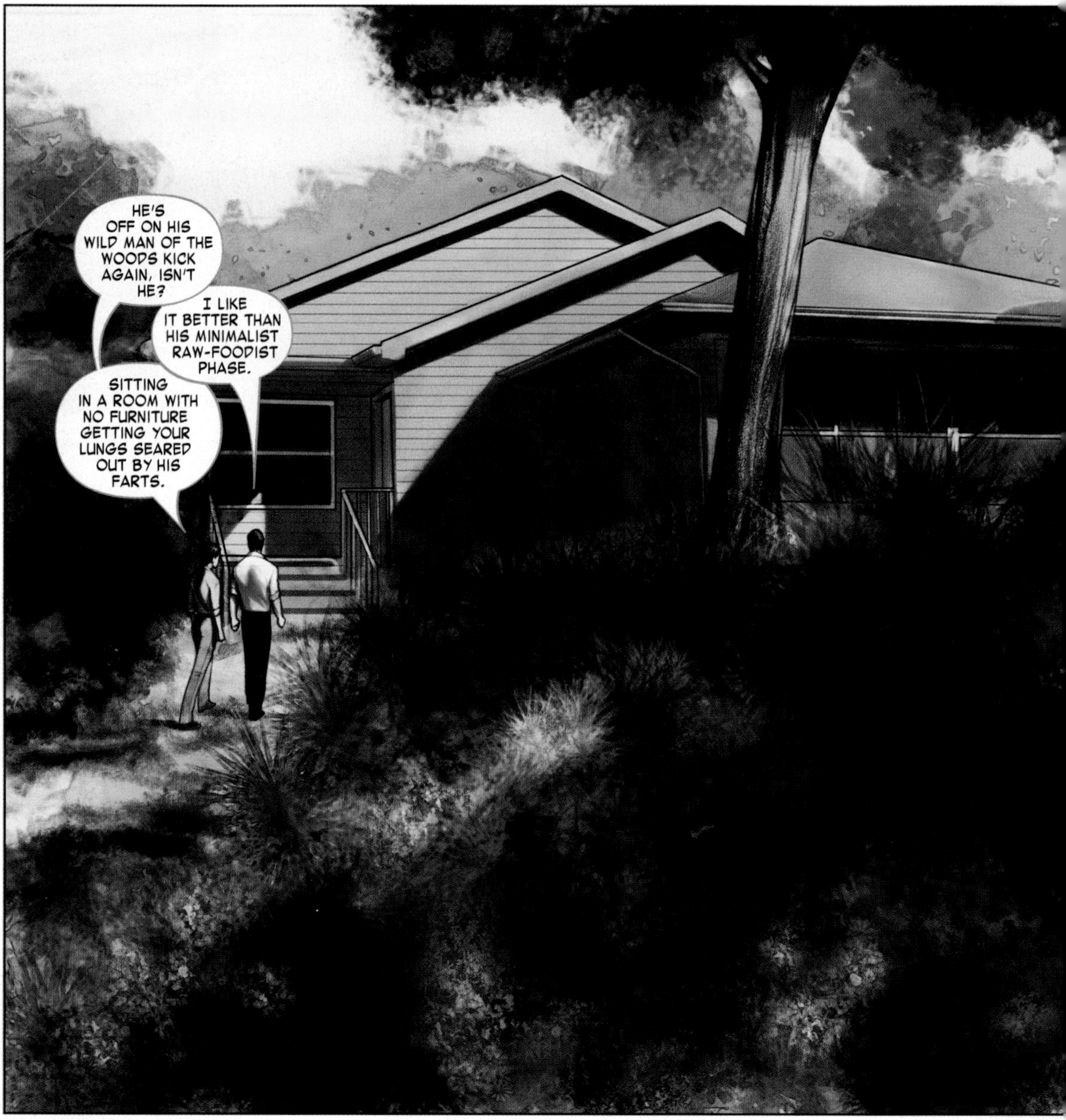
HE'S OFF ON HIS WILD MAN OF THE WOODS KICK AGAIN, ISN'T HE?
I LIKE IT BETTER THAN HIS MINIMALIST RAW-FOODIST PHASE.
SITTING IN A ROOM WITH NO FURNITURE GETTING YOUR LUNGS SEARED OUT BY HIS FARTS.

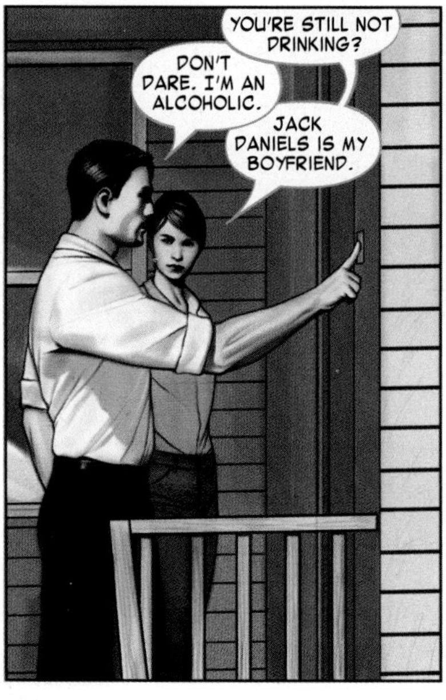
YOU'RE STILL NOT DRINKING?
DON'T DARE. I'M AN ALCOHOLIC.
JACK DANIELS IS MY BOYFRIEND.

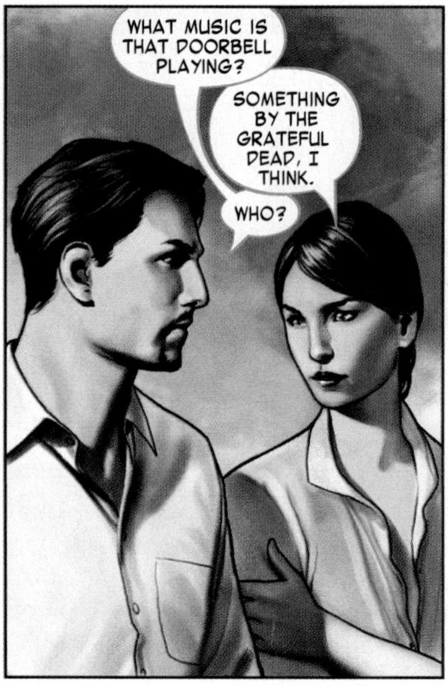
WHAT MUSIC IS THAT DOORBELL PLAYING?
SOMETHING BY THE GRATEFUL DEAD, I THINK.
WHO?

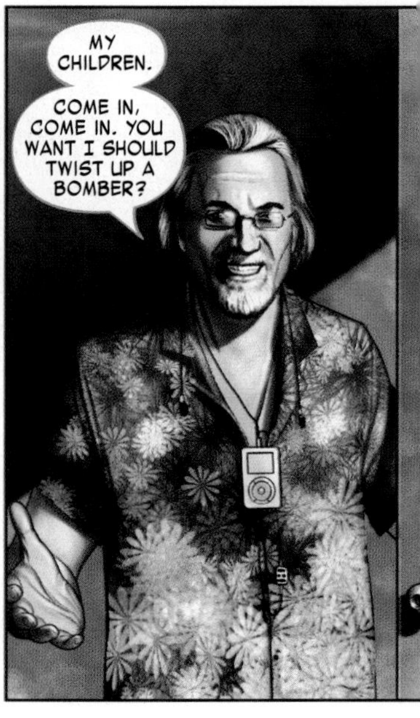
MY CHILDREN.
COME IN, COME IN. YOU WANT I SHOULD TWIST UP A BOMBER?

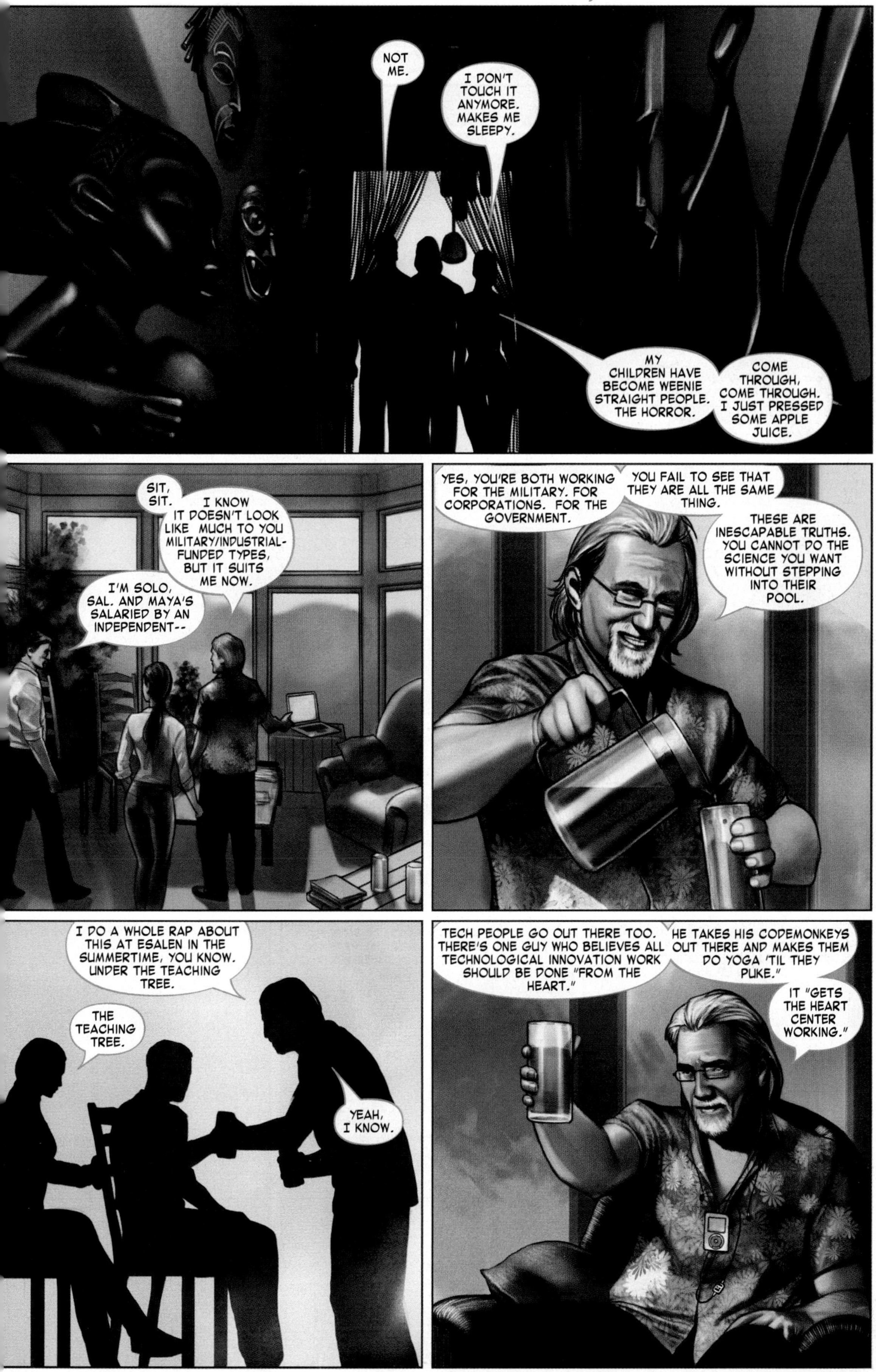
NOT ME.
I DON'T TOUCH IT ANYMORE. MAKES ME SLEEPY.
MY CHILDREN HAVE BECOME WEENIE STRAIGHT PEOPLE. THE HORROR.
COME THROUGH, COME THROUGH. I JUST PRESSED SOME APPLE JUICE.
SIT, SIT.
I KNOW IT DOESN'T LOOK LIKE MUCH TO YOU MILITARY/INDUSTRIAL-FUNDED TYPES, BUT IT SUITS ME NOW.
I'M SOLO, SAL. AND MAYA'S SALARIED BY AN INDEPENDENT--
YES, YOU'RE BOTH WORKING FOR THE MILITARY. FOR CORPORATIONS. FOR THE GOVERNMENT.
YOU FAIL TO SEE THAT THEY ARE ALL THE SAME THING.
THESE ARE INESCAPABLE TRUTHS. YOU CANNOT DO THE SCIENCE YOU WANT WITHOUT STEPPING INTO THEIR POOL.
I DO A WHOLE RAP ABOUT THIS AT ESALEN IN THE SUMMERTIME, YOU KNOW. UNDER THE TEACHING TREE.
THE TEACHING TREE.
YEAH, I KNOW.
TECH PEOPLE GO OUT THERE TOO. THERE'S ONE GUY WHO BELIEVES ALL TECHNOLOGICAL INNOVATION WORK SHOULD BE DONE "FROM THE HEART."
HE TAKES HIS CODEMONKEYS OUT THERE AND MAKES THEM DO YOGA 'TIL THEY PUKE."
IT "GETS THE HEART CENTER WORKING."

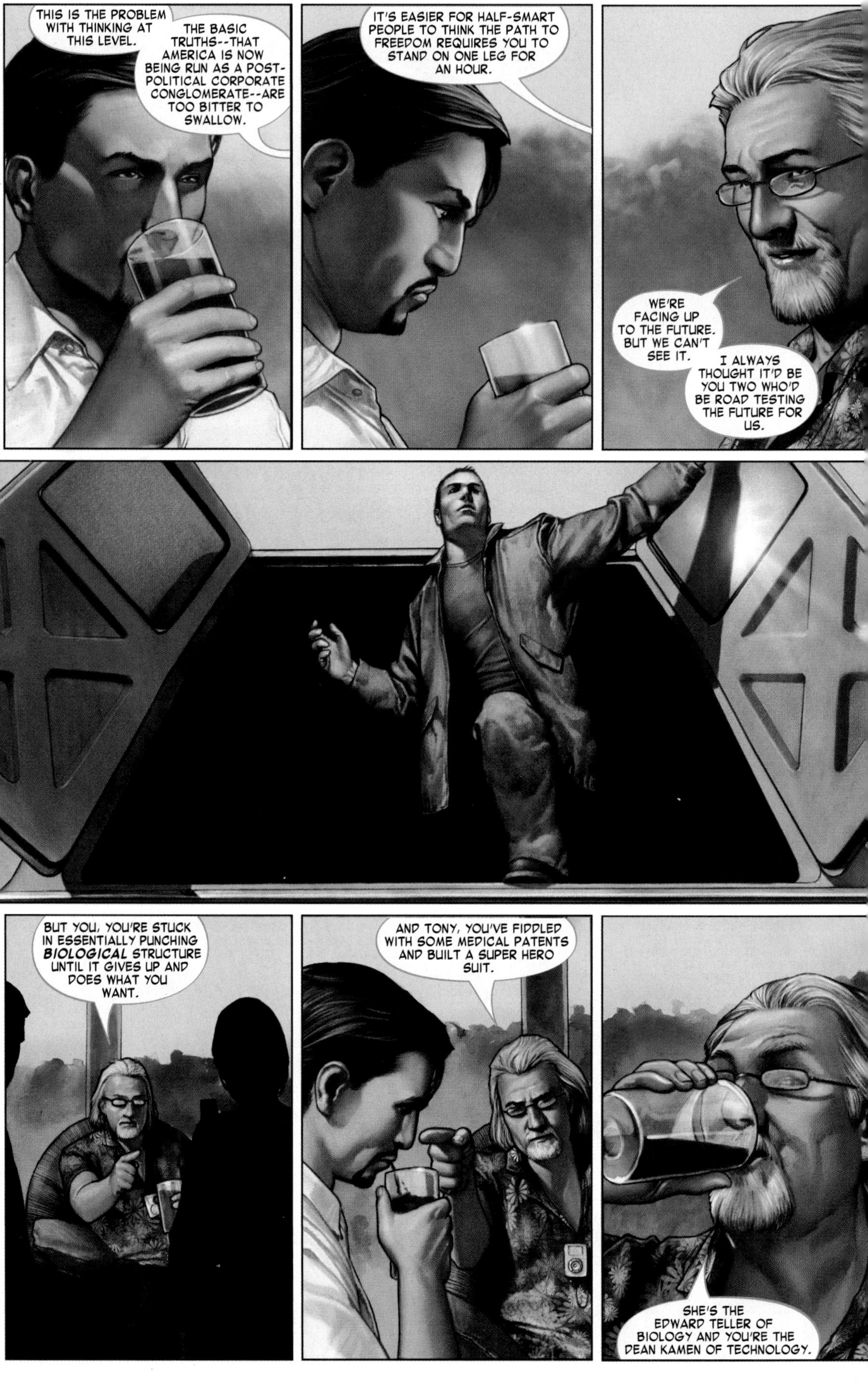
THIS IS THE PROBLEM WITH THINKING AT THIS LEVEL.
THE BASIC TRUTHS--THAT AMERICA IS NOW BEING RUN AS A POST-POLITICAL CORPORATE CONGLOMERATE--ARE TOO BITTER TO SWALLOW.
IT'S EASIER FOR HALF-SMART PEOPLE TO THINK THE PATH TO FREEDOM REQUIRES YOU TO STAND ON ONE LEG FOR AN HOUR.
WE'RE FACING UP TO THE FUTURE. BUT WE CAN'T SEE IT.
I ALWAYS THOUGHT IT'D BE YOU TWO WHO'D BE ROAD TESTING THE FUTURE FOR US.
BUT YOU, YOU'RE STUCK IN ESSENTIALLY PUNCHING *BIOLOGICAL* STRUCTURE UNTIL IT GIVES UP AND DOES WHAT YOU WANT.
AND TONY, YOU'VE FIDDLED WITH SOME MEDICAL PATENTS AND BUILT A SUPER HERO SUIT.
SHE'S THE EDWARD TELLER OF BIOLOGY AND YOU'RE THE DEAN KAMEN OF TECHNOLOGY.

THAT'S NOT FAIR. DEAN KAMEN'S DONE GOOD, USEFUL WORK.

YEAH, BUT HE ALSO MADE THE SEGWAY.

CLIVE SINCLAIR MADE BRITAIN A CENTER OF EXCELLENCE FOR CONSUMER MICROCOMPUTING, BUT ALL HE'S REMEMBERED FOR IS THE C5, WHICH WAS A SEGWAY WITH PEDALS.

YOU TWO ARE GOING TO YOUR GRAVES WITH THE EPITAPH "ALMOST USEFUL."

BUT THEN, SO AM I.

WHAT ARE YOU WORKING ON RIGHT NOW?

MOSTLY, I'M TAKING DRUGS. I SPEND MY DAYS COOKING DOWN ILLINOIS BUNDLEWEED INTO DMT AND RAISING MUSHROOMS.

YOU AND YOUR DAMN PSYCHEDELICS.

YOU NEVER WOULD DROP LSD, WOULD YOU?

I LIKED WHISKY BETTER.

GOOD FOR YOU. I'VE COME TO CONSIDER LSD AS ABRASIVELY PSYCHIATRIC.

IT REALLY JUST RERUNS ALL YOUR MEMORY STORES AT RANDOM. DMT AND MUSHROOMS ARE MUCH MORE INTERESTING AND ALIVE.

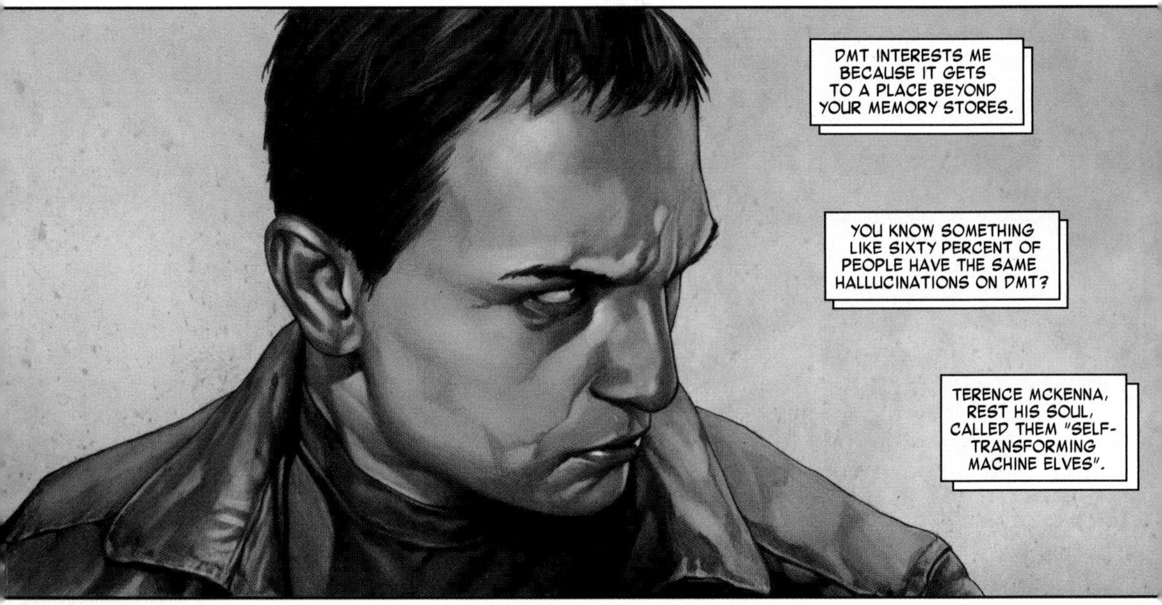
DMT INTERESTS ME BECAUSE IT GETS TO A PLACE BEYOND YOUR MEMORY STORES.
YOU KNOW SOMETHING LIKE SIXTY PERCENT OF PEOPLE HAVE THE SAME HALLUCINATIONS ON DMT?
TERENCE MCKENNA, REST HIS SOUL, CALLED THEM "SELF-TRANSFORMING MACHINE ELVES".

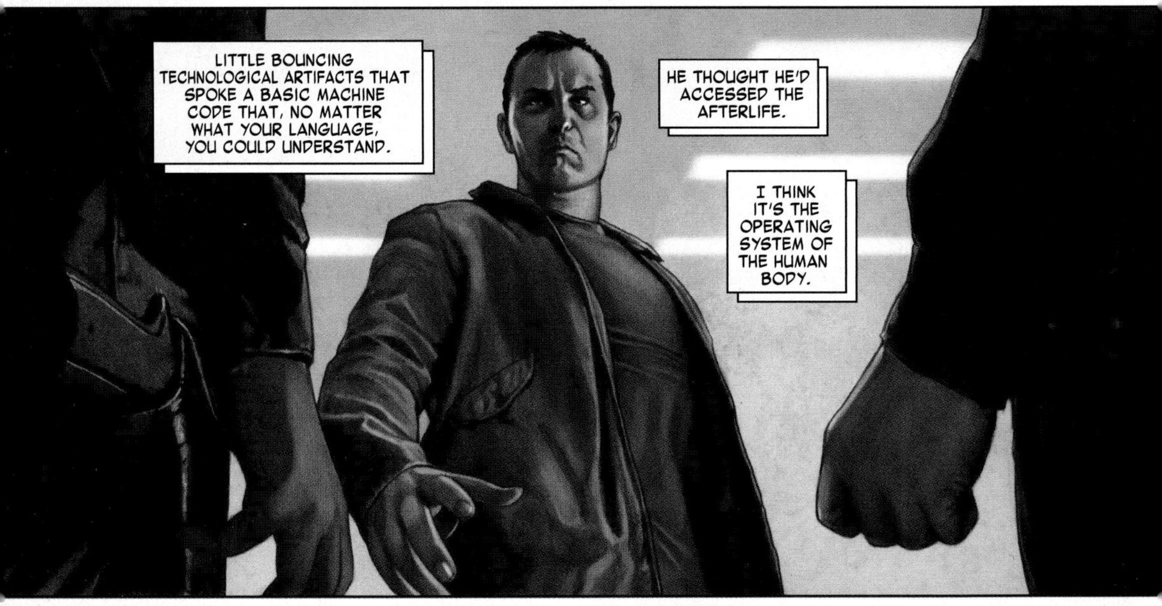
LITTLE BOUNCING TECHNOLOGICAL ARTIFACTS THAT SPOKE A BASIC MACHINE CODE THAT, NO MATTER WHAT YOUR LANGUAGE, YOU COULD UNDERSTAND.
HE THOUGHT HE'D ACCESSED THE AFTERLIFE.
I THINK IT'S THE OPERATING SYSTEM OF THE HUMAN BODY.

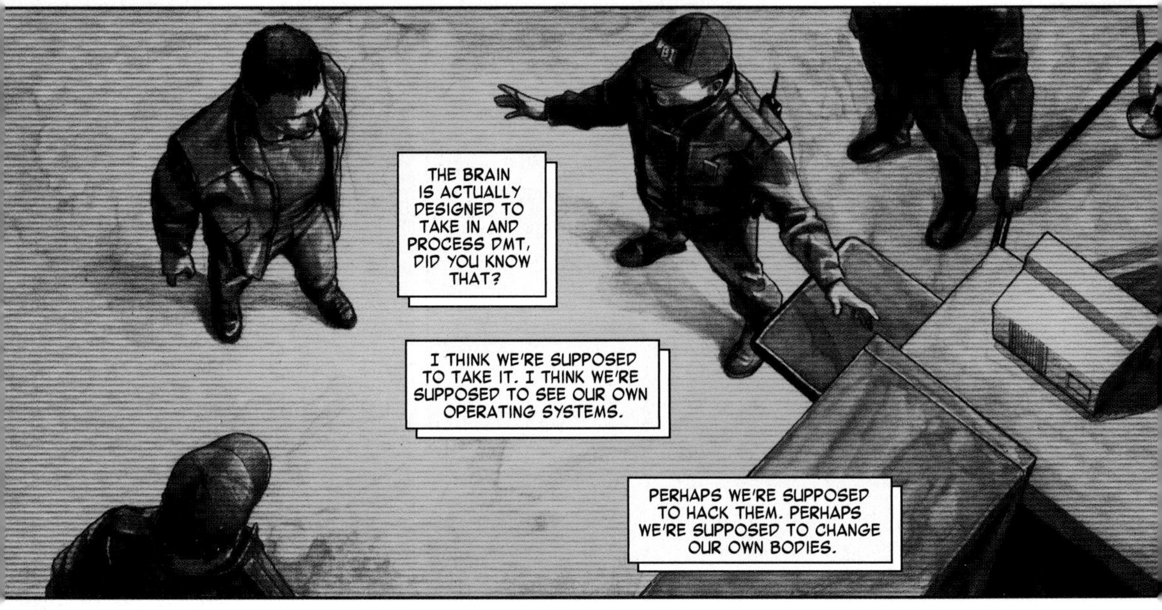
FBI
THE BRAIN IS ACTUALLY DESIGNED TO TAKE IN AND PROCESS DMT, DID YOU KNOW THAT?
I THINK WE'RE SUPPOSED TO TAKE IT. I THINK WE'RE SUPPOSED TO SEE OUR OWN OPERATING SYSTEMS.
PERHAPS WE'RE SUPPOSED TO HACK THEM. PERHAPS WE'RE SUPPOSED TO CHANGE OUR OWN BODIES.

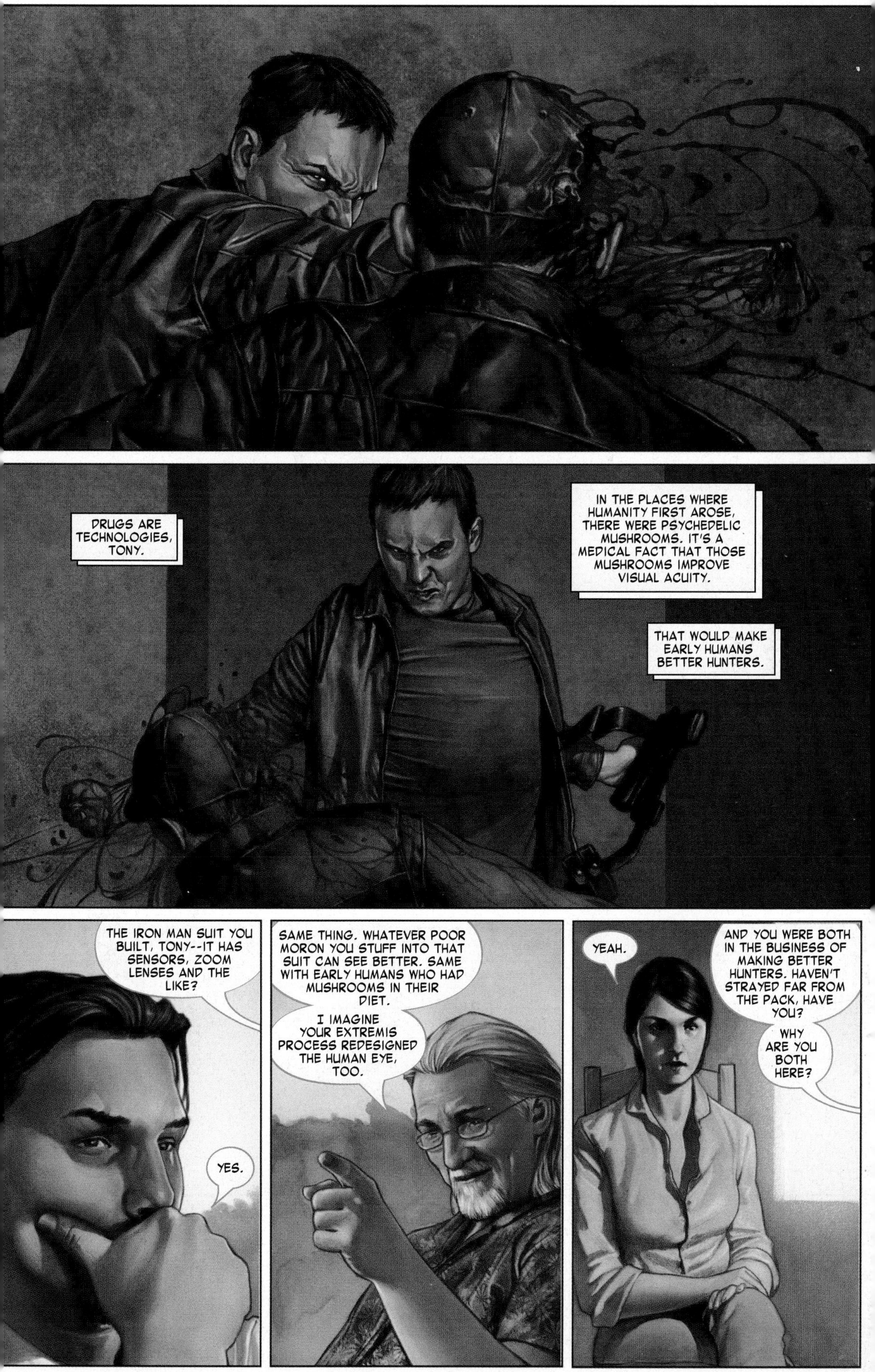

DRUGS ARE TECHNOLOGIES, TONY.
IN THE PLACES WHERE HUMANITY FIRST AROSE, THERE WERE PSYCHEDELIC MUSHROOMS. IT'S A MEDICAL FACT THAT THOSE MUSHROOMS IMPROVE VISUAL ACUITY.
THAT WOULD MAKE EARLY HUMANS BETTER HUNTERS.
THE IRON MAN SUIT YOU BUILT, TONY--IT HAS SENSORS, ZOOM LENSES AND THE LIKE?
YES.
SAME THING. WHATEVER POOR MORON YOU STUFF INTO THAT SUIT CAN SEE BETTER. SAME WITH EARLY HUMANS WHO HAD MUSHROOMS IN THEIR DIET.
I IMAGINE YOUR EXTREMIS PROCESS REDESIGNED THE HUMAN EYE, TOO.
YEAH.
AND YOU WERE BOTH IN THE BUSINESS OF MAKING BETTER HUNTERS. HAVEN'T STRAYED FAR FROM THE PACK, HAVE YOU?
WHY ARE YOU BOTH HERE?

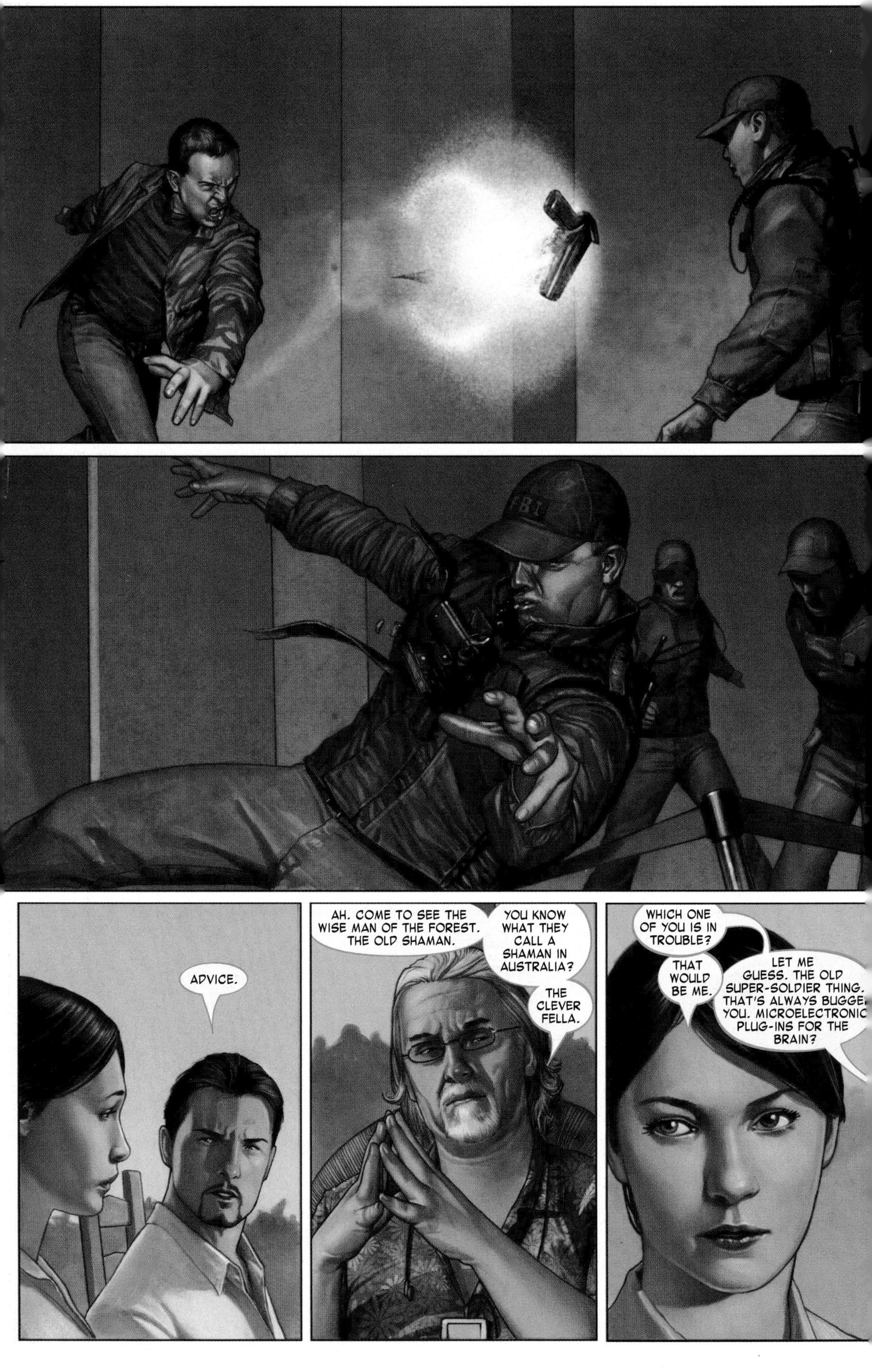
ADVICE.
AH. COME TO SEE THE WISE MAN OF THE FOREST. THE OLD SHAMAN.
YOU KNOW WHAT THEY CALL A SHAMAN IN AUSTRALIA?
THE CLEVER FELLA.
WHICH ONE OF YOU IS IN TROUBLE?
THAT WOULD BE ME.
LET ME GUESS. THE OLD SUPER-SOLDIER THING. THAT'S ALWAYS BUGGE YOU. MICROELECTRONIC PLUG-INS FOR THE BRAIN?

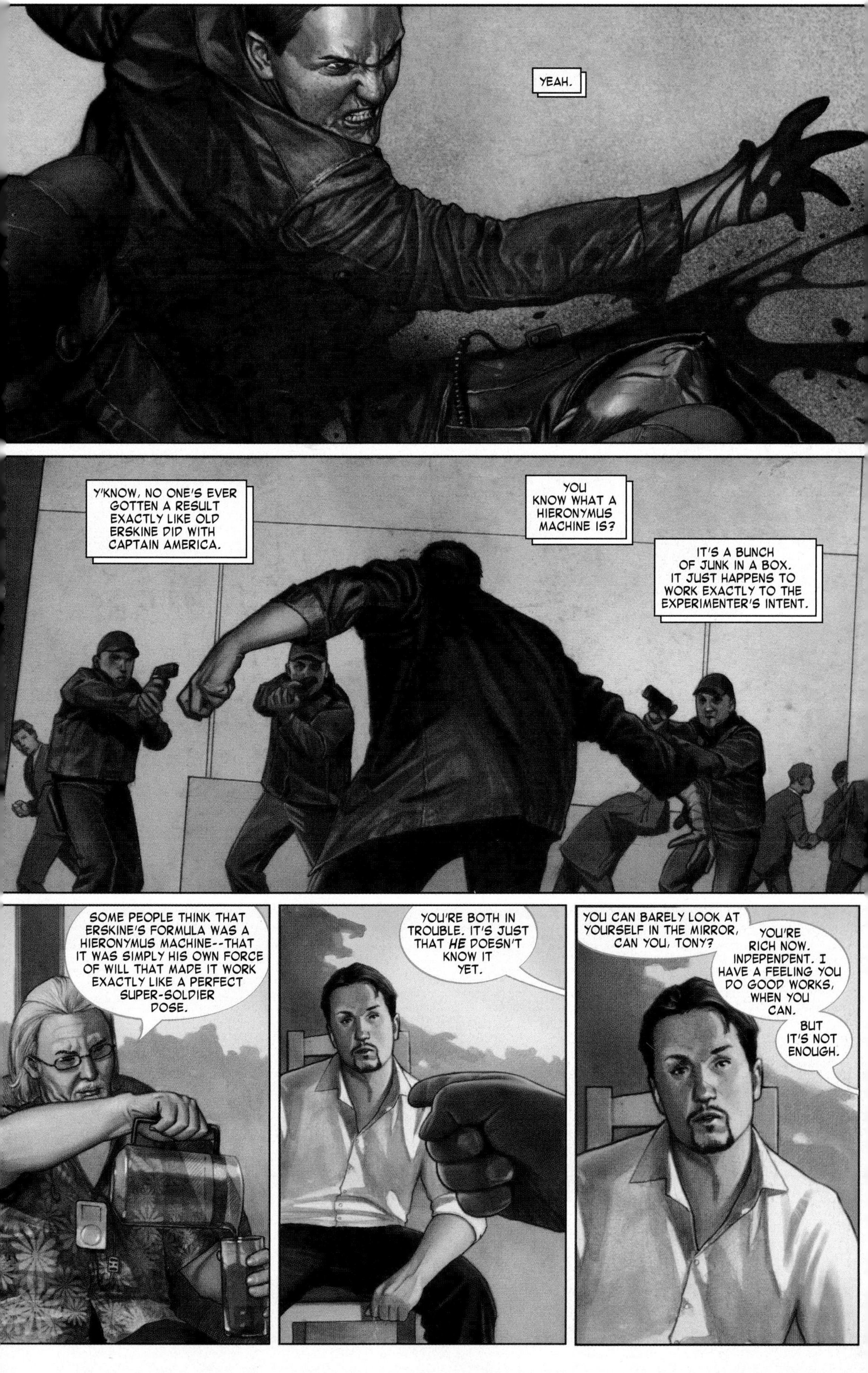
YEAH.
Y'KNOW, NO ONE'S EVER GOTTEN A RESULT EXACTLY LIKE OLD ERSKINE DID WITH CAPTAIN AMERICA.
YOU KNOW WHAT A HIERONYMUS MACHINE IS?
IT'S A BUNCH OF JUNK IN A BOX. IT JUST HAPPENS TO WORK EXACTLY TO THE EXPERIMENTER'S INTENT.
SOME PEOPLE THINK THAT ERSKINE'S FORMULA WAS A HIERONYMUS MACHINE--THAT IT WAS SIMPLY HIS OWN FORCE OF WILL THAT MADE IT WORK EXACTLY LIKE A PERFECT SUPER-SOLDIER DOSE.
YOU'RE BOTH IN TROUBLE. IT'S JUST THAT *HE* DOESN'T KNOW IT YET.
YOU CAN BARELY LOOK AT YOURSELF IN THE MIRROR, CAN YOU, TONY?
YOU'RE RICH NOW. INDEPENDENT. I HAVE A FEELING YOU DO GOOD WORKS, WHEN YOU CAN.
BUT IT'S NOT ENOUGH.

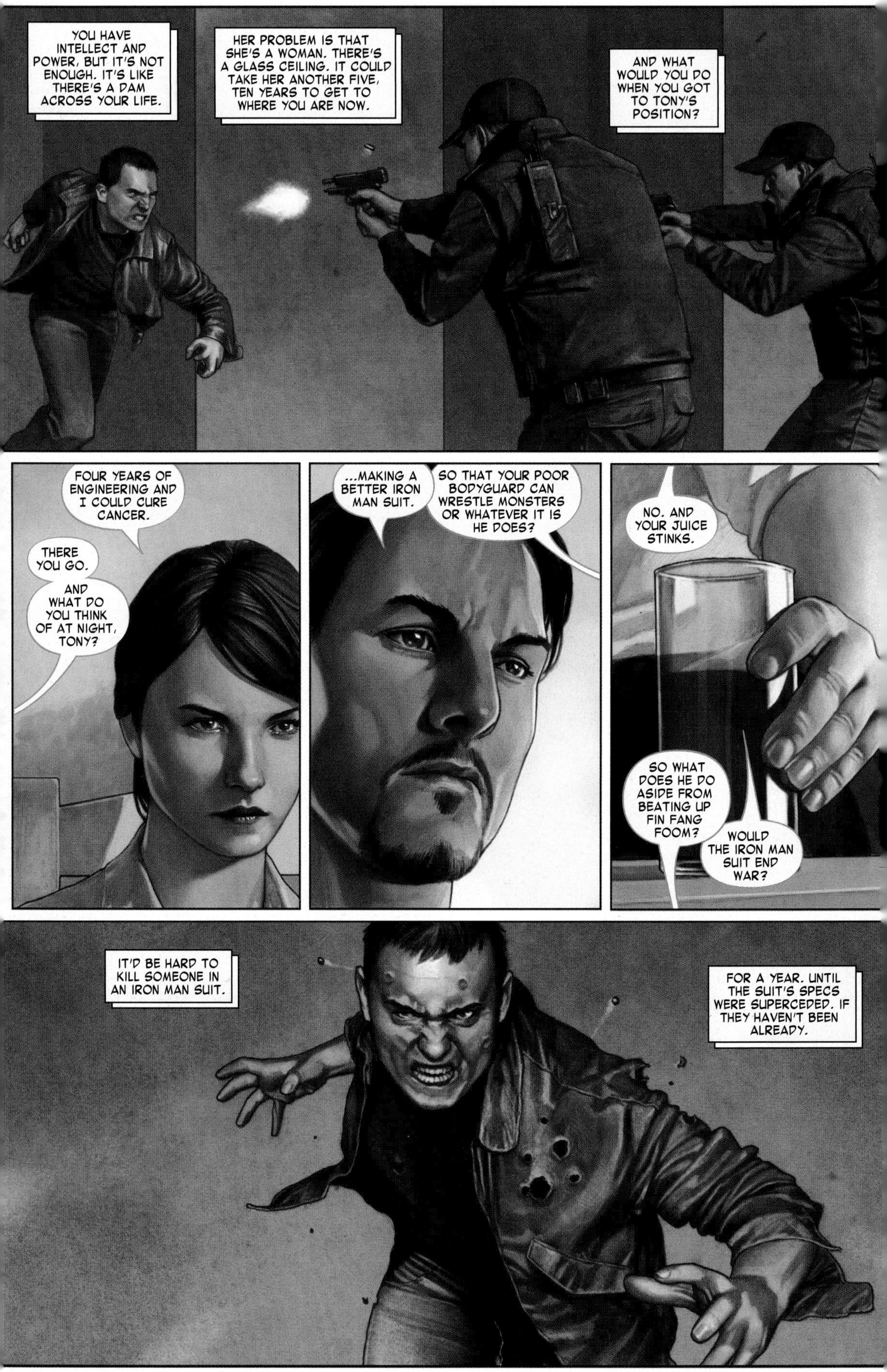
YOU HAVE INTELLECT AND POWER, BUT IT'S NOT ENOUGH. IT'S LIKE THERE'S A DAM ACROSS YOUR LIFE.
HER PROBLEM IS THAT SHE'S A WOMAN. THERE'S A GLASS CEILING. IT COULD TAKE HER ANOTHER FIVE, TEN YEARS TO GET TO WHERE YOU ARE NOW.
AND WHAT WOULD YOU DO WHEN YOU GOT TO TONY'S POSITION?
FOUR YEARS OF ENGINEERING AND I COULD CURE CANCER.
THERE YOU GO.
AND WHAT DO YOU THINK OF AT NIGHT, TONY?
...MAKING A BETTER IRON MAN SUIT.
SO THAT YOUR POOR BODYGUARD CAN WRESTLE MONSTERS OR WHATEVER IT IS HE DOES?
NO. AND YOUR JUICE STINKS.
SO WHAT DOES HE DO ASIDE FROM BEATING UP FIN FANG FOOM?
WOULD THE IRON MAN SUIT END WAR?
IT'D BE HARD TO KILL SOMEONE IN AN IRON MAN SUIT.
FOR A YEAR. UNTIL THE SUIT'S SPECS WERE SUPERCEDED. IF THEY HAVEN'T BEEN ALREADY.

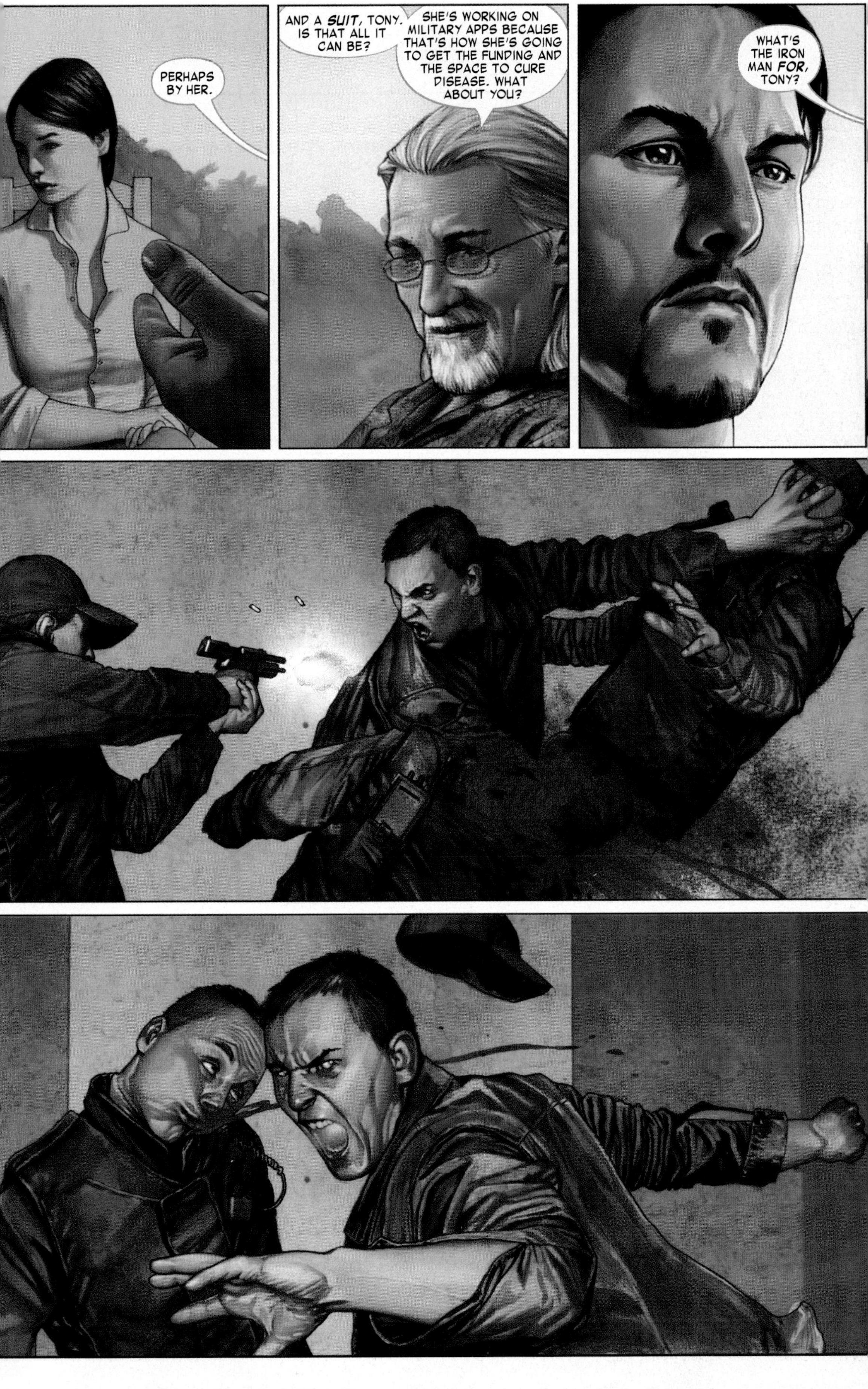
PERHAPS BY HER.
AND A SUIT, TONY. IS THAT ALL IT CAN BE?
SHE'S WORKING ON MILITARY APPS BECAUSE THAT'S HOW SHE'S GOING TO GET THE FUNDING AND THE SPACE TO CURE DISEASE. WHAT ABOUT YOU?
WHAT'S THE IRON MAN FOR, TONY?

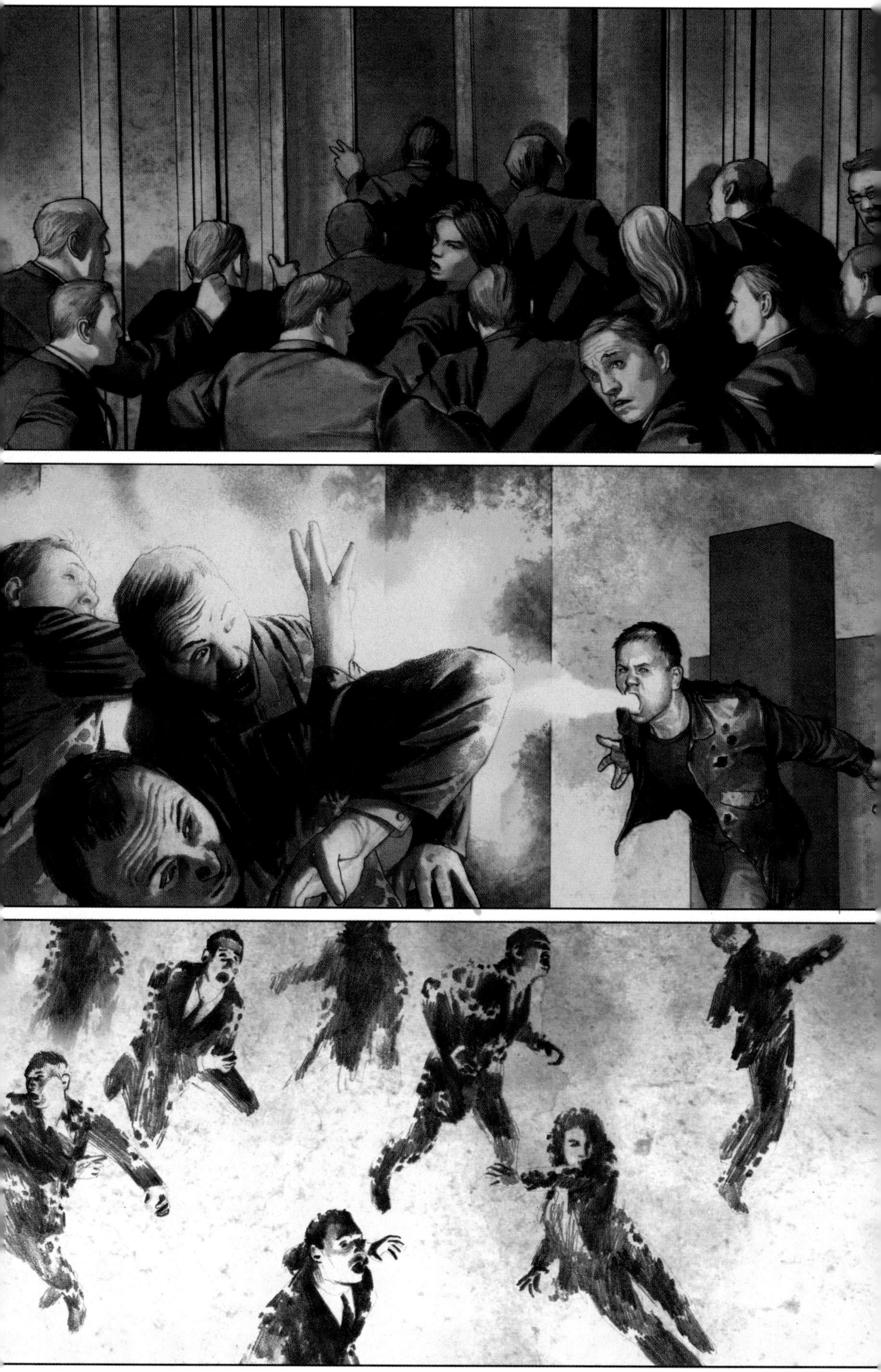

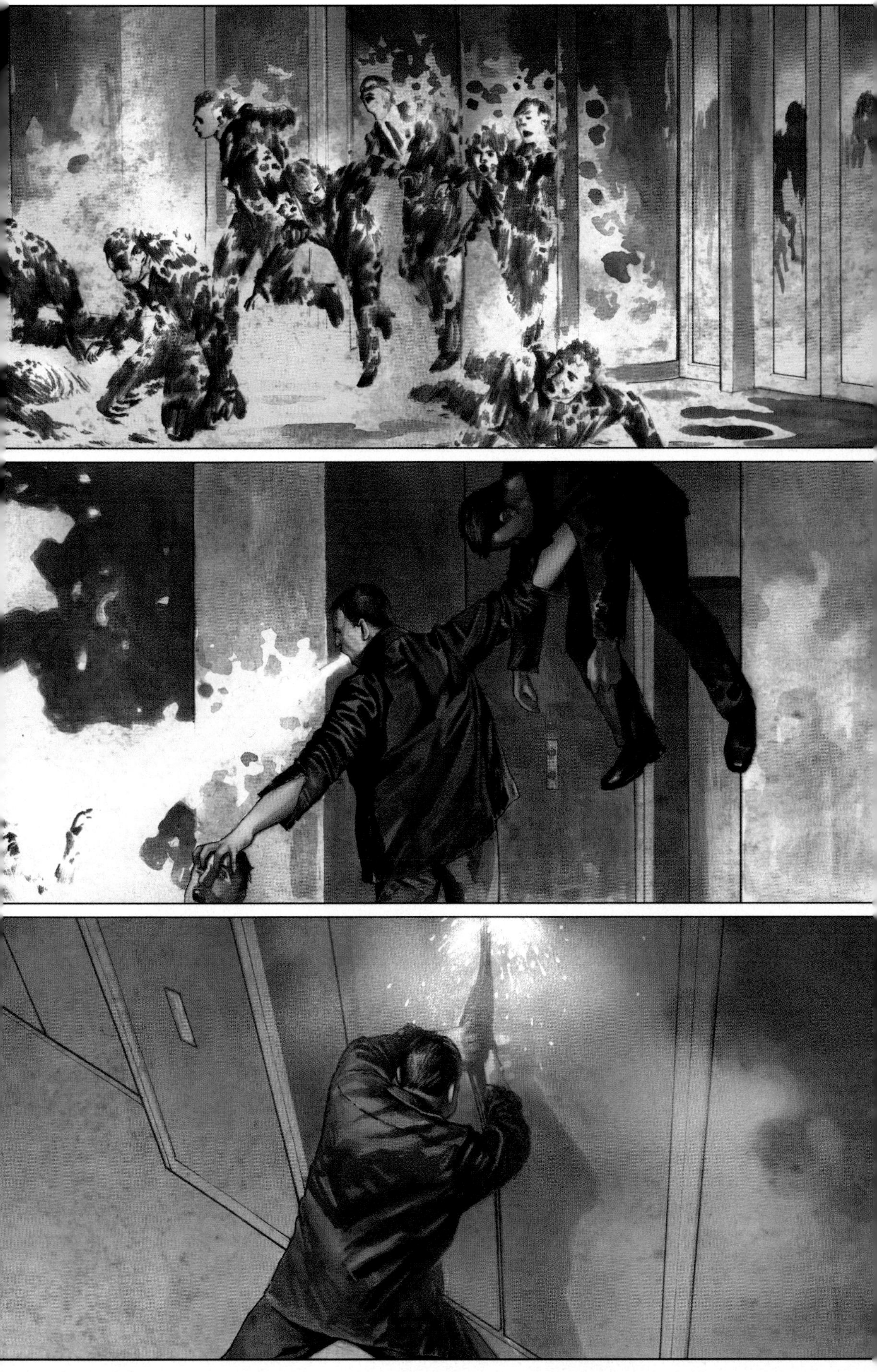

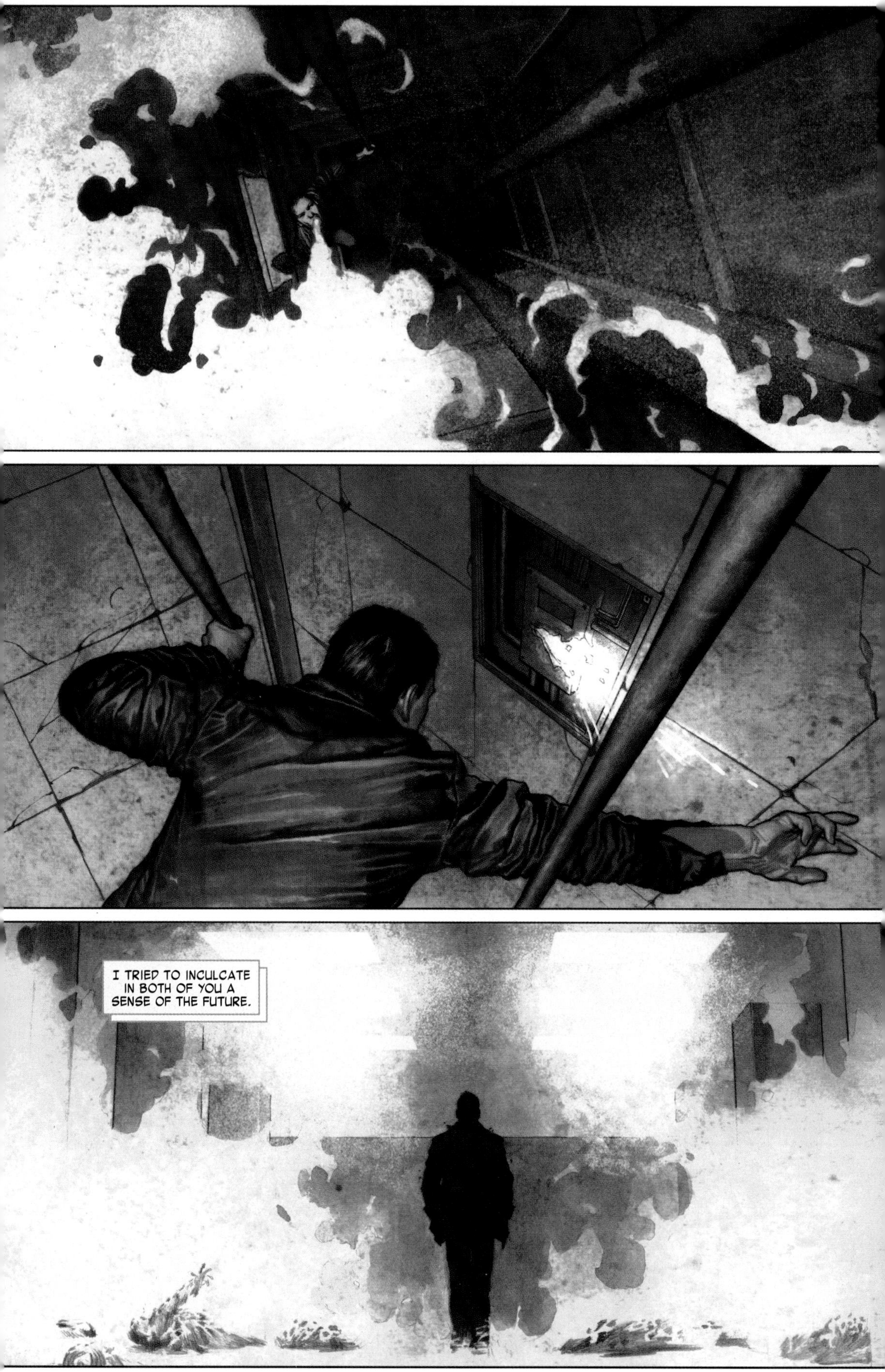
I TRIED TO INCULCATE IN BOTH OF YOU A SENSE OF THE FUTURE.

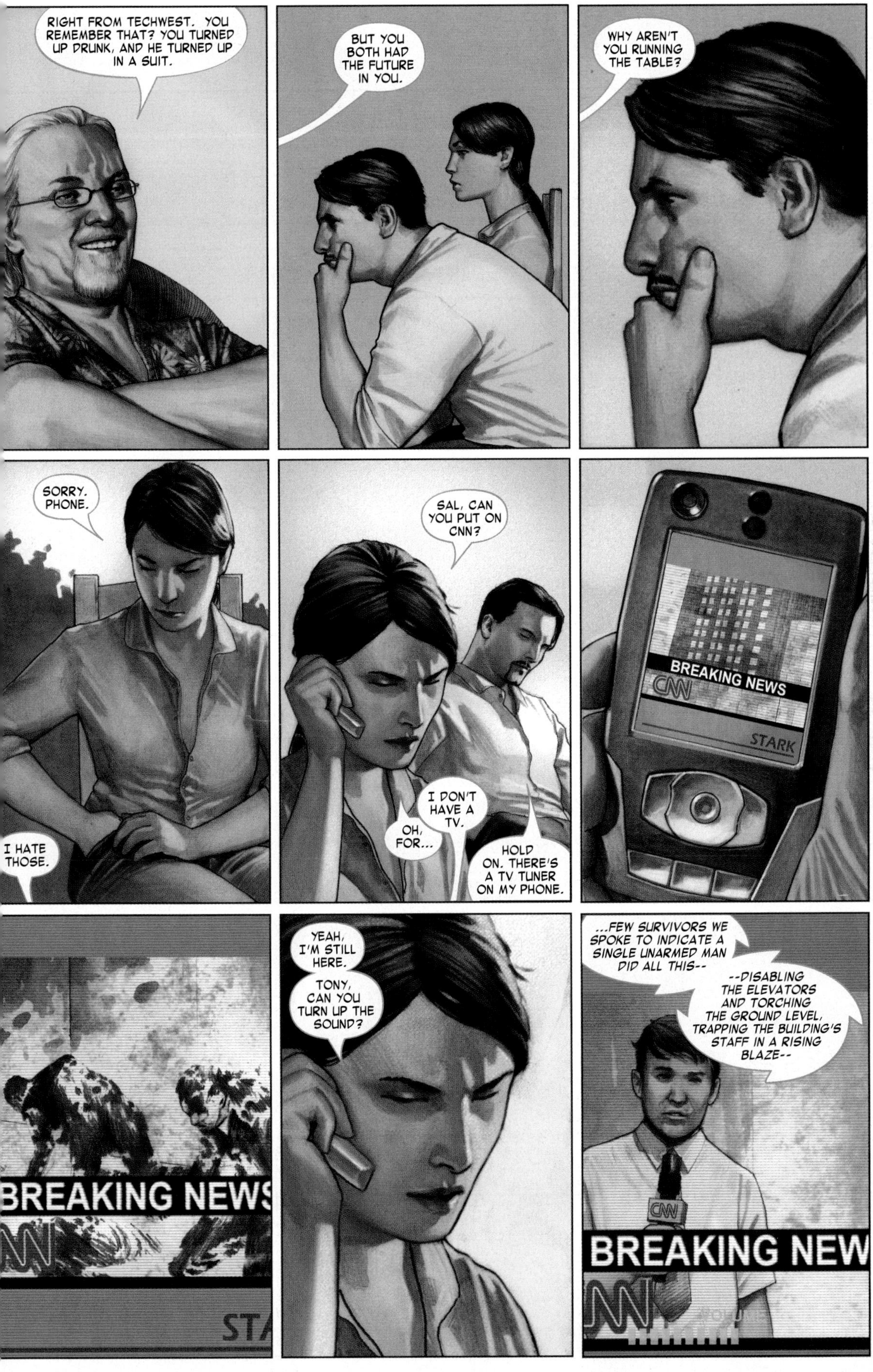
RIGHT FROM TECHWEST. YOU REMEMBER THAT? YOU TURNED UP DRUNK, AND HE TURNED UP IN A SUIT.
BUT YOU BOTH HAD THE FUTURE IN YOU.
WHY AREN'T YOU RUNNING THE TABLE?
SORRY. PHONE.
I HATE THOSE.
SAL, CAN YOU PUT ON CNN?
I DON'T HAVE A TV.
OH, FOR...
HOLD ON. THERE'S A TV TUNER ON MY PHONE.
BREAKING NEWS
CNN
STARK
BREAKING NEWS
STA
YEAH, I'M STILL HERE.
TONY, CAN YOU TURN UP THE SOUND?
...FEW SURVIVORS WE SPOKE TO INDICATE A SINGLE UNARMED MAN DID ALL THIS--
--DISABLING THE ELEVATORS AND TORCHING THE GROUND LEVEL, TRAPPING THE BUILDING'S STAFF IN A RISING BLAZE--
CNN
BREAKING NEW

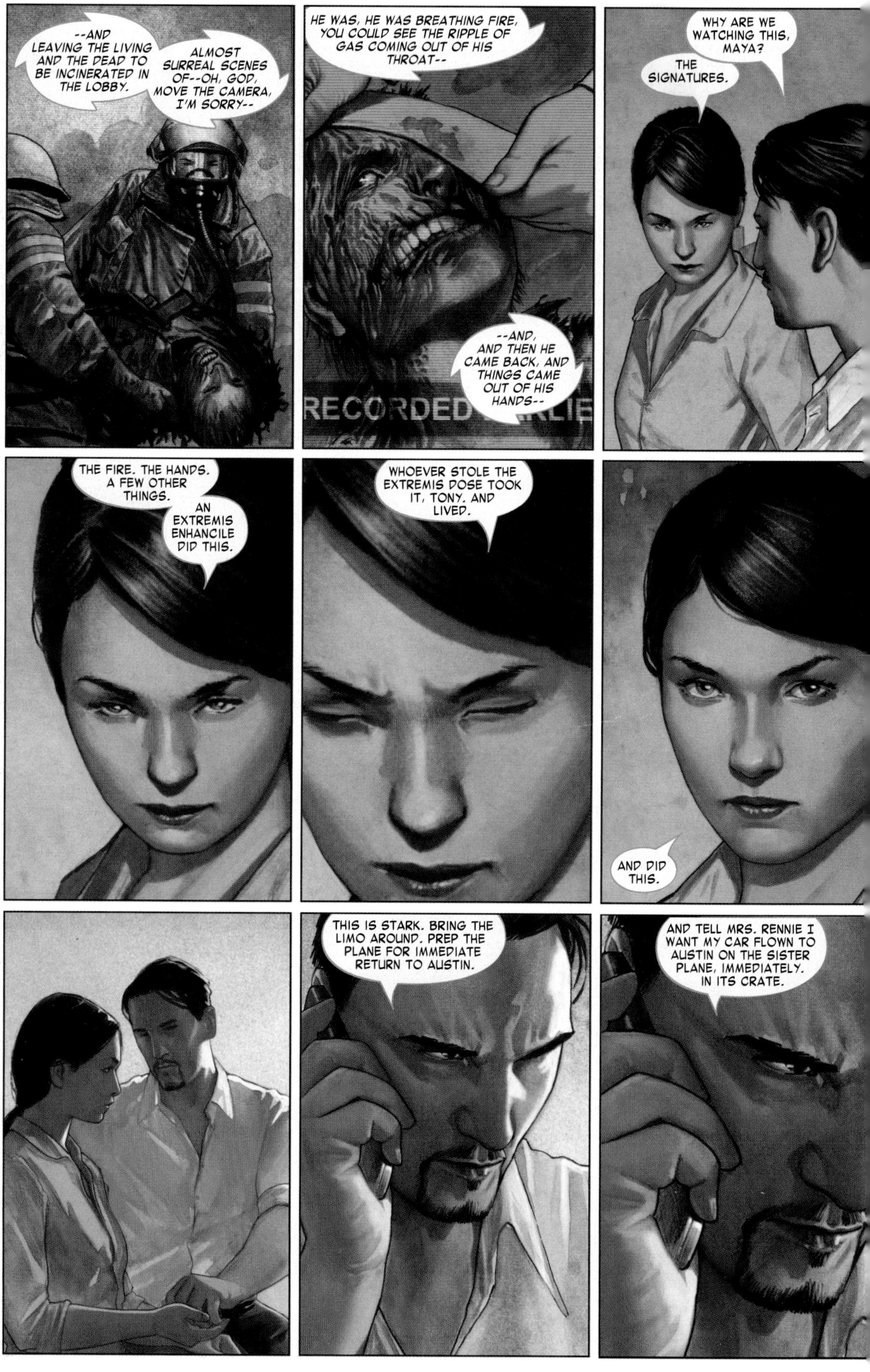
--AND LEAVING THE LIVING AND THE DEAD TO BE INCINERATED IN THE LOBBY.
ALMOST SURREAL SCENES OF--OH, GOD, MOVE THE CAMERA, I'M SORRY--
HE WAS, HE WAS BREATHING FIRE, YOU COULD SEE THE RIPPLE OF GAS COMING OUT OF HIS THROAT--
--AND, AND THEN HE CAME BACK, AND THINGS CAME OUT OF HIS HANDS--
RECORDED
WHY ARE WE WATCHING THIS, MAYA?
THE SIGNATURES.
THE FIRE. THE HANDS. A FEW OTHER THINGS.
AN EXTREMIS ENHANCILE DID THIS.
WHOEVER STOLE THE EXTREMIS DOSE TOOK IT, TONY. AND LIVED.
AND DID THIS.
THIS IS STARK. BRING THE LIMO AROUND. PREP THE PLANE FOR IMMEDIATE RETURN TO AUSTIN.
AND TELL MRS. RENNIE I WANT MY CAR FLOWN TO AUSTIN ON THE SISTER PLANE, IMMEDIATELY. IN ITS CRATE.

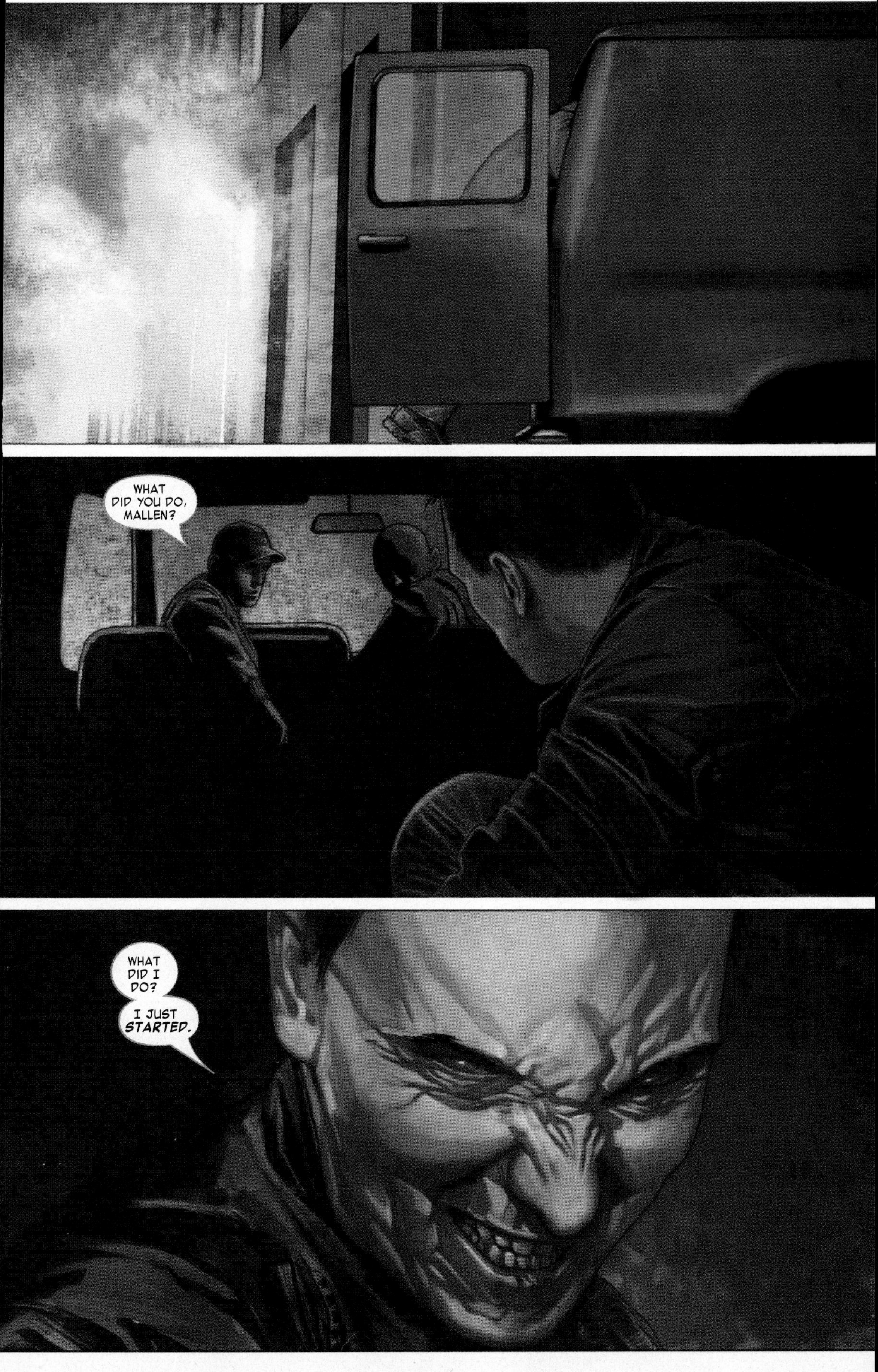
WHAT DID YOU DO, MALLEN?
WHAT DID I DO?
I JUST STARTED.

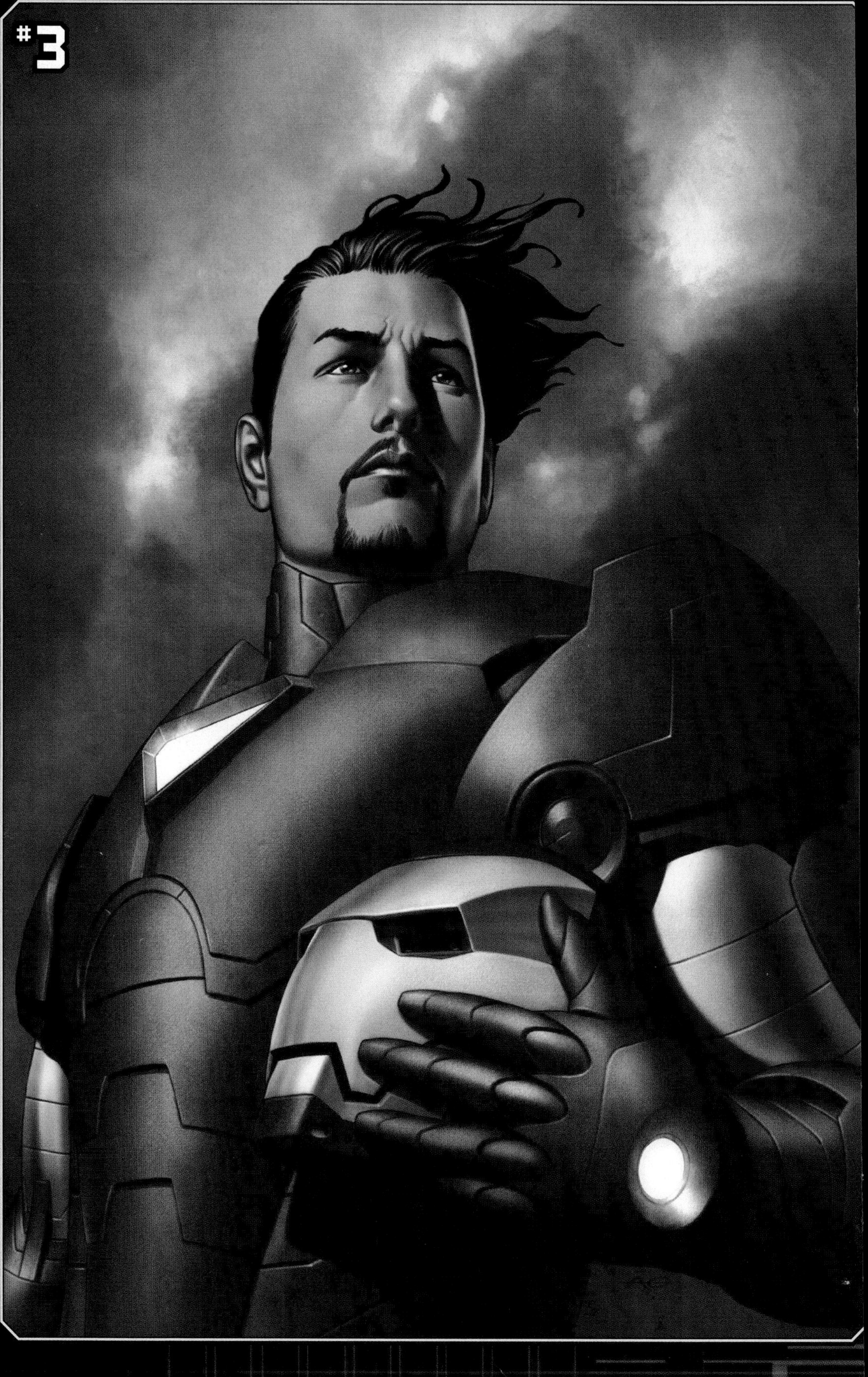
#3

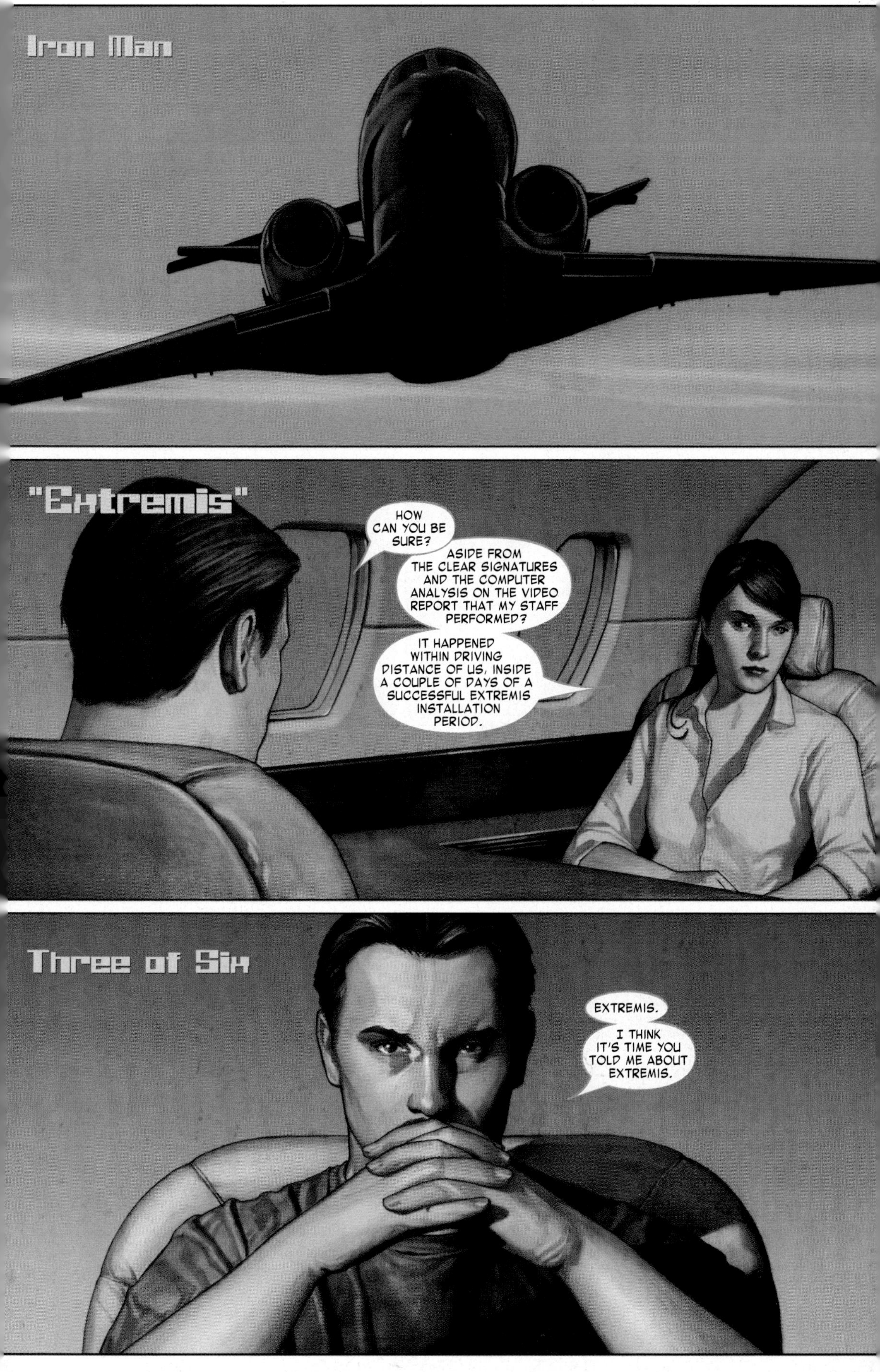
Iron Man
"Extremis"
HOW CAN YOU BE SURE?
ASIDE FROM THE CLEAR SIGNATURES AND THE COMPUTER ANALYSIS ON THE VIDEO REPORT THAT MY STAFF PERFORMED?
IT HAPPENED WITHIN DRIVING DISTANCE OF US, INSIDE A COUPLE OF DAYS OF A SUCCESSFUL EXTREMIS INSTALLATION PERIOD.
Three of Six
EXTREMIS.
I THINK IT'S TIME YOU TOLD ME ABOUT EXTREMIS.

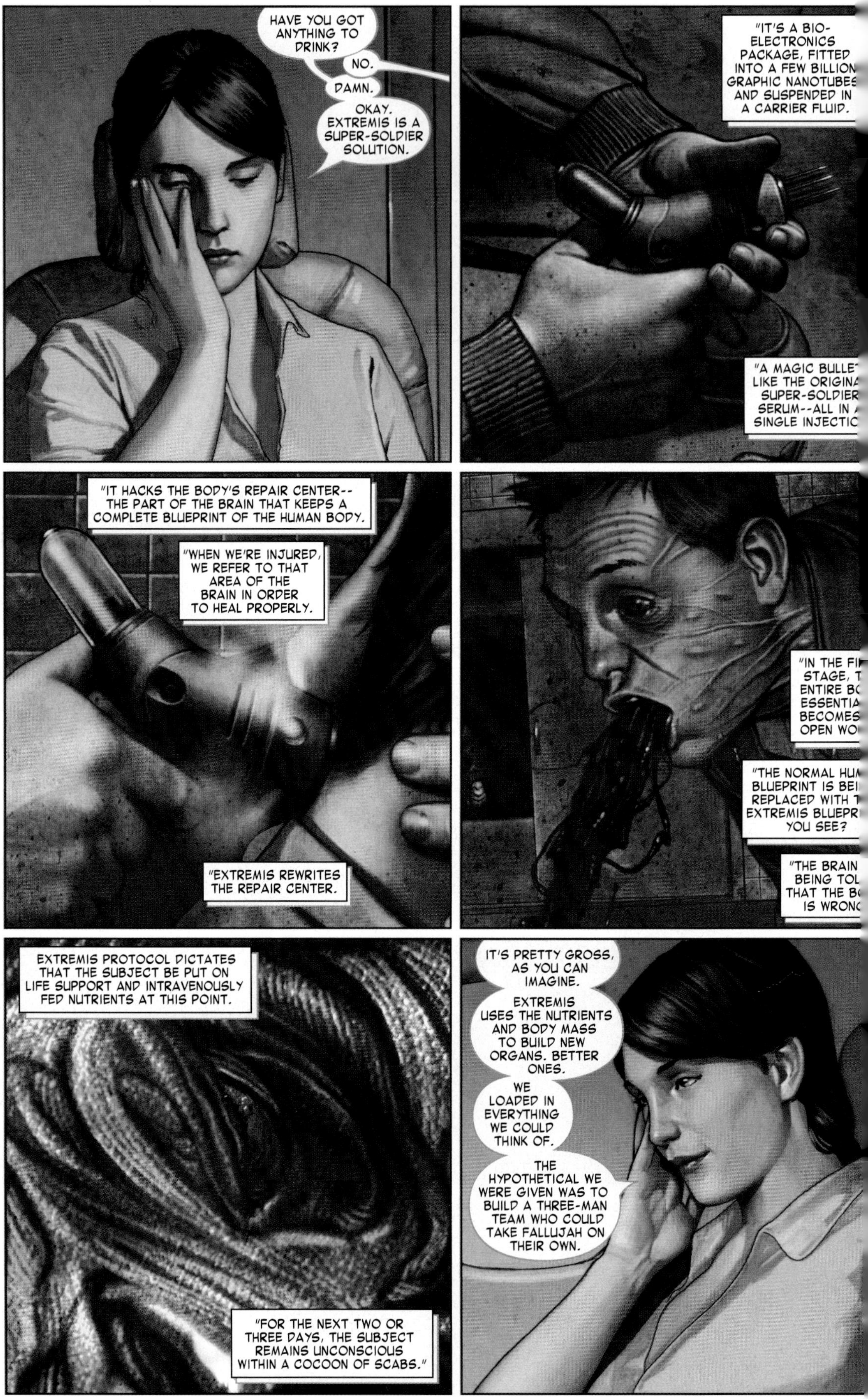
HAVE YOU GOT ANYTHING TO DRINK?
NO.
DAMN.
OKAY. EXTREMIS IS A SUPER-SOLDIER SOLUTION.
"IT'S A BIO-ELECTRONICS PACKAGE, FITTED INTO A FEW BILLION GRAPHIC NANOTUBES AND SUSPENDED IN A CARRIER FLUID.
"A MAGIC BULLET LIKE THE ORIGINA SUPER-SOLDIER SERUM--ALL IN A SINGLE INJECTIO
"IT HACKS THE BODY'S REPAIR CENTER-- THE PART OF THE BRAIN THAT KEEPS A COMPLETE BLUEPRINT OF THE HUMAN BODY.
"WHEN WE'RE INJURED, WE REFER TO THAT AREA OF THE BRAIN IN ORDER TO HEAL PROPERLY.
"EXTREMIS REWRITES THE REPAIR CENTER.
"IN THE FI STAGE, T ENTIRE BO ESSENTIA BECOMES OPEN WO
"THE NORMAL HUM BLUEPRINT IS BEI REPLACED WITH T EXTREMIS BLUEPR YOU SEE?
"THE BRAIN BEING TOL THAT THE BO IS WRONG
EXTREMIS PROTOCOL DICTATES THAT THE SUBJECT BE PUT ON LIFE SUPPORT AND INTRAVENOUSLY FED NUTRIENTS AT THIS POINT.
"FOR THE NEXT TWO OR THREE DAYS, THE SUBJECT REMAINS UNCONSCIOUS WITHIN A COCOON OF SCABS."
IT'S PRETTY GROSS, AS YOU CAN IMAGINE.
EXTREMIS USES THE NUTRIENTS AND BODY MASS TO BUILD NEW ORGANS. BETTER ONES.
WE LOADED IN EVERYTHING WE COULD THINK OF.
THE HYPOTHETICAL WE WERE GIVEN WAS TO BUILD A THREE-MAN TEAM WHO COULD TAKE FALLUJAH ON THEIR OWN.

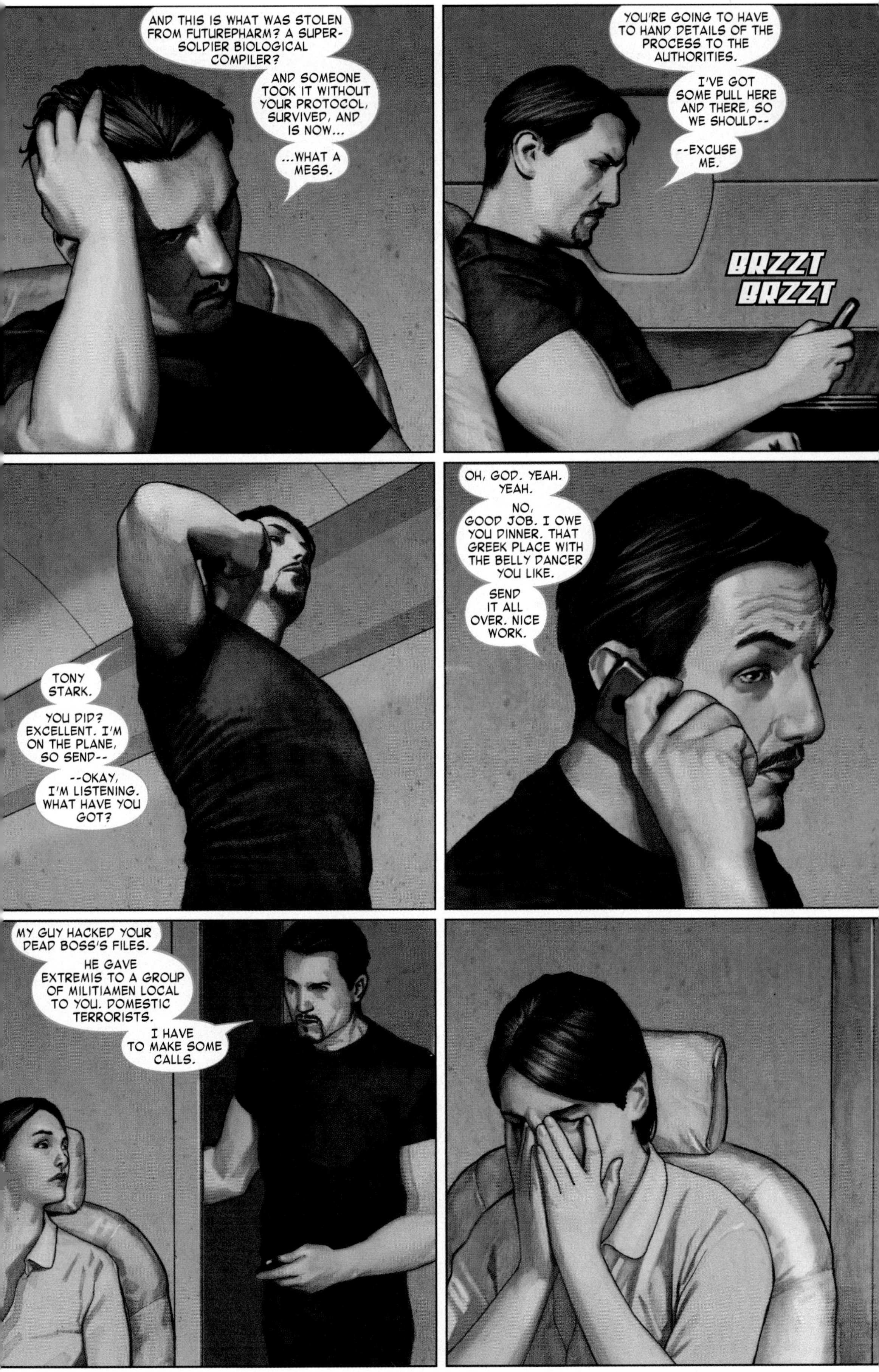
AND THIS IS WHAT WAS STOLEN FROM FUTUREPHARM? A SUPER-SOLDIER BIOLOGICAL COMPILER?
AND SOMEONE TOOK IT WITHOUT YOUR PROTOCOL, SURVIVED, AND IS NOW...
...WHAT A MESS.
YOU'RE GOING TO HAVE TO HAND DETAILS OF THE PROCESS TO THE AUTHORITIES.
I'VE GOT SOME PULL HERE AND THERE, SO WE SHOULD--
--EXCUSE ME.
BRZZT
BRZZT
TONY STARK.
YOU DID? EXCELLENT. I'M ON THE PLANE, SO SEND--
--OKAY, I'M LISTENING. WHAT HAVE YOU GOT?
OH, GOD. YEAH. YEAH.
NO, GOOD JOB. I OWE YOU DINNER. THAT GREEK PLACE WITH THE BELLY DANCER YOU LIKE.
SEND IT ALL OVER. NICE WORK.
MY GUY HACKED YOUR DEAD BOSS'S FILES.
HE GAVE EXTREMIS TO A GROUP OF MILITIAMEN LOCAL TO YOU. DOMESTIC TERRORISTS.
I HAVE TO MAKE SOME CALLS.

AVENGERS LIAISON CHANNEL. PRIORITY A-1. IRON MAN.

INFORMATION REGARDING ATTACK ON F.B.I. STATION, HOUSTON.

FORWARD TO ALL RELEVANT LAW ENFORCEMENT ENTITIES.

UPLOAD OF RELATED FILES TO FOLLOW TWO MINUTES BEHIND THIS MESSAGE.

PERPETRATOR IS IN SUPERHUMAN ASPECT, POSSIBLY SUFFERING SIDE-EFFECTS OF PROCESS.

PERPETRATOR AND ASSOCIATES LIKELY TO BE IN TRANSIT FROM HOUSTON TO BASTROP AT THIS TIME.

DETAILS OF SUPERHUMAN ASPECT PENDING AT THIS TIME.

IRON MAN REMOTE WARM-UP SEQUENCE ENGAGED...

IRON MAN IS AVAILABLE FOR INTERCEPT AND ENGAGEMENT.

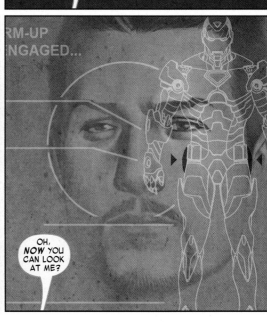

RM-UP NGAGED...

OH, NOW YOU CAN LOOK AT ME?

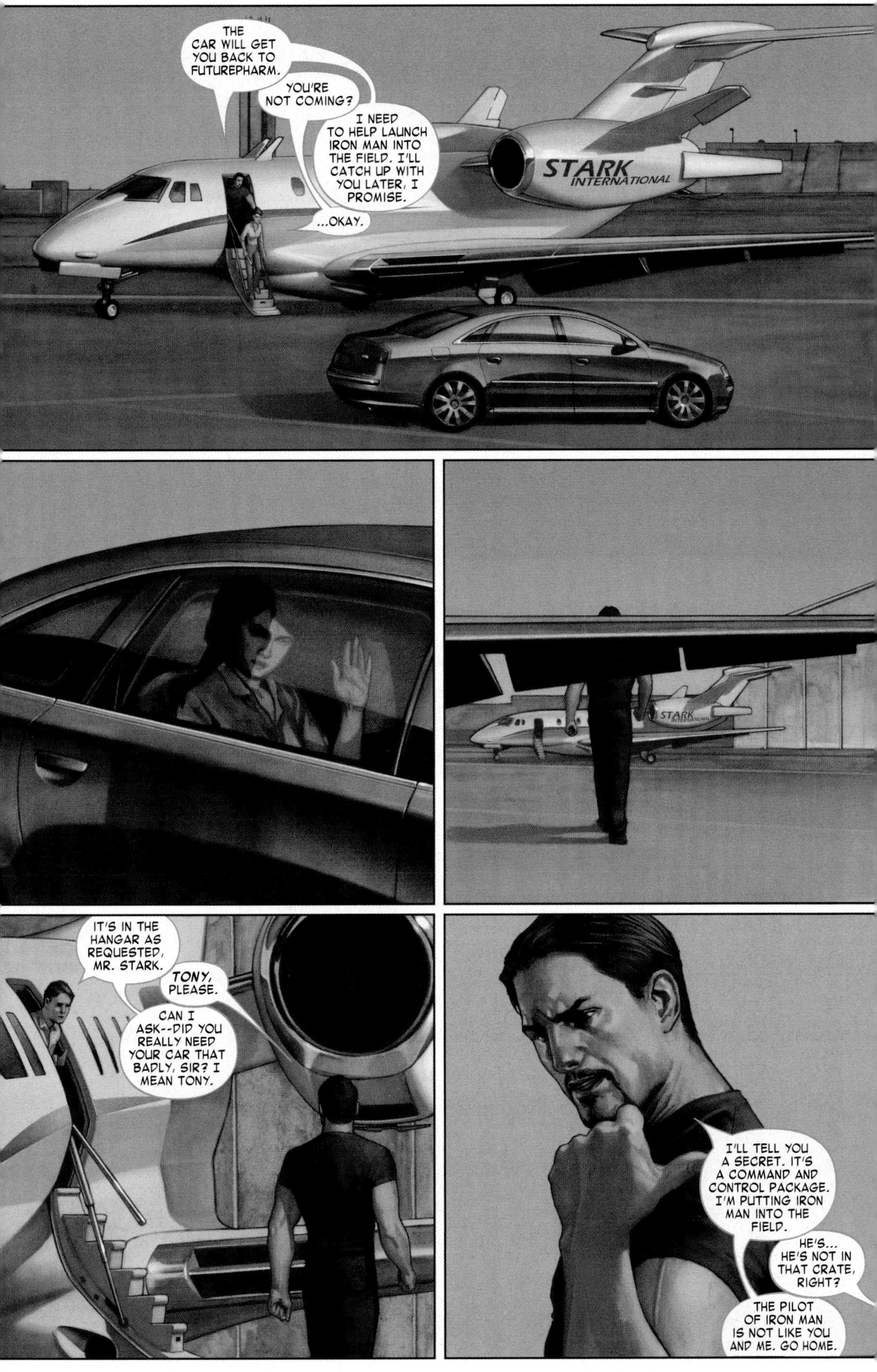
THE CAR WILL GET YOU BACK TO FUTUREPHARM.
YOU'RE NOT COMING?
I NEED TO HELP LAUNCH IRON MAN INTO THE FIELD. I'LL CATCH UP WITH YOU LATER, I PROMISE.
...OKAY.
STARK INTERNATIONAL
STARK INTERNATIONAL
IT'S IN THE HANGAR AS REQUESTED, MR. STARK.
TONY, PLEASE.
CAN I ASK--DID YOU REALLY NEED YOUR CAR THAT BADLY, SIR? I MEAN TONY.
I'LL TELL YOU A SECRET. IT'S A COMMAND AND CONTROL PACKAGE. I'M PUTTING IRON MAN INTO THE FIELD.
HE'S... HE'S NOT IN THAT CRATE, RIGHT?
THE PILOT OF IRON MAN IS NOT LIKE YOU AND ME. GO HOME.

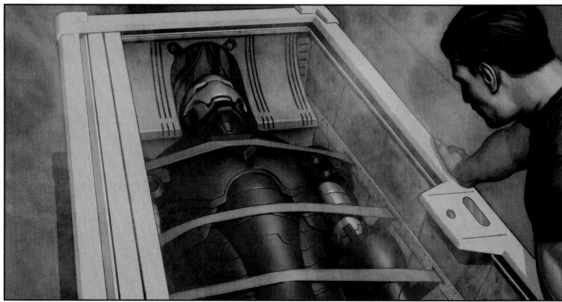

I MUST BE CRAZY.

OKAY. FOR MY NEXT TRICK: SNEAKING OUT OF A HANGAR AND LAUNCHING WITHOUT ANYONE NOTICING.

I TRY TO BUY THE MORE REMOTE HANGARS, BUT THERE'S ALWAYS SOME KID WITH A DIGITAL CAMERA.

USUALLY A STARK CAMERA.

NO. FOR MY NEXT TRICK: LOCKING THE DAMN DOOR SO NO ONE ACCIDENTALLY GETS TO SEE IRON MAN BUTT NAKED.

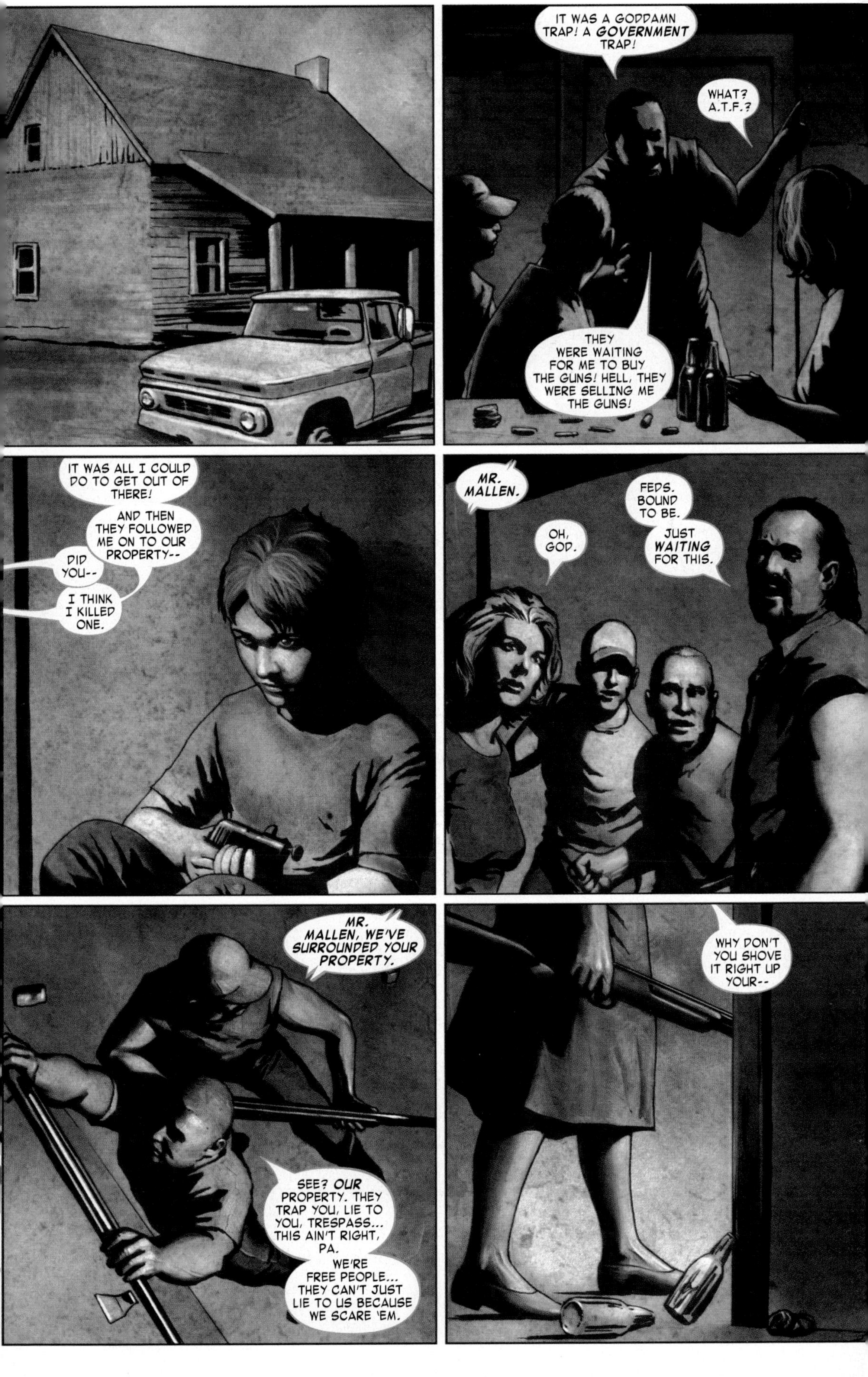
IT WAS A GODDAMN TRAP! A GOVERNMENT TRAP!
WHAT? A.T.F.?
THEY WERE WAITING FOR ME TO BUY THE GUNS! HELL, THEY WERE SELLING ME THE GUNS!
IT WAS ALL I COULD DO TO GET OUT OF THERE!
AND THEN THEY FOLLOWED ME ON TO OUR PROPERTY--
DID YOU--
I THINK I KILLED ONE.
MR. MALLEN.
OH, GOD.
FEDS. BOUND TO BE.
JUST WAITING FOR THIS.
MR. MALLEN, WE'VE SURROUNDED YOUR PROPERTY.
SEE? OUR PROPERTY. THEY TRAP YOU, LIE TO YOU, TRESPASS... THIS AIN'T RIGHT, PA.
WE'RE FREE PEOPLE... THEY CAN'T JUST LIE TO US BECAUSE WE SCARE 'EM.
WHY DON'T YOU SHOVE IT RIGHT UP YOUR--

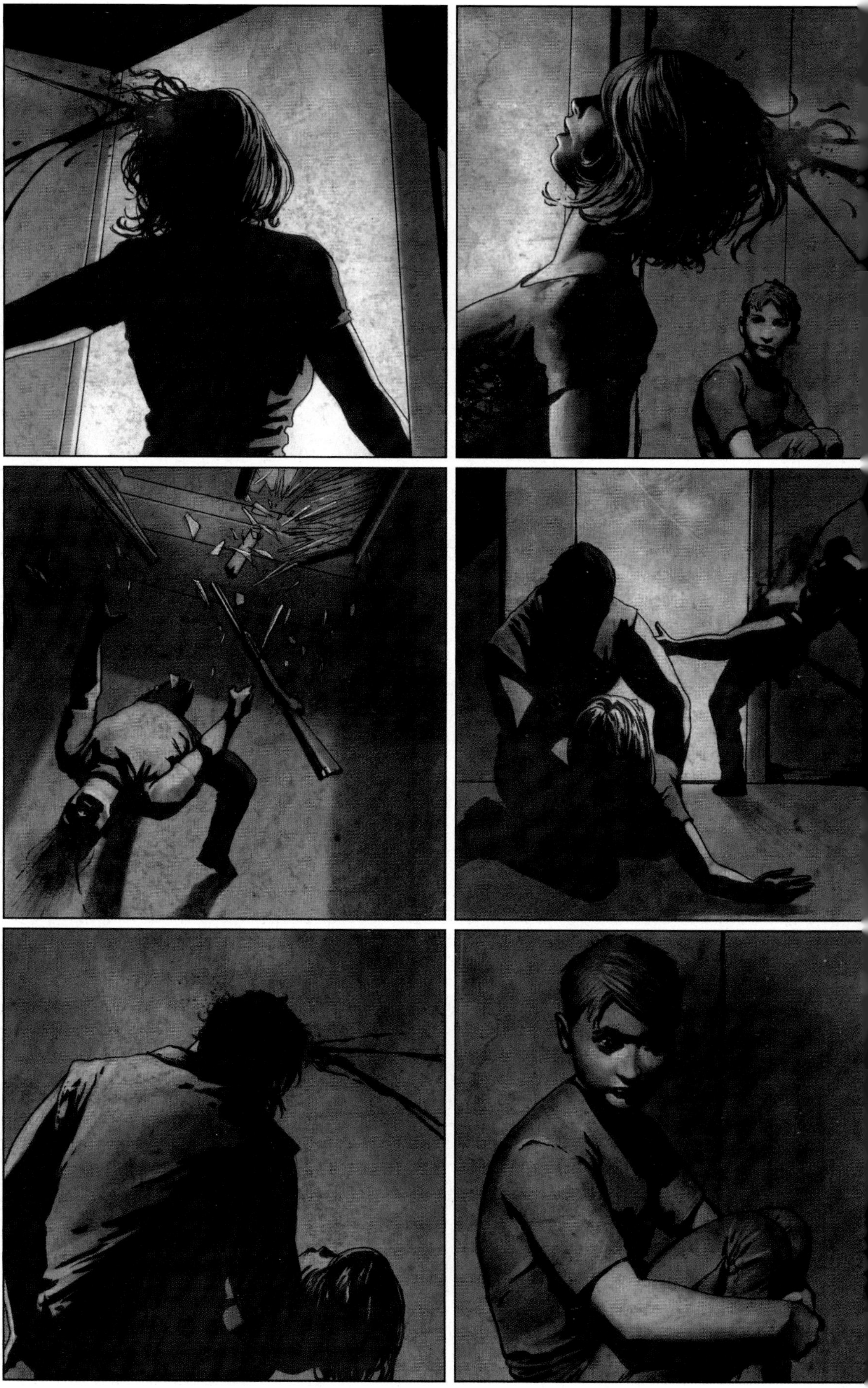

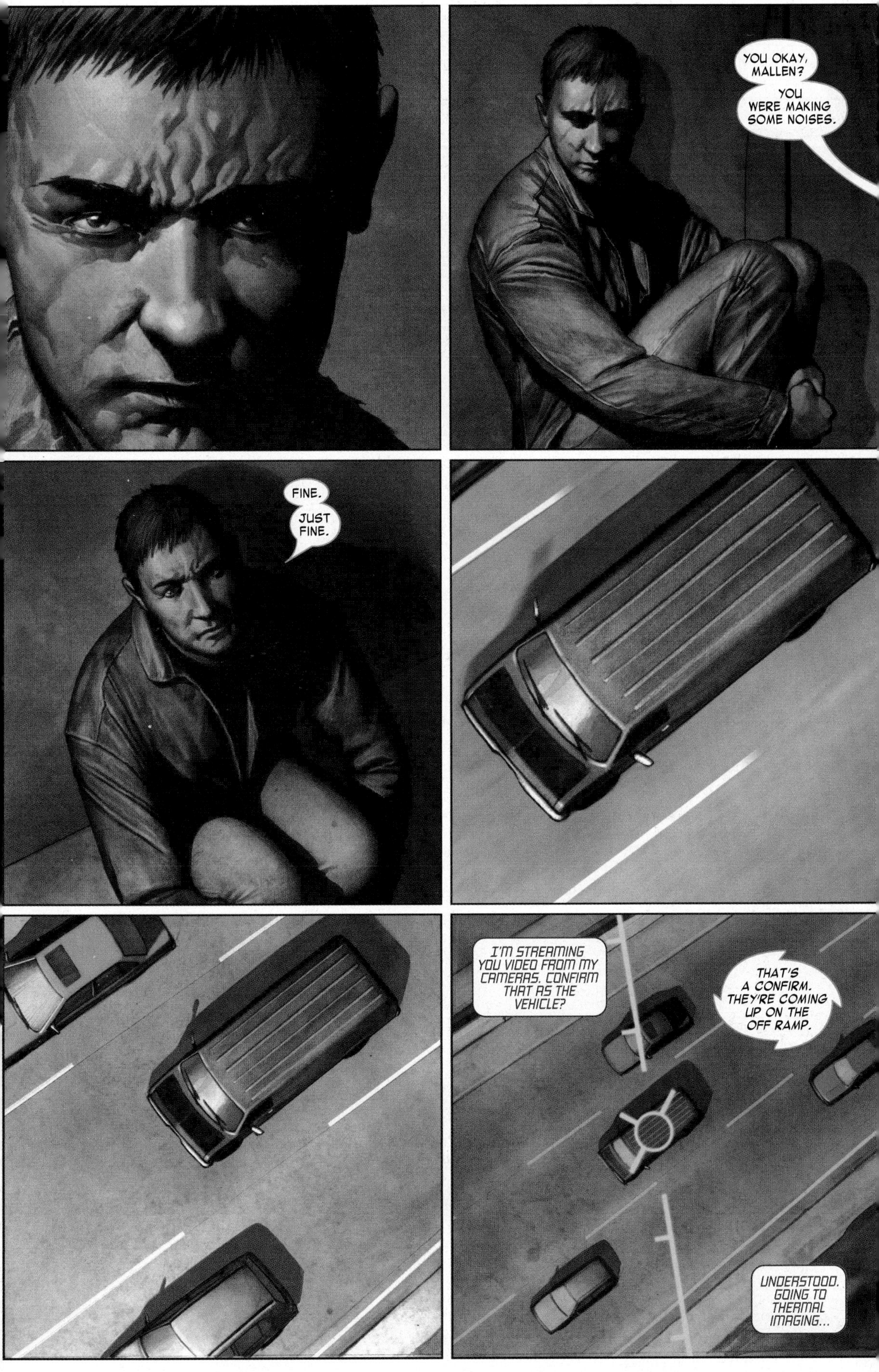
YOU OKAY, MALLEN?
YOU WERE MAKING SOME NOISES.
FINE.
JUST FINE.
I'M STREAMING YOU VIDEO FROM MY CAMERAS. CONFIRM THAT AS THE VEHICLE?
THAT'S A CONFIRM. THEY'RE COMING UP ON THE OFF RAMP.
UNDERSTOOD. GOING TO THERMAL IMAGING...

OKAY... ONE DRIVER, ONE FRONT PASSENGER... VERY HOT SPOT IN THE BACK...

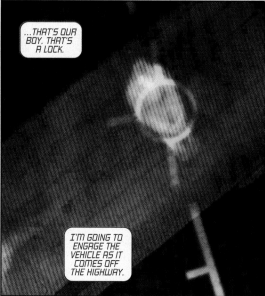

...THAT'S OUR BOY. THAT'S A LOCK.

I'M GOING TO ENGAGE THE VEHICLE AS IT COMES OFF THE HIGHWAY.

NOW LISTEN UP: I'M GOING TO BE ENGAGING WITH REPULSOR WEAPONS.

REPULSORS ARE REACTIONLES FORCE PROJECTION--ONE-WA PUSH. GET IN THE WAY OF ON AND YOU'RE RISKING BROKEN BON AND INTERNAL ORGAN DAMAG

I WANT ALL POLICE OFFICERS PULLED W BACK UNTIL I'VE SUBDUED THE TARG

I'M GOING TO ATTEMPT TO FREE UP THE TWO IN THE FRONT FOR YOU.

STAND BY.

MUNITIONS
REPULSORS 40%
PRIMARY

THAT SHOULD BE
ENOUGH...DON'T
WANT TO VAPORIZE
THEM...

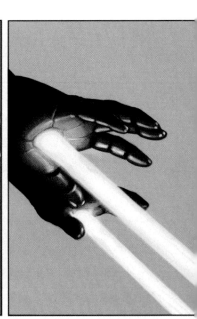

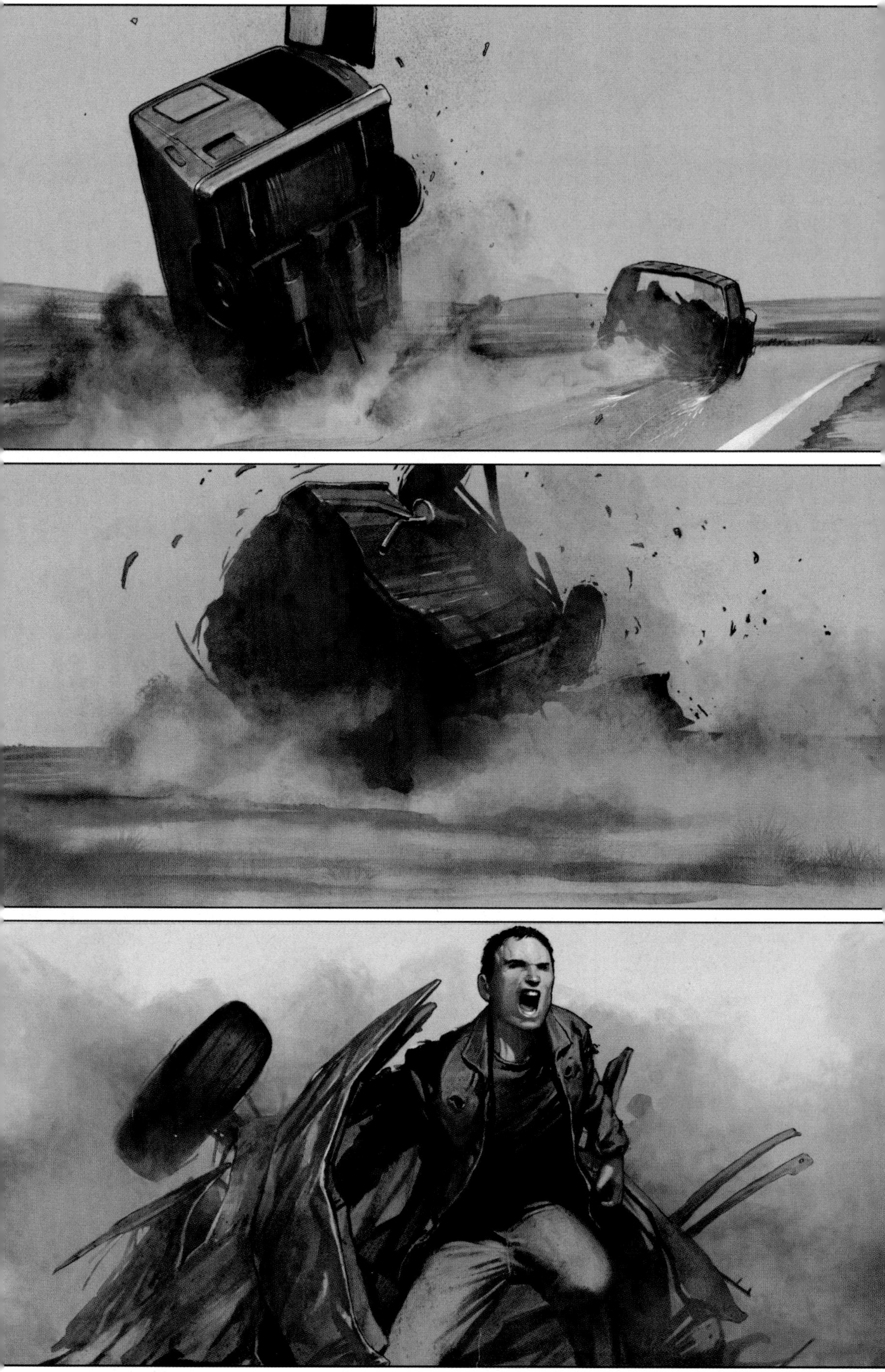

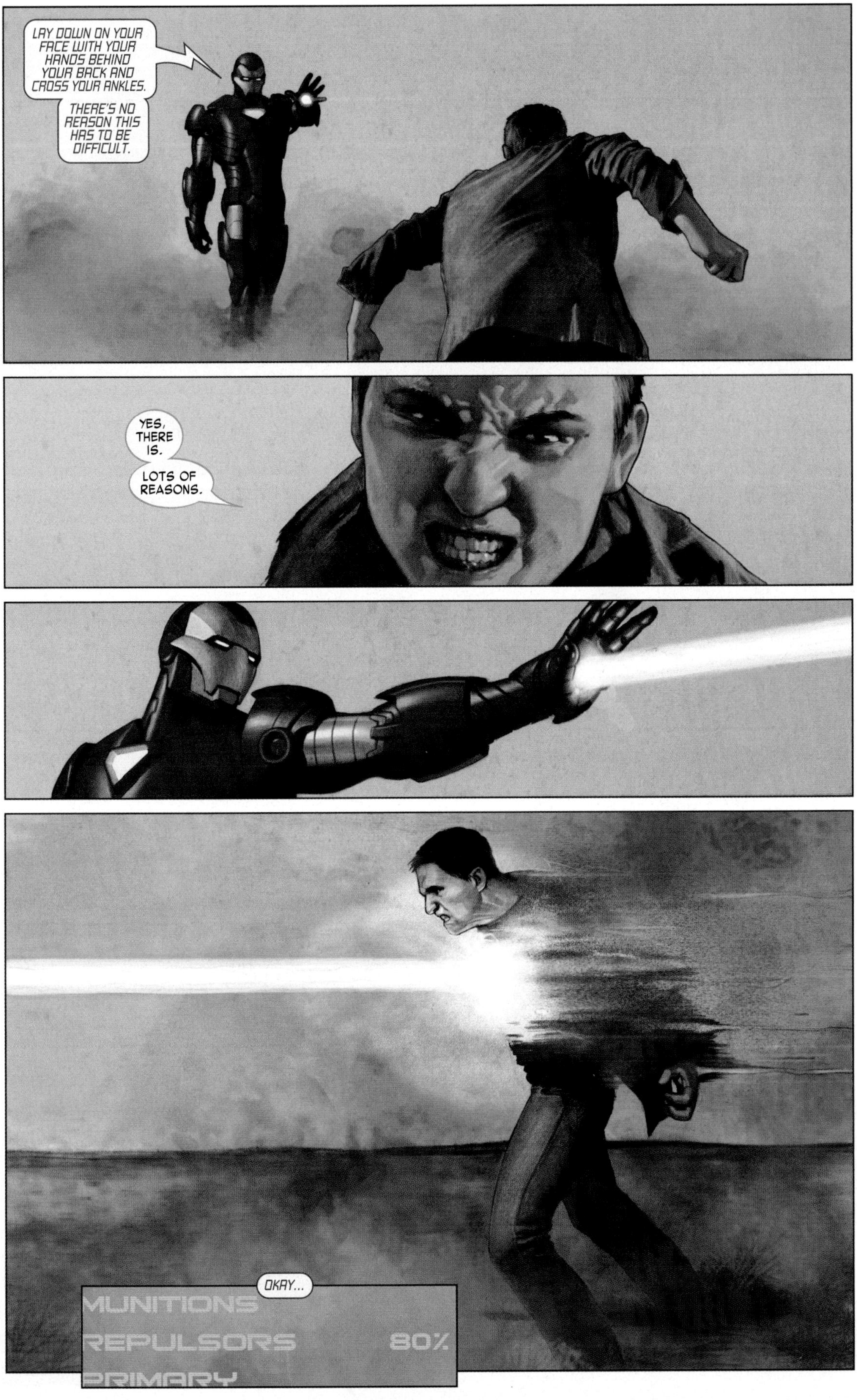
LAY DOWN ON YOUR FACE WITH YOUR HANDS BEHIND YOUR BACK AND CROSS YOUR ANKLES.
THERE'S NO REASON THIS HAS TO BE DIFFICULT.
YES, THERE IS.
LOTS OF REASONS.
OKAY...
MUNITIONS
REPULSORS 80%
PRIMARY

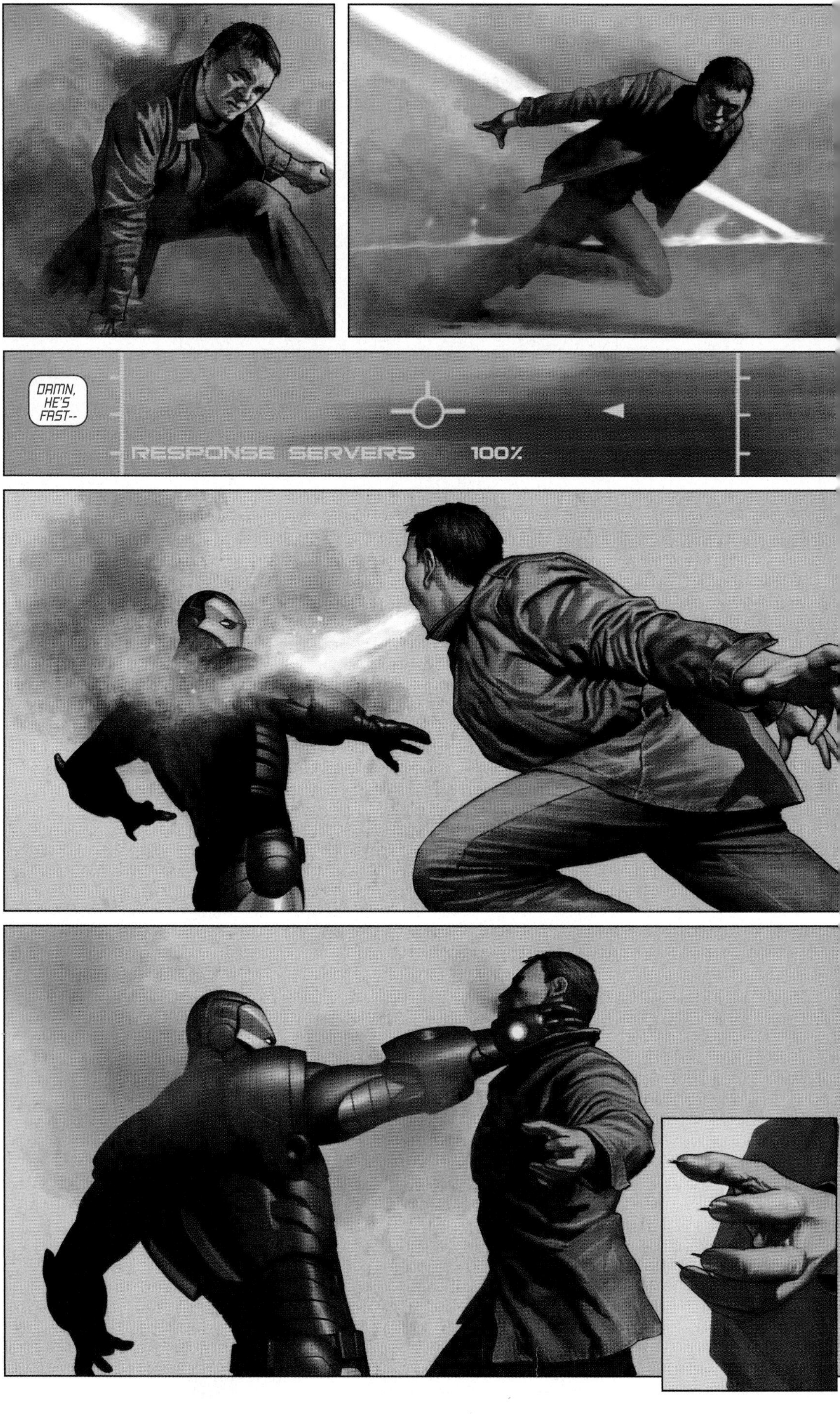
DAMN, HE'S FAST--
RESPONSE SERVERS 100%

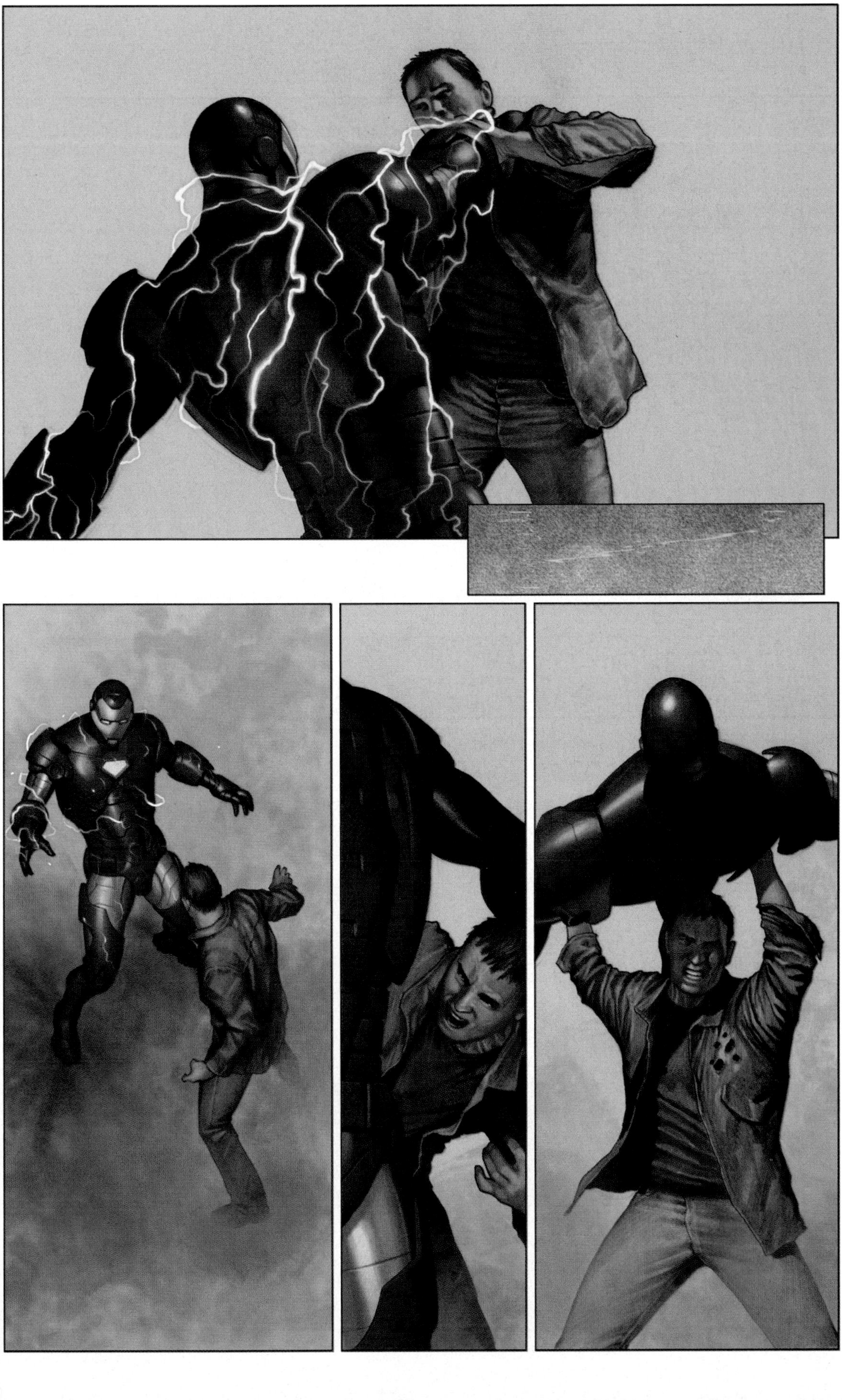

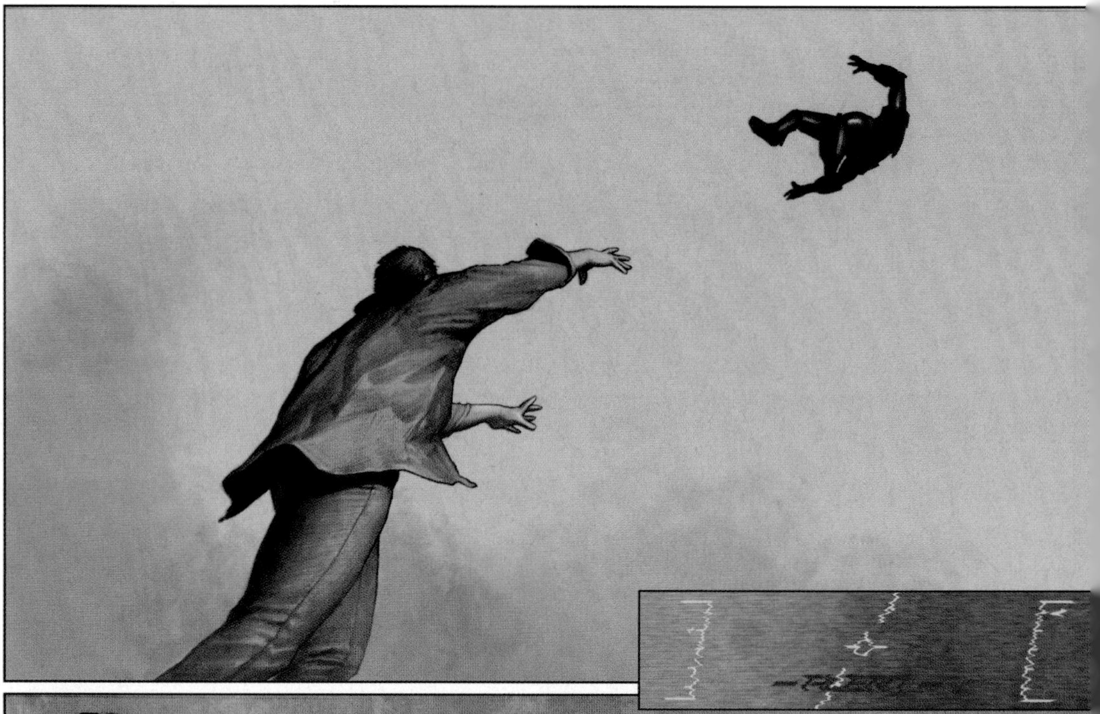

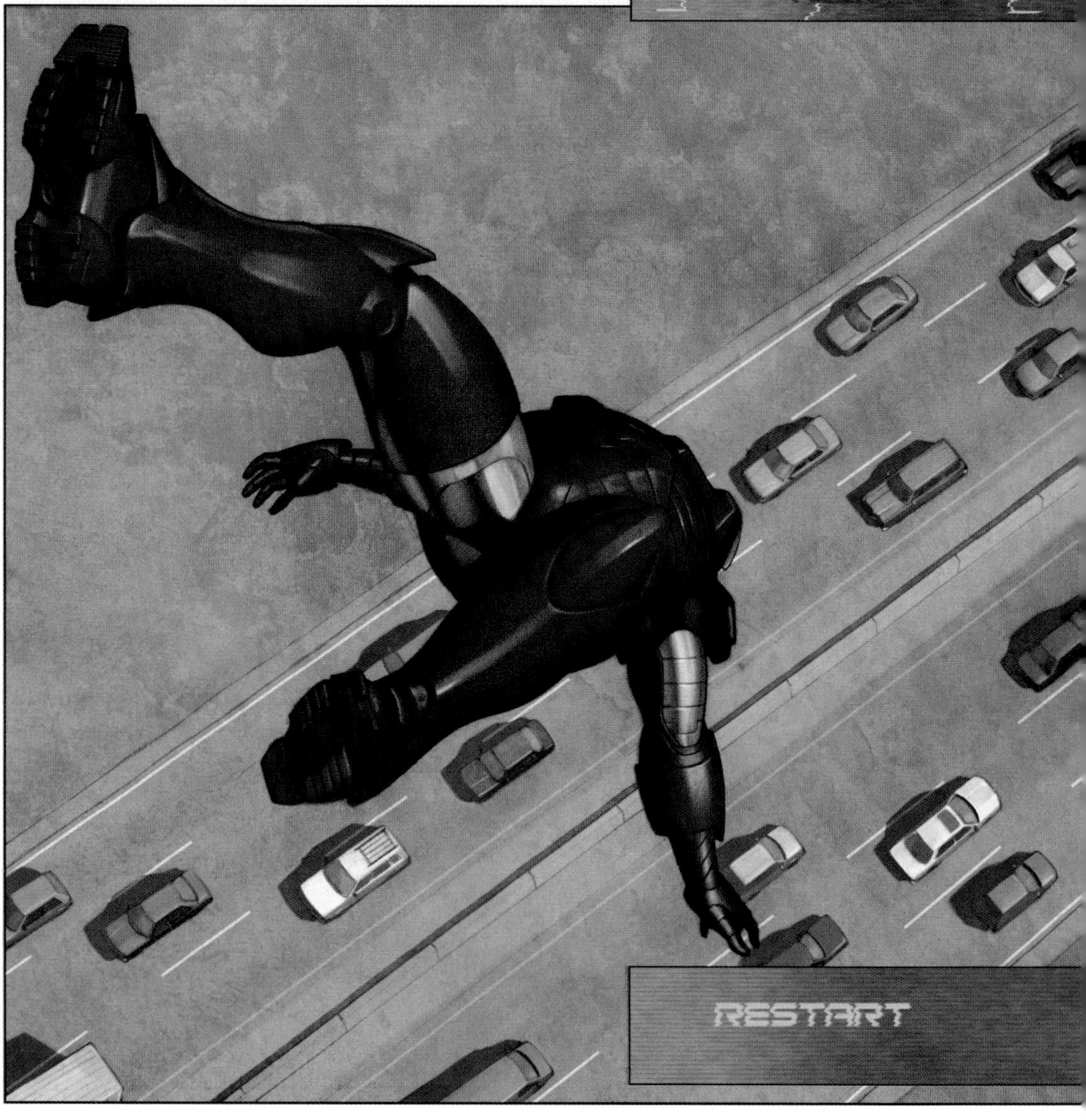
RESTART

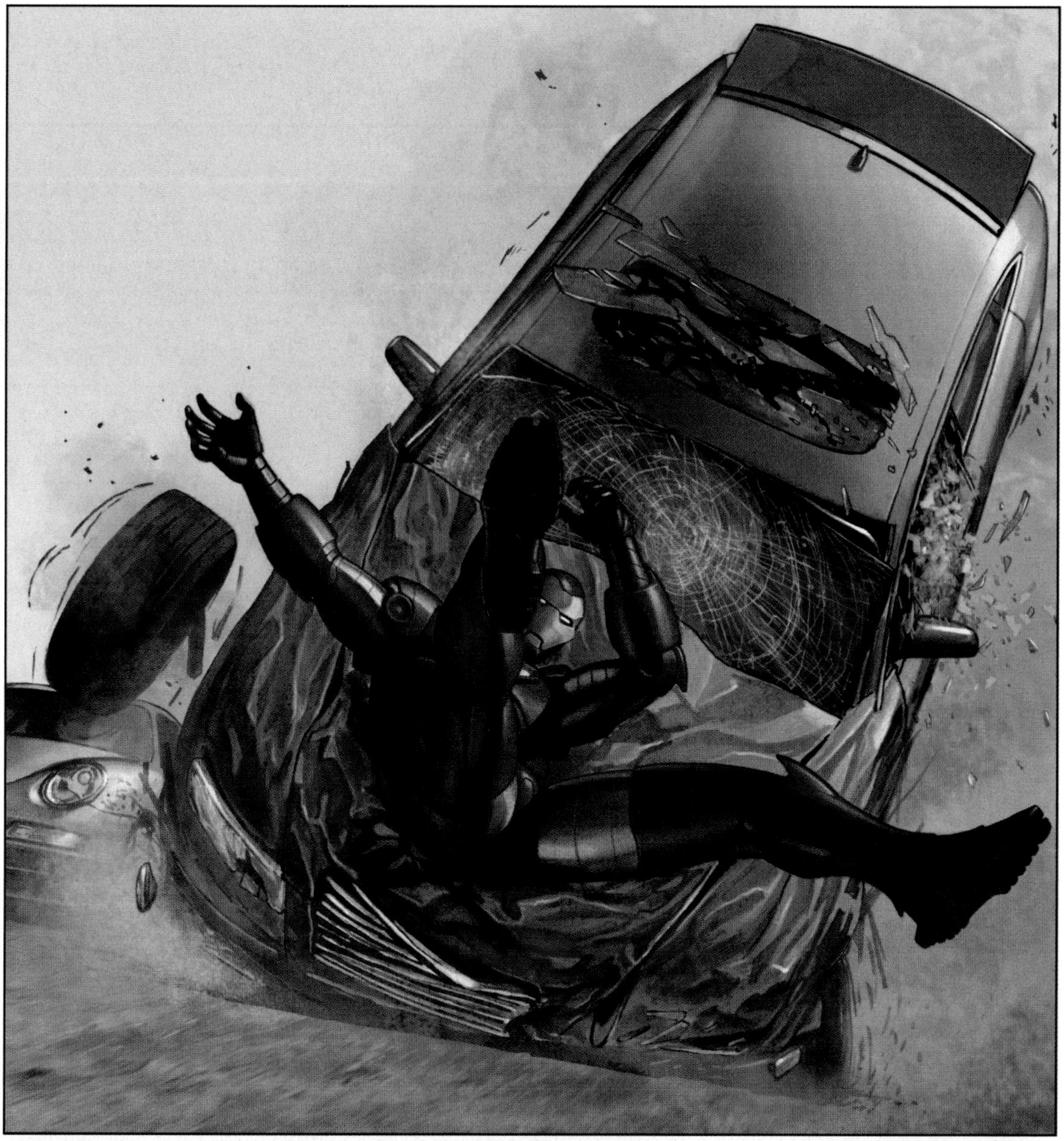

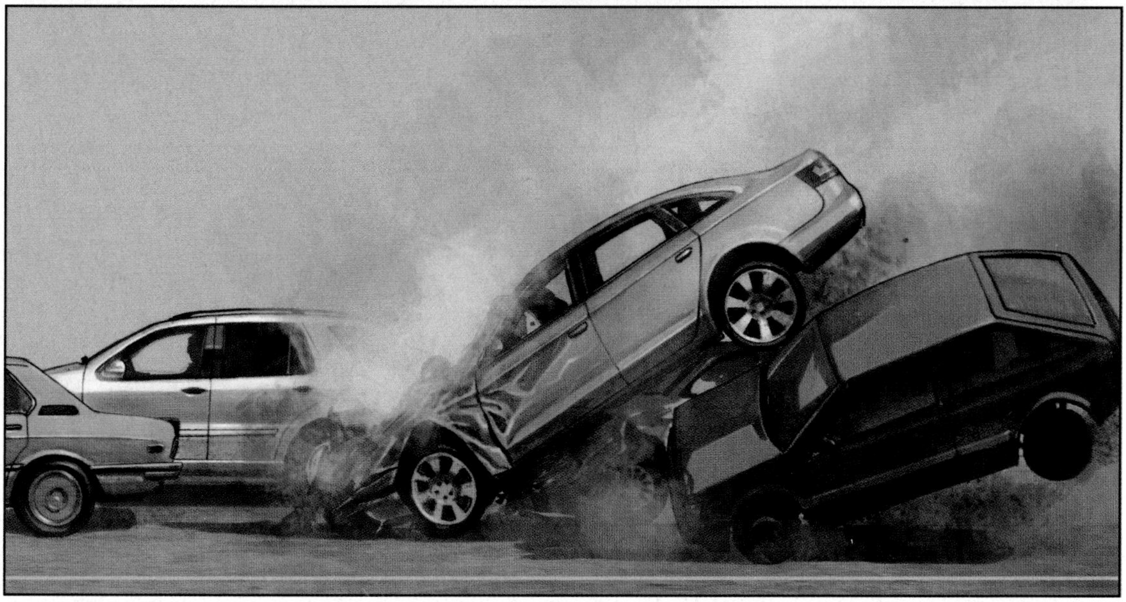

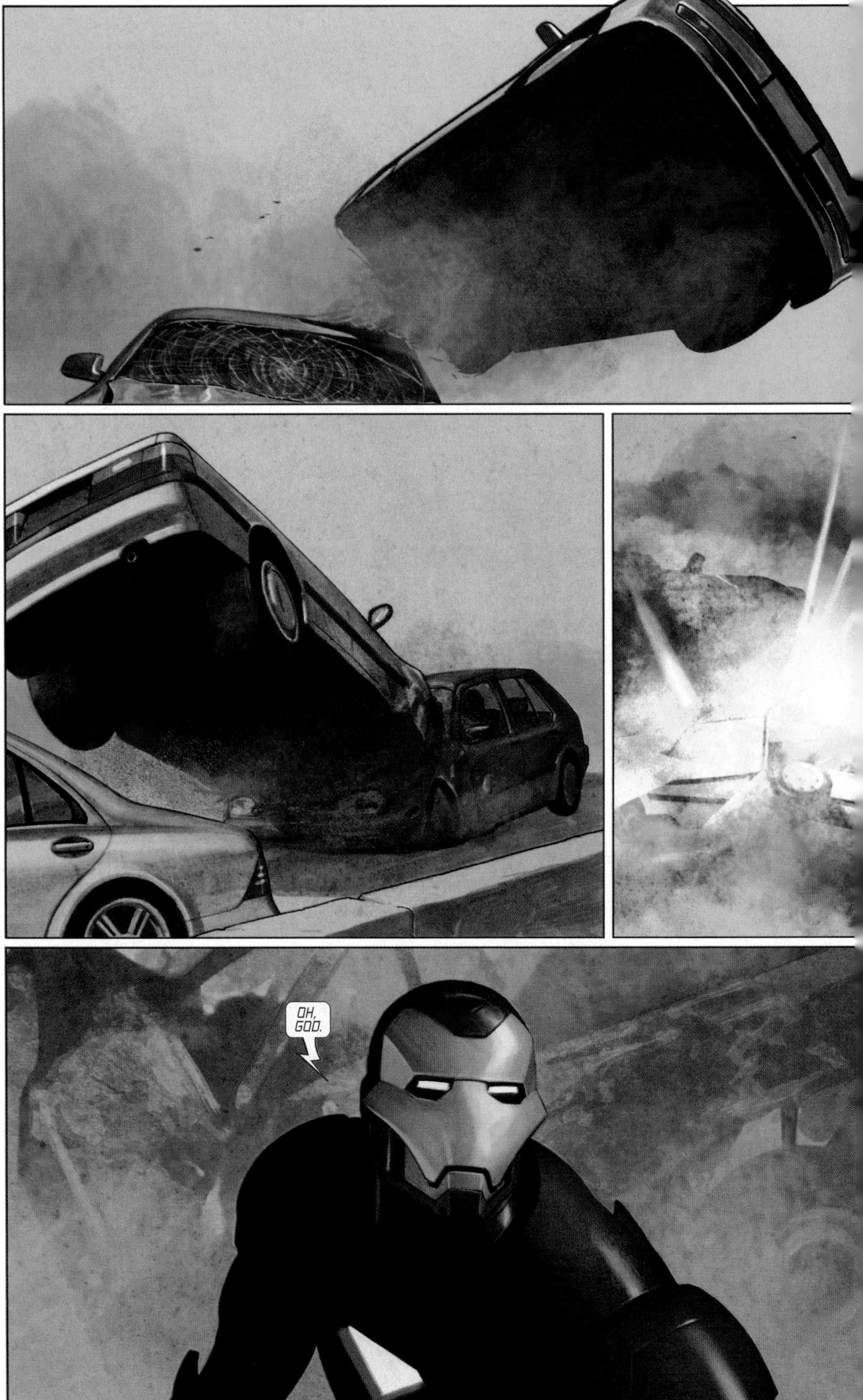
OH, GOD.

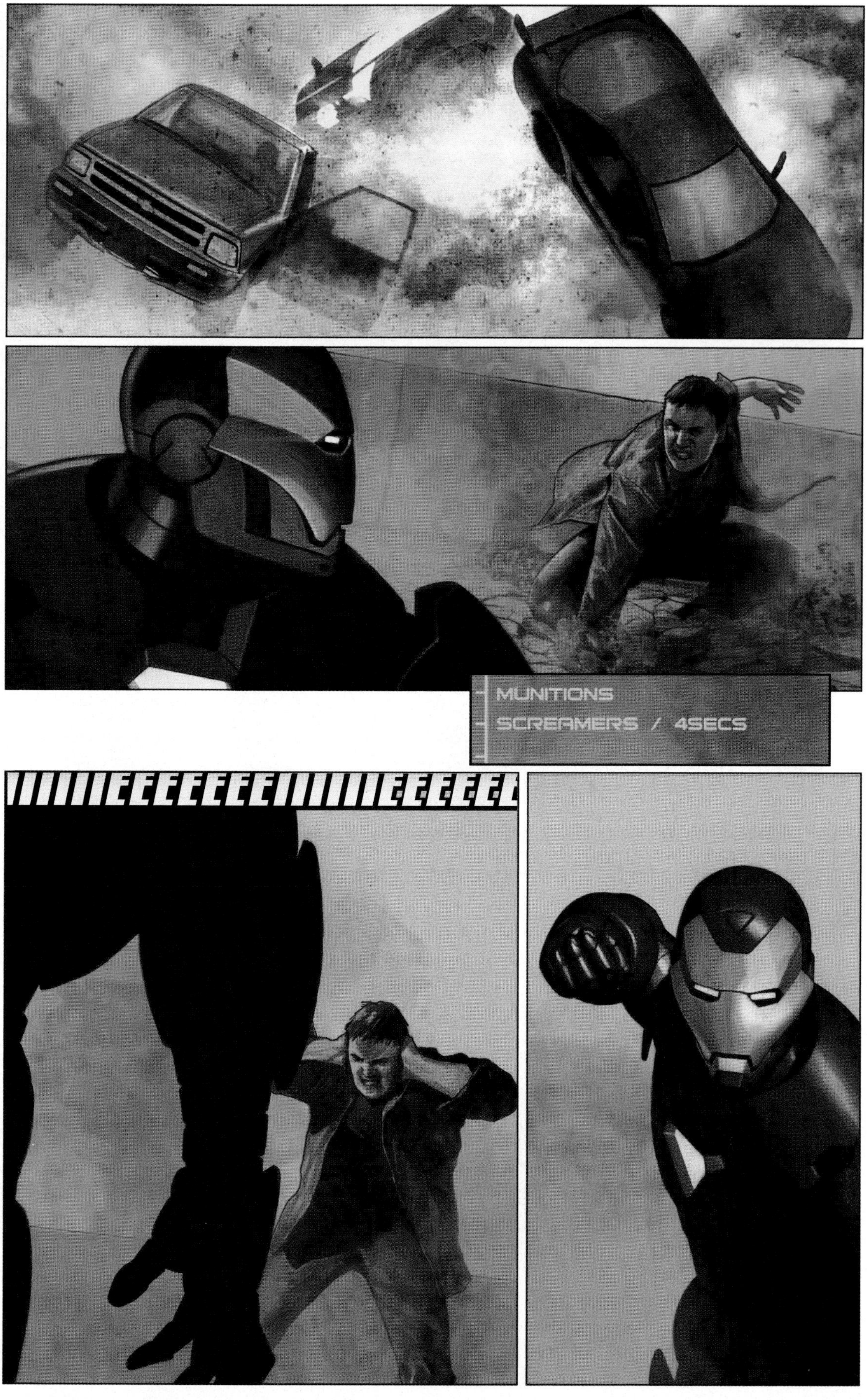
MUNITIONS
SCREAMERS / 4SECS
IIIIIEEEEEEEIIIIIIEEEEEE

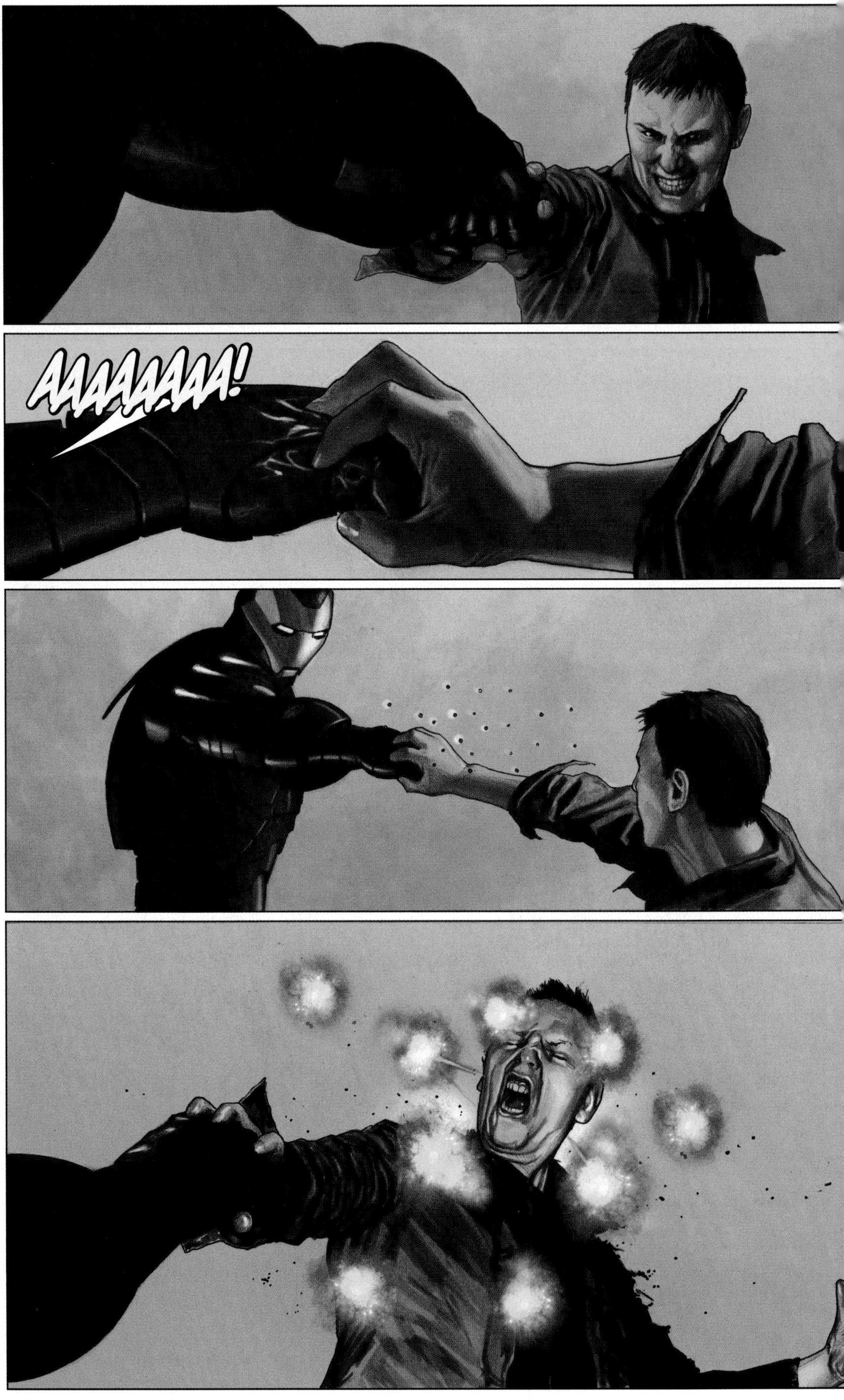
AAAAAAAA!

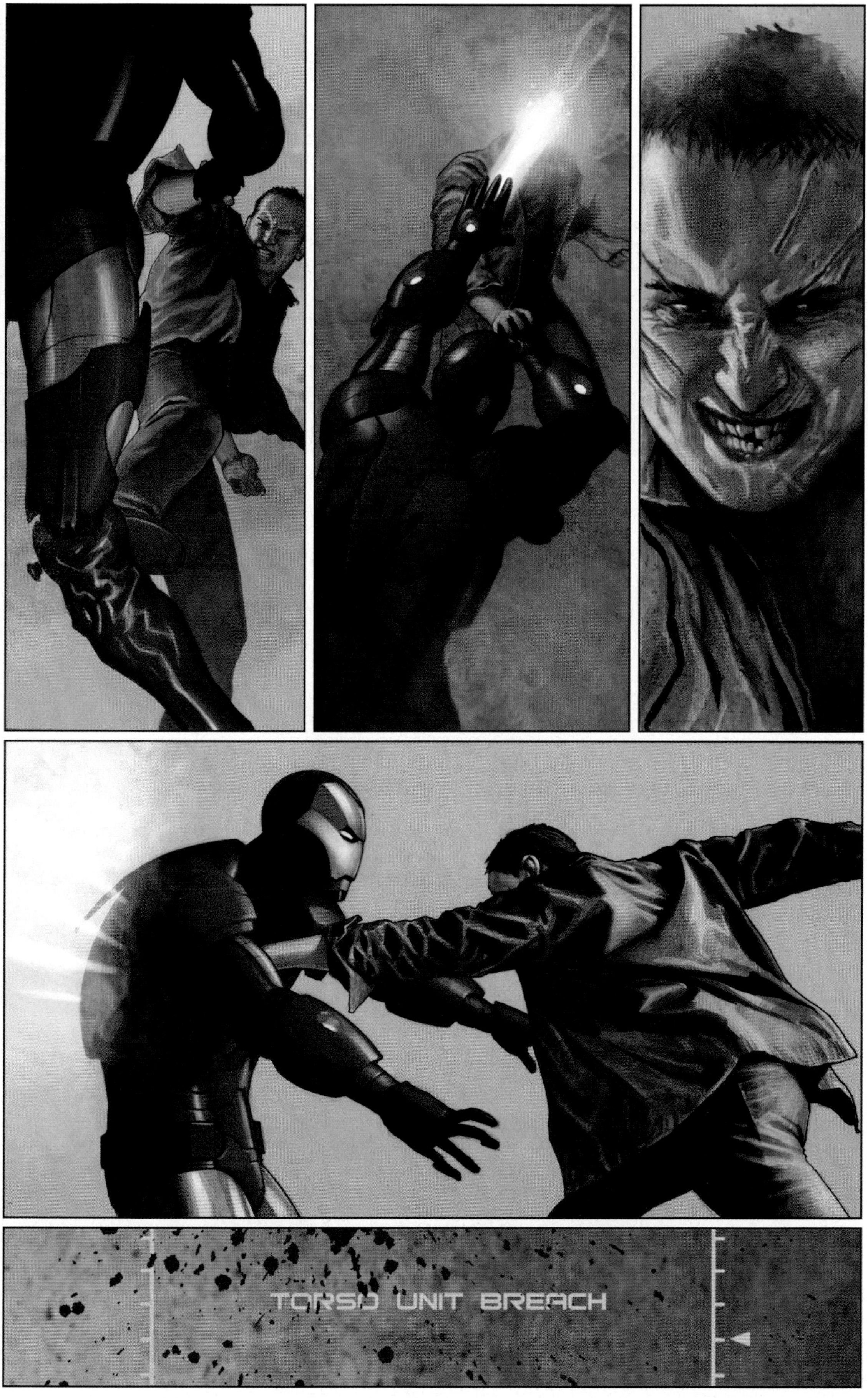
TORSO UNIT BREACH

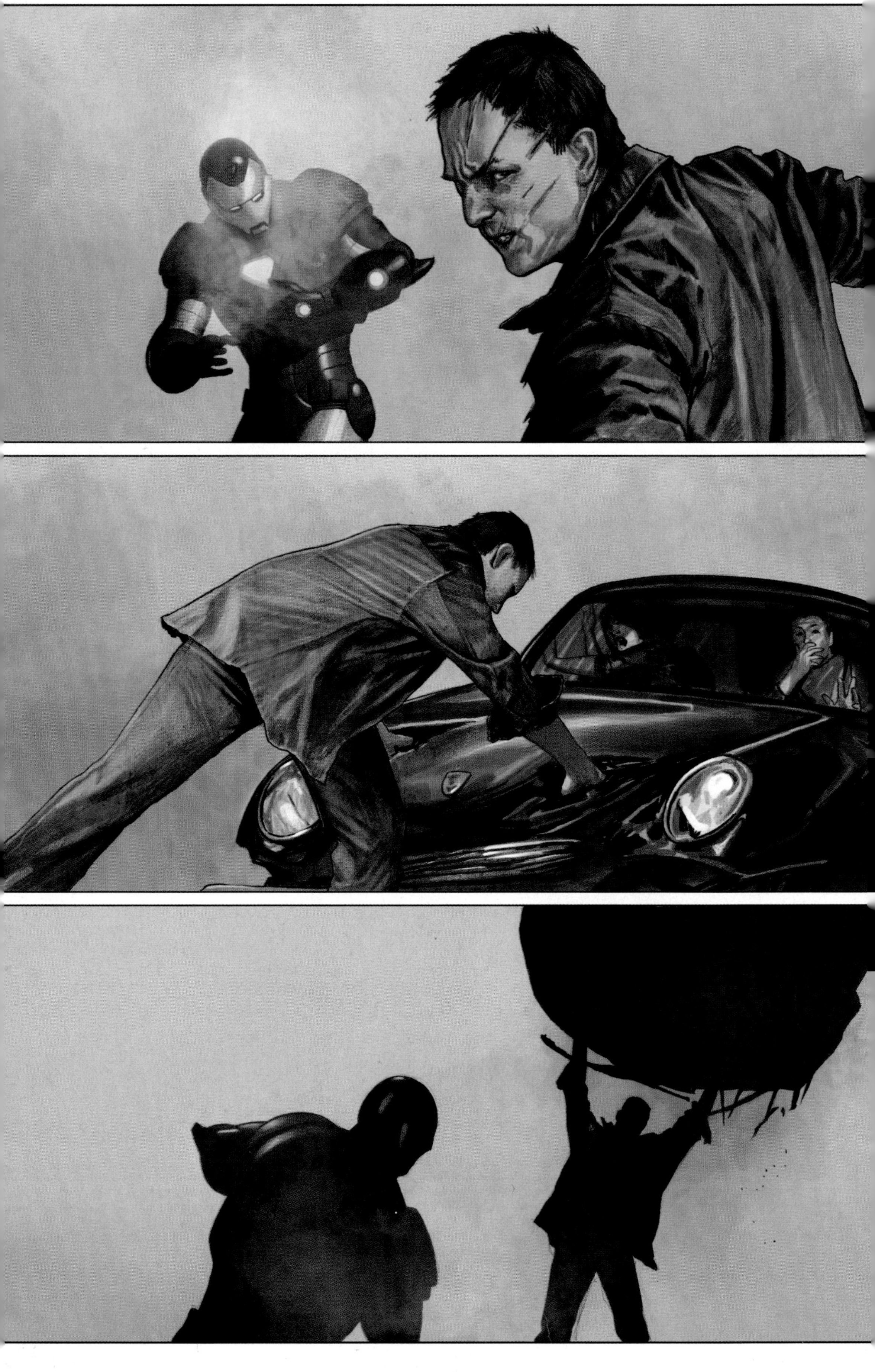

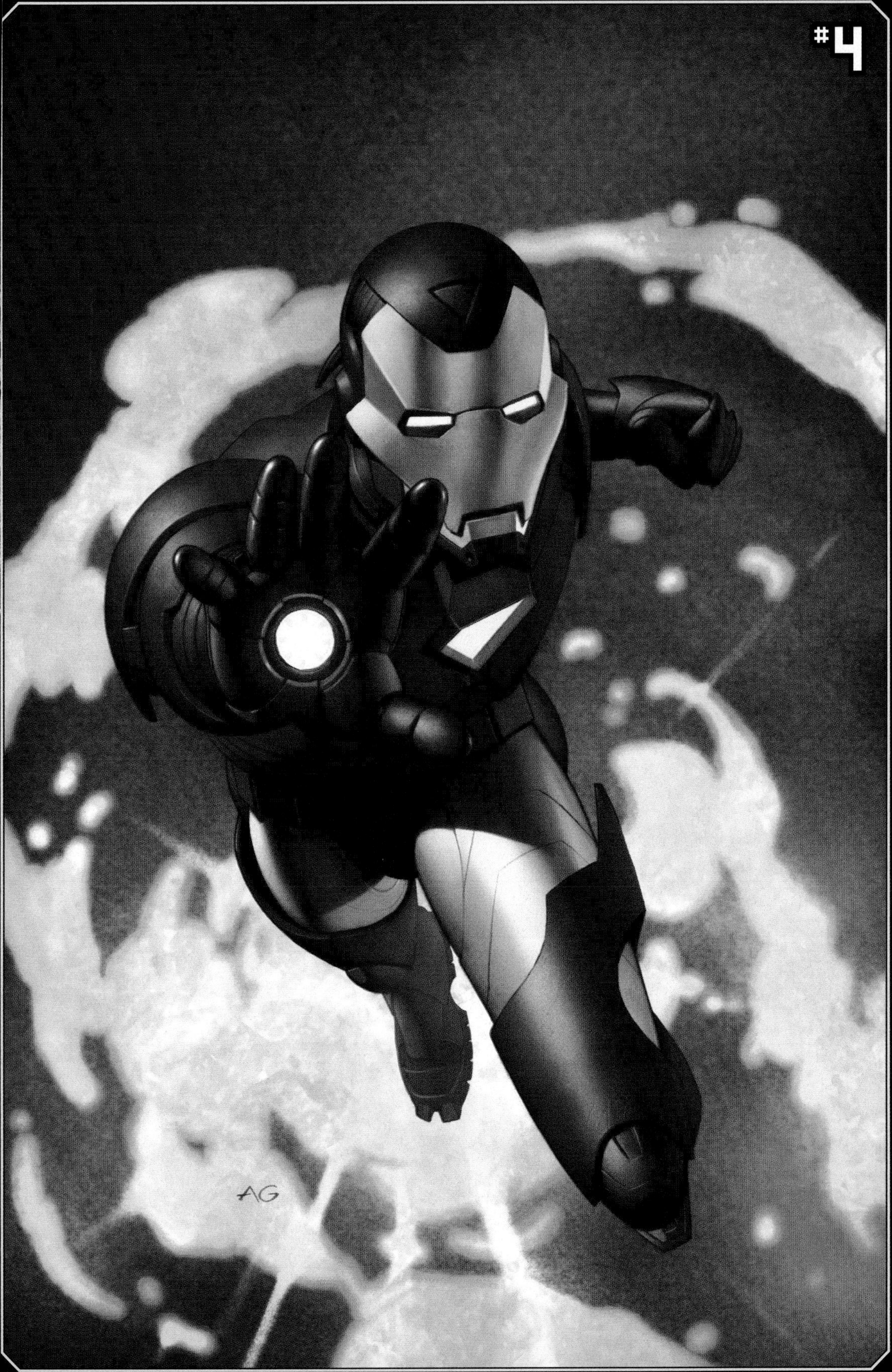
#4
AG

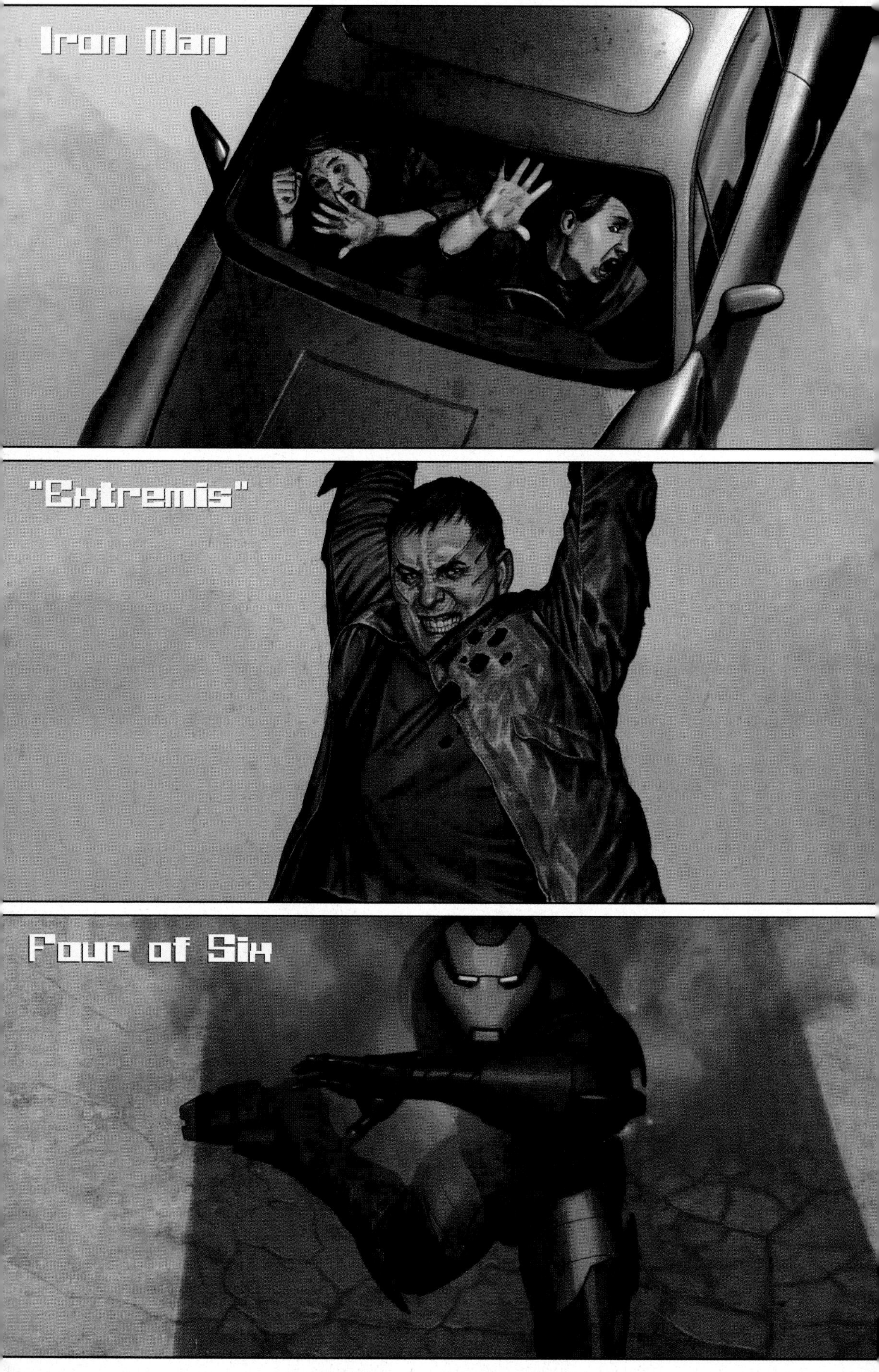
Iron Man
"Extremis"
Four of Six

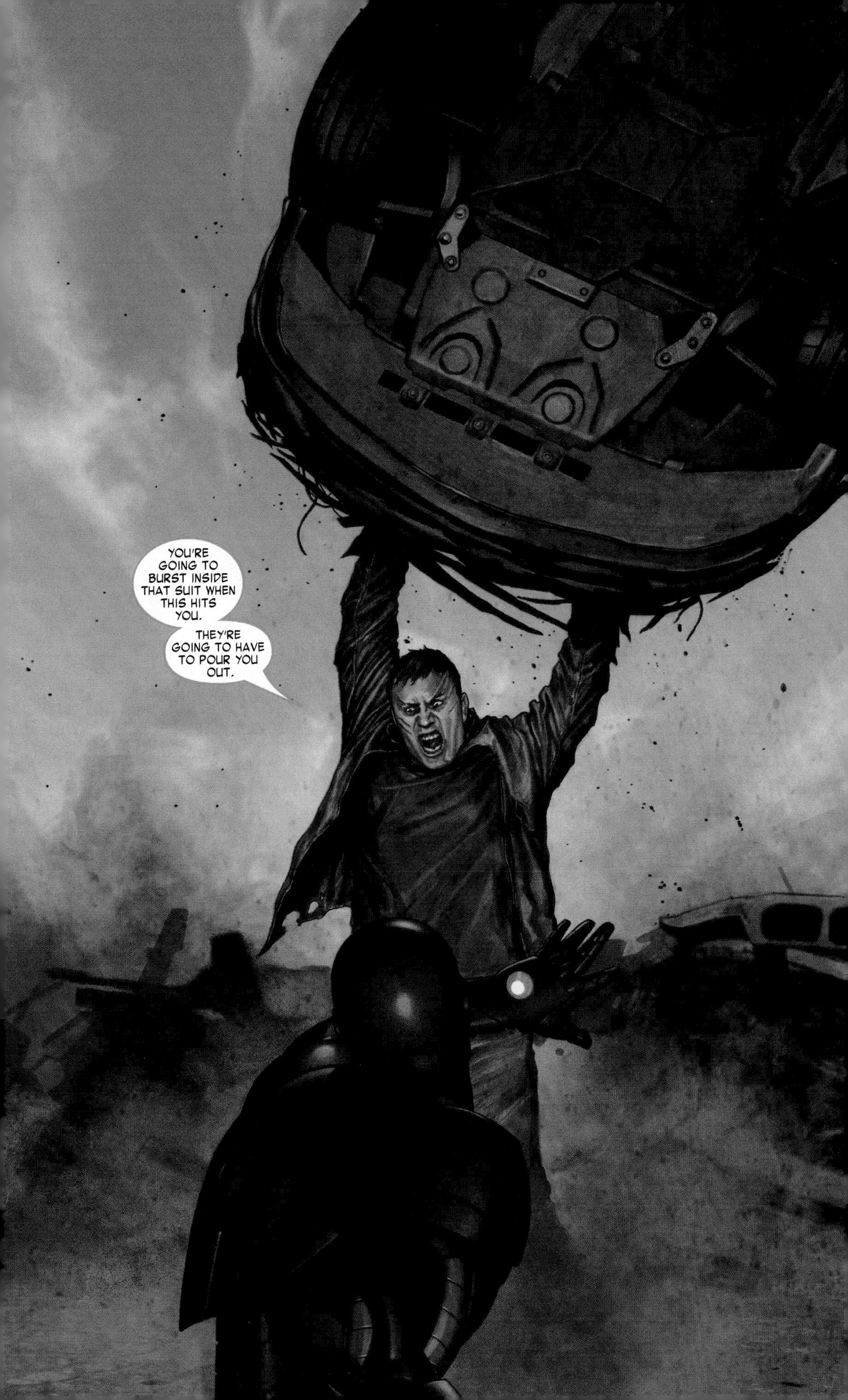
YOU'RE GOING TO BURST INSIDE THAT SUIT WHEN THIS HITS YOU.
THEY'RE GOING TO HAVE TO POUR YOU OUT.

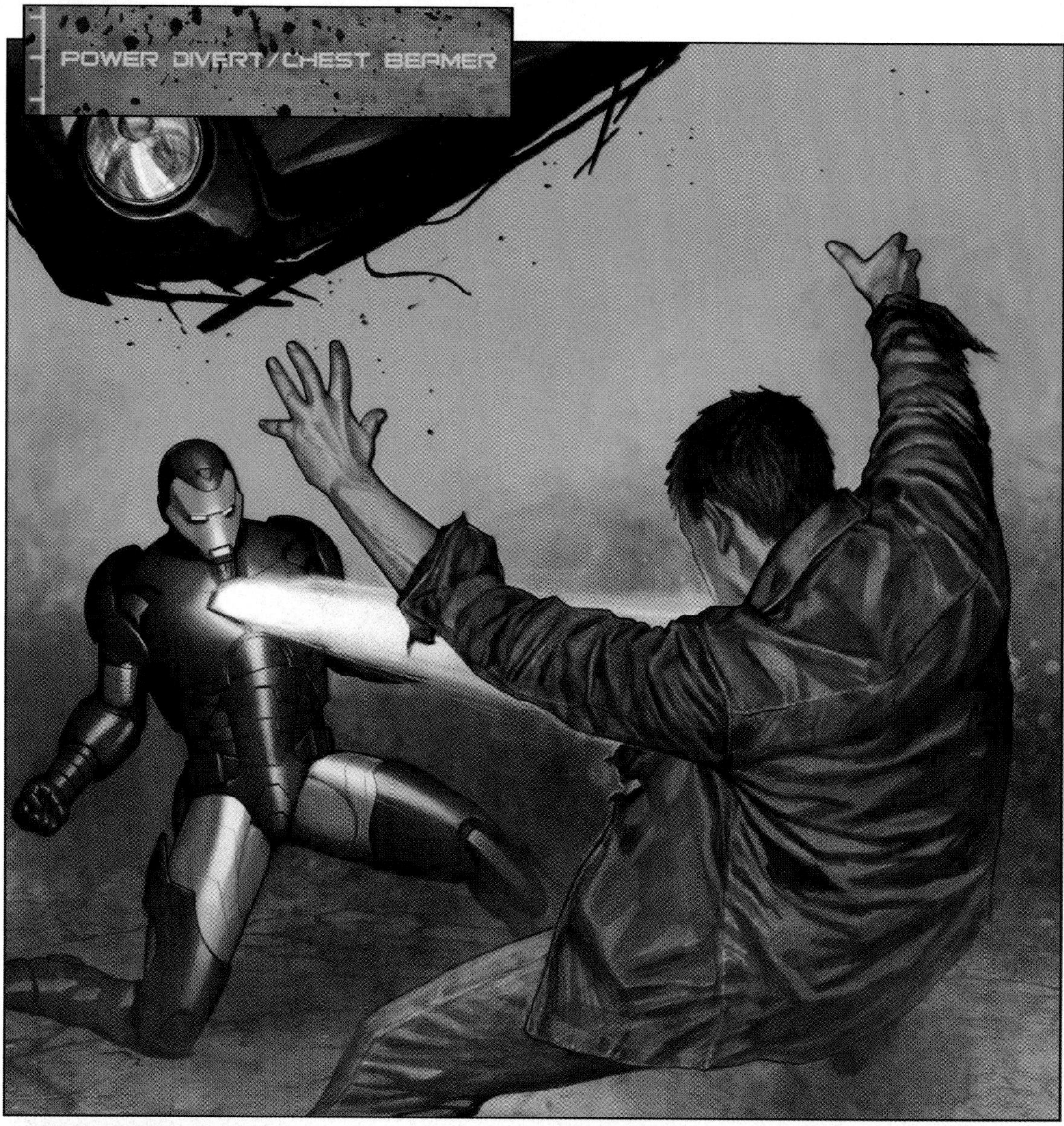
POWER DIVERT/CHEST BEAMER

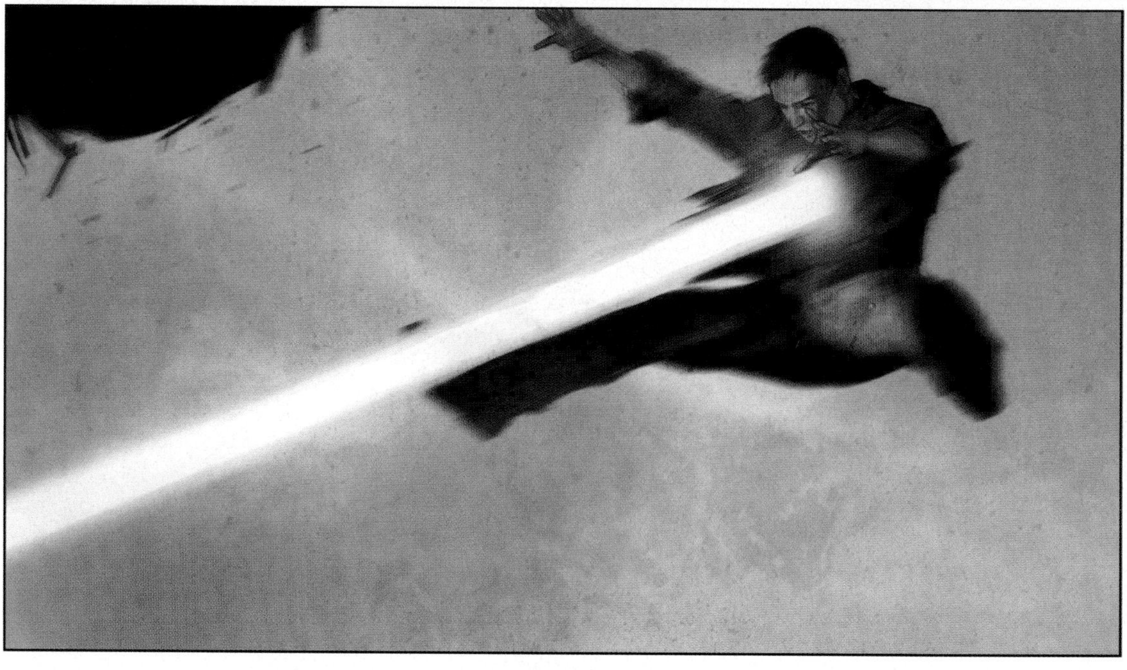

OH, HELL...

CHUNG!

POWER TRANSMISSION 0%

NO NO NO. DON'T YOU DARE.

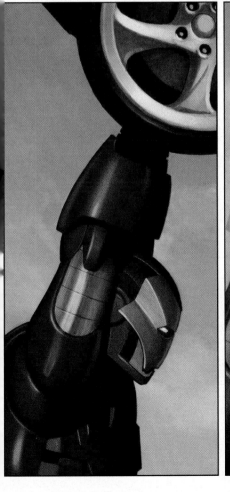

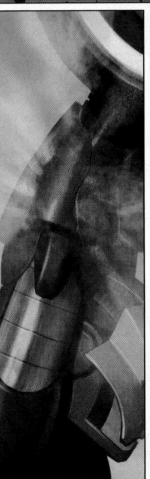

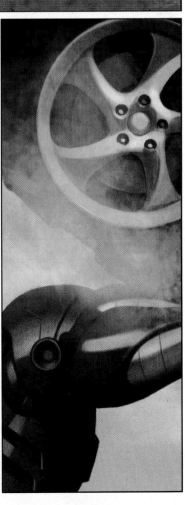

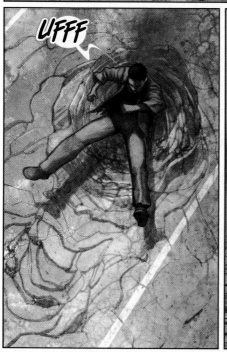

UFFF

OWW. YOU BASTARD....

DOESN'T MATTER. NOT IMPORTANT.

I HAVE ALL THE TIME IN THE WORLD NOW.

LEAVE THE LITTLE THINGS BEHIND.

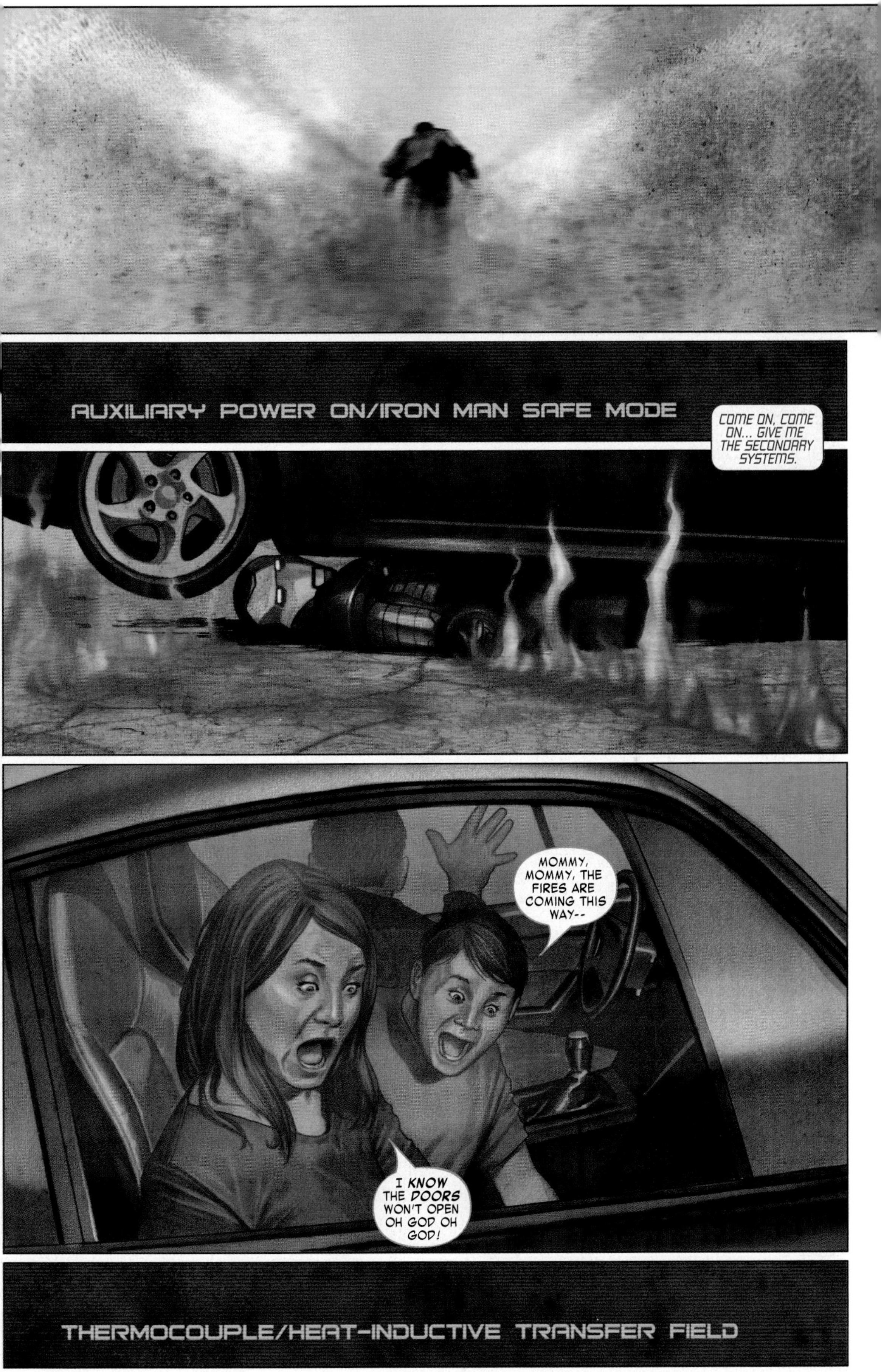
AUXILIARY POWER ON/IRON MAN SAFE MODE
COME ON, COME ON... GIVE ME THE SECONDARY SYSTEMS.
MOMMY, MOMMY, THE FIRES ARE COMING THIS WAY--
I KNOW THE DOORS WON'T OPEN OH GOD OH GOD!
THERMOCOUPLE/HEAT-INDUCTIVE TRANSFER FIELD

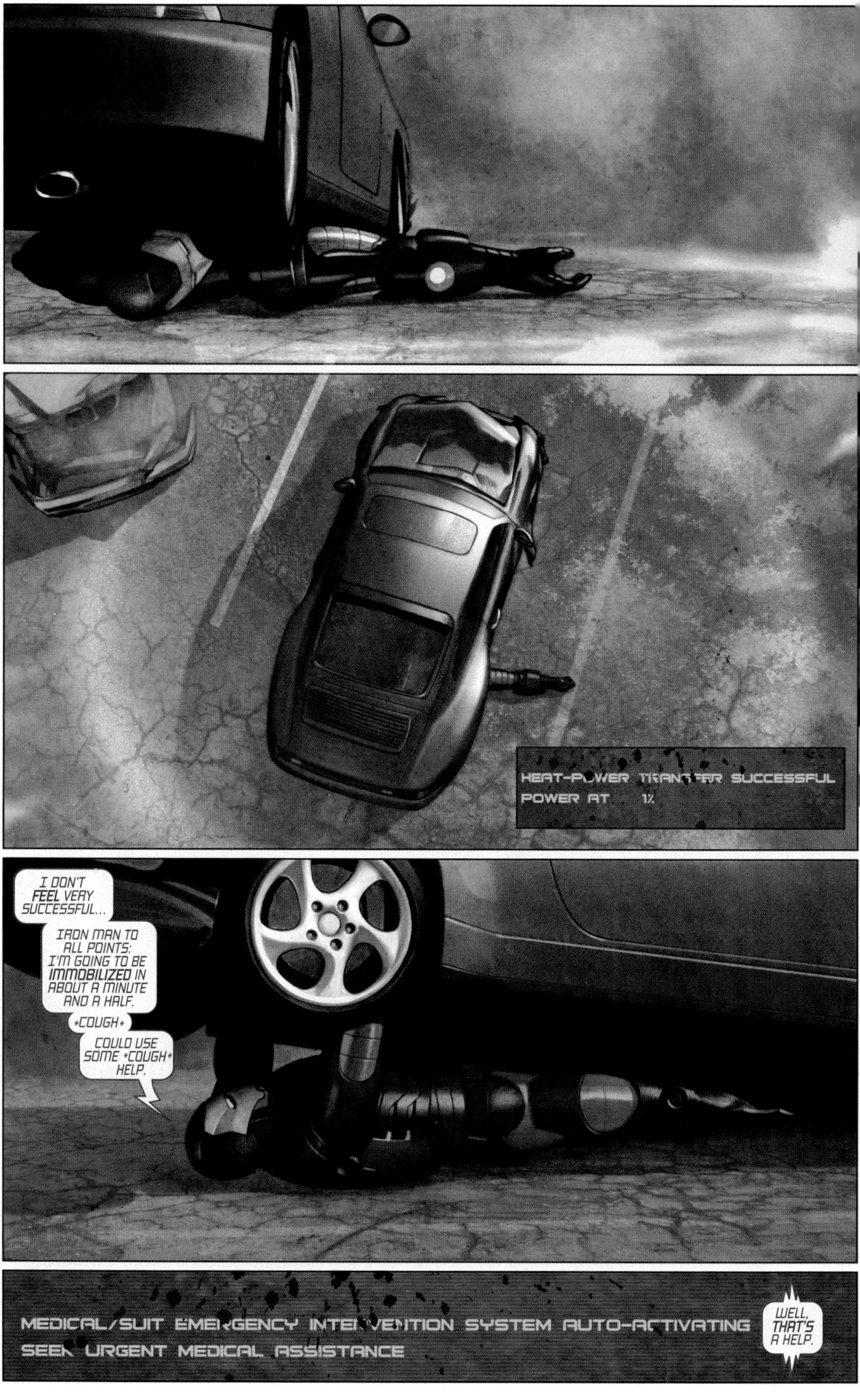
HEAT-POWER TRANSFER SUCCESSFUL
POWER AT 1%
I DON'T FEEL VERY SUCCESSFUL...
IRON MAN TO ALL POINTS: I'M GOING TO BE IMMOBILIZED IN ABOUT A MINUTE AND A HALF.
COUGH
COULD USE SOME *COUGH* HELP.
MEDICAL/SUIT EMERGENCY INTERVENTION SYSTEM AUTO-ACTIVATING
SEEK URGENT MEDICAL ASSISTANCE
WELL, THAT'S A HELP.

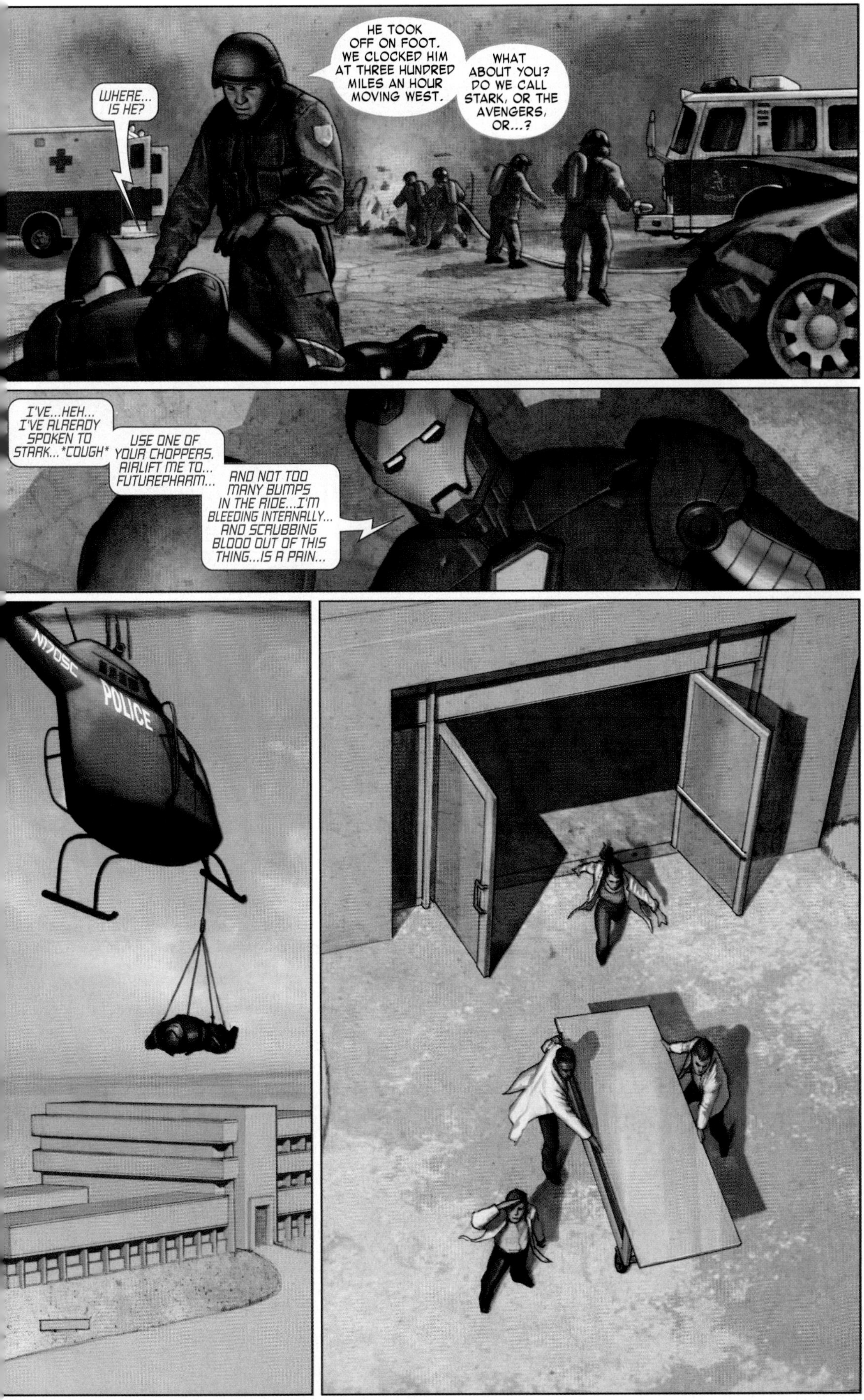
WHERE... IS HE?
HE TOOK OFF ON FOOT. WE CLOCKED HIM AT THREE HUNDRED MILES AN HOUR MOVING WEST.
WHAT ABOUT YOU? DO WE CALL STARK, OR THE AVENGERS, OR...?
I'VE...HEH... I'VE ALREADY SPOKEN TO STARK...*COUGH*
USE ONE OF YOUR CHOPPERS. AIRLIFT ME TO... FUTUREPHARM...
AND NOT TOO MANY BUMPS IN THE RIDE...I'M BLEEDING INTERNALLY... AND SCRUBBING BLOOD OUT OF THIS THING...IS A PAIN...
N170SC
POLICE

SORRY IT'S NOT A PROPER GURNEY, BUT I FIGURED YOUR ARMOR'S WEIGHT WOULD COLLAPSE IT.

WE USE THIS FOR MOVING HEAVY LAB EQUIPMENT AROUND.

THAT'S OKAY... I AM HEAVY LAB EQUIPMENT...

I STILL DON'T UNDERSTAND WHY YOU WANTED TO COME HERE. WE'RE NOT A HOSPITAL.

BUT YOU DO HAVE...MEDICAL FACILITIES...

AND THIS... IS ABOUT EXTREMIS...

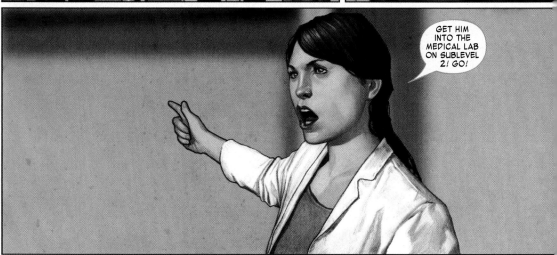

GET HIM INTO THE MEDICAL LAB ON SUBLEVEL 2! GO!

GET...RID OF THEM...

PARK HIM AND GO. I'LL TAKE IT FROM HERE.

OKAY, IT'S JUST US.

TONY SENT YOU?

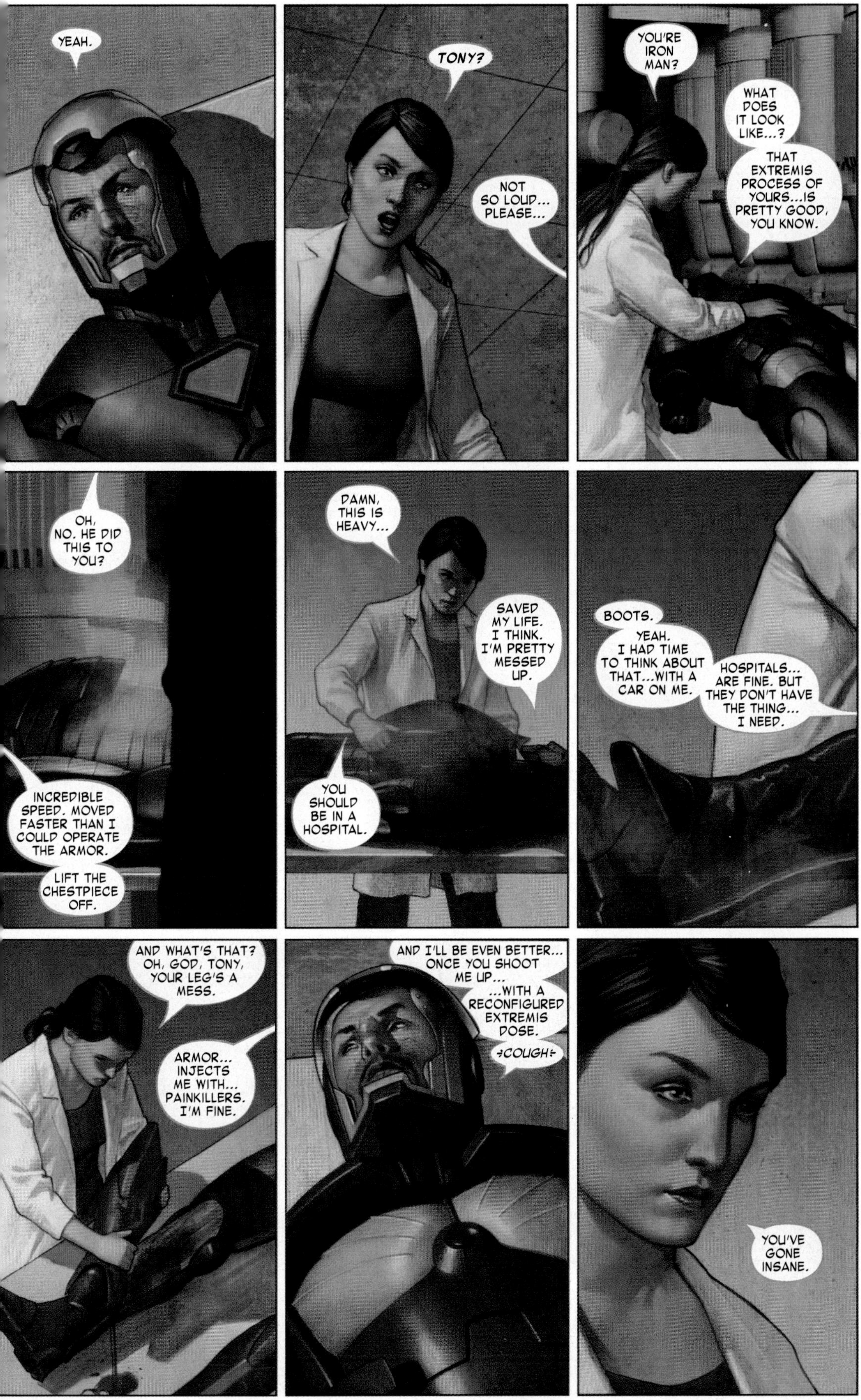
YEAH.
TONY?
NOT SO LOUD... PLEASE...
YOU'RE IRON MAN?
WHAT DOES IT LOOK LIKE...?
THAT EXTREMIS PROCESS OF YOURS...IS PRETTY GOOD, YOU KNOW.
OH, NO. HE DID THIS TO YOU?
INCREDIBLE SPEED. MOVED FASTER THAN I COULD OPERATE THE ARMOR.
LIFT THE CHESTPIECE OFF.
DAMN, THIS IS HEAVY...
SAVED MY LIFE. I THINK. I'M PRETTY MESSED UP.
YOU SHOULD BE IN A HOSPITAL.
BOOTS.
YEAH. I HAD TIME TO THINK ABOUT THAT...WITH A CAR ON ME.
HOSPITALS... ARE FINE. BUT THEY DON'T HAVE THE THING... I NEED.
AND WHAT'S THAT? OH, GOD, TONY, YOUR LEG'S A MESS.
ARMOR... INJECTS ME WITH... PAINKILLERS. I'M FINE.
AND I'LL BE EVEN BETTER... ONCE YOU SHOOT ME UP...
...WITH A RECONFIGURED EXTREMIS DOSE.
COUGH
YOU'VE GONE INSANE.

HE'S A BIOLOGICAL COMBAT MACHINE...AND I'M JUST A MAN IN AN IRON SUIT.

I'VE SPENT MONTHS IN MY GARAGE TRYING TO INCREASE THE ARMOR'S RESPONSE TIME. AND IT'S STILL. NOT. FAST. ENOUGH.

I NEED TO WIRE THE ARMOR DIRECTLY INTO MY BRAIN. EXTREMIS COULD DO THAT.

MAYBE WE COULD WORK IN SOME KIND OF TIVO THING WHILE WE'RE AT IT. MY COMPANY BOARD WOULD LOVE BRAIN TELEVISION.

EXTREMIS IS UNTESTED EVEN IN ITS CURRENT CONFIGURATION--

SEEMS TO WORK FINE. JUST LOOK AT MY FACE.

--AND THE GUY WAS PRESUMABLY HEALTHY WHEN HE TOOK THE DOSE. *YOU* LOOK LIKE YOU'VE BEEN PUSHED THROUGH A WOODCHIPPER.

GAK!

EXTREMIS WORKS THROUGH THE HEALING CENTER, YOU SAID.

IT'LL FIX ME WHILE IT'S WORKING.

I DON'T NEED THE POWERS. IF ANYTHING, WE'RE TALKING ABOUT SIMPLIFYING THE PAYLOAD.

I NEED TO *BE* THE SUIT. INSTEAD OF GROWING NEW ORGANS...I NEED TO GROW NEW CONNECTIONS...

THIS THING'S GOTTEN TOO HEAVY. AND TOO SLOW.

I'M TALKING ABOUT SPEED OF DEPLOYMENT. SPEED OF OPERATION...

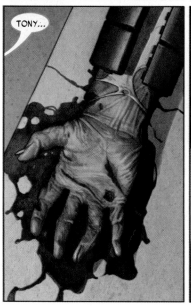

TONY...

THANK GOD FOR PAINKILLERS, EH?

GET A COMPUTER IN HERE...

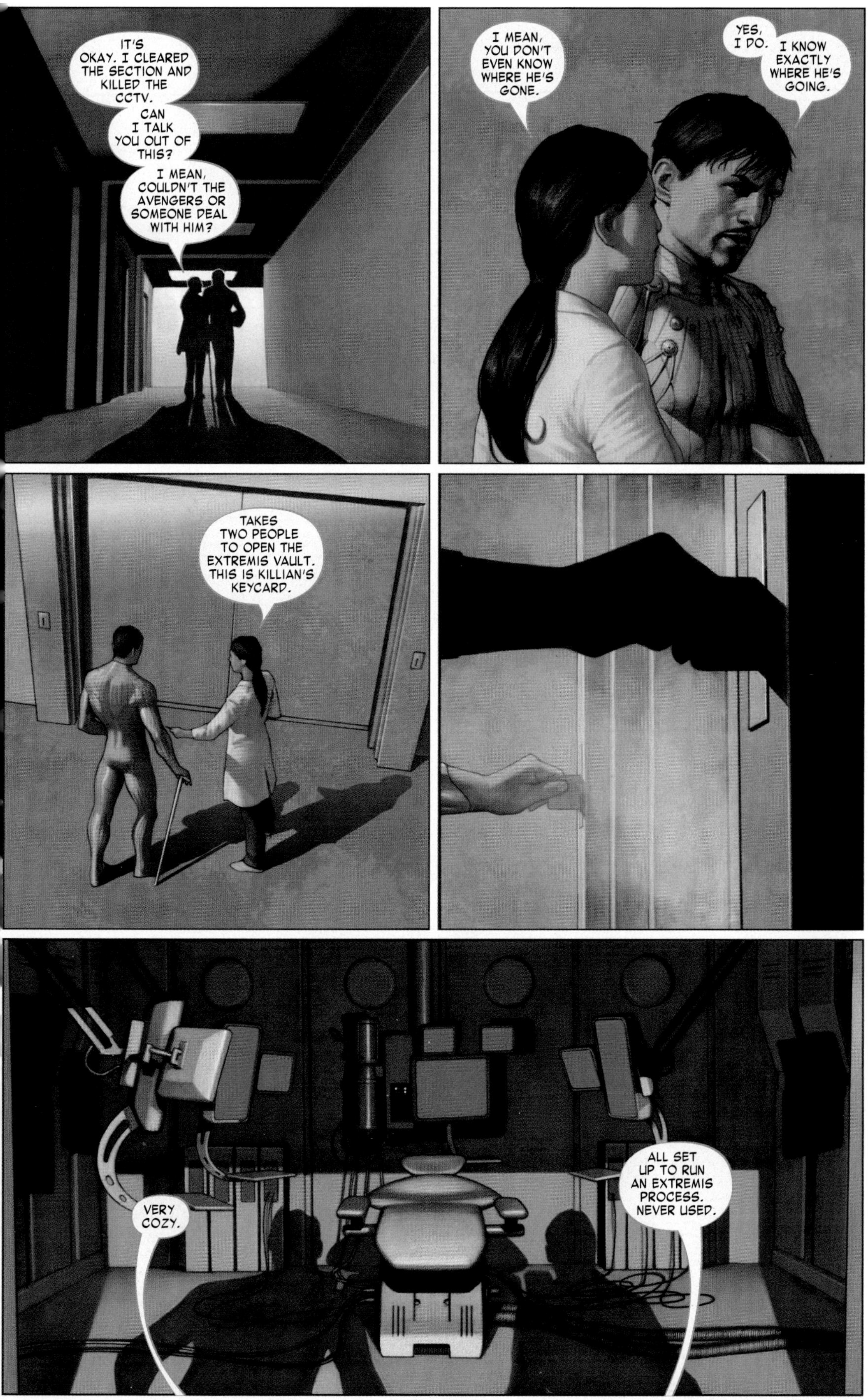
IT'S OKAY. I CLEARED THE SECTION AND KILLED THE CCTV.
CAN I TALK YOU OUT OF THIS?
I MEAN, COULDN'T THE AVENGERS OR SOMEONE DEAL WITH HIM?
I MEAN, YOU DON'T EVEN KNOW WHERE HE'S GONE.
YES, I DO.
I KNOW EXACTLY WHERE HE'S GOING.
TAKES TWO PEOPLE TO OPEN THE EXTREMIS VAULT. THIS IS KILLIAN'S KEYCARD.
VERY COZY.
ALL SET UP TO RUN AN EXTREMIS PROCESS. NEVER USED.

WELL, IT WILL BE.

UZZT!

EXCUSE ME.

MAYA HANSEN.

OH. I'LL BE RIGHT THERE.

HOW MUCH DO YOU SPEND ON PLANES? A PACKAGE FROM CONEY ISLAND HAS ARRIVED FOR YOU.

I'LL BE RIGHT BACK. MAKE YOURSELF... COMFORTABLE, I GUESS.

ONE OF THE ITEMS WILL BE A CASE. BRING IT BACK?

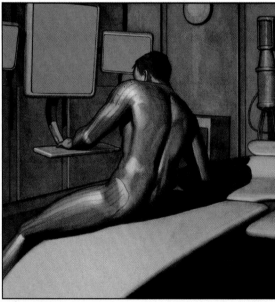

Iron Man Hud Playback

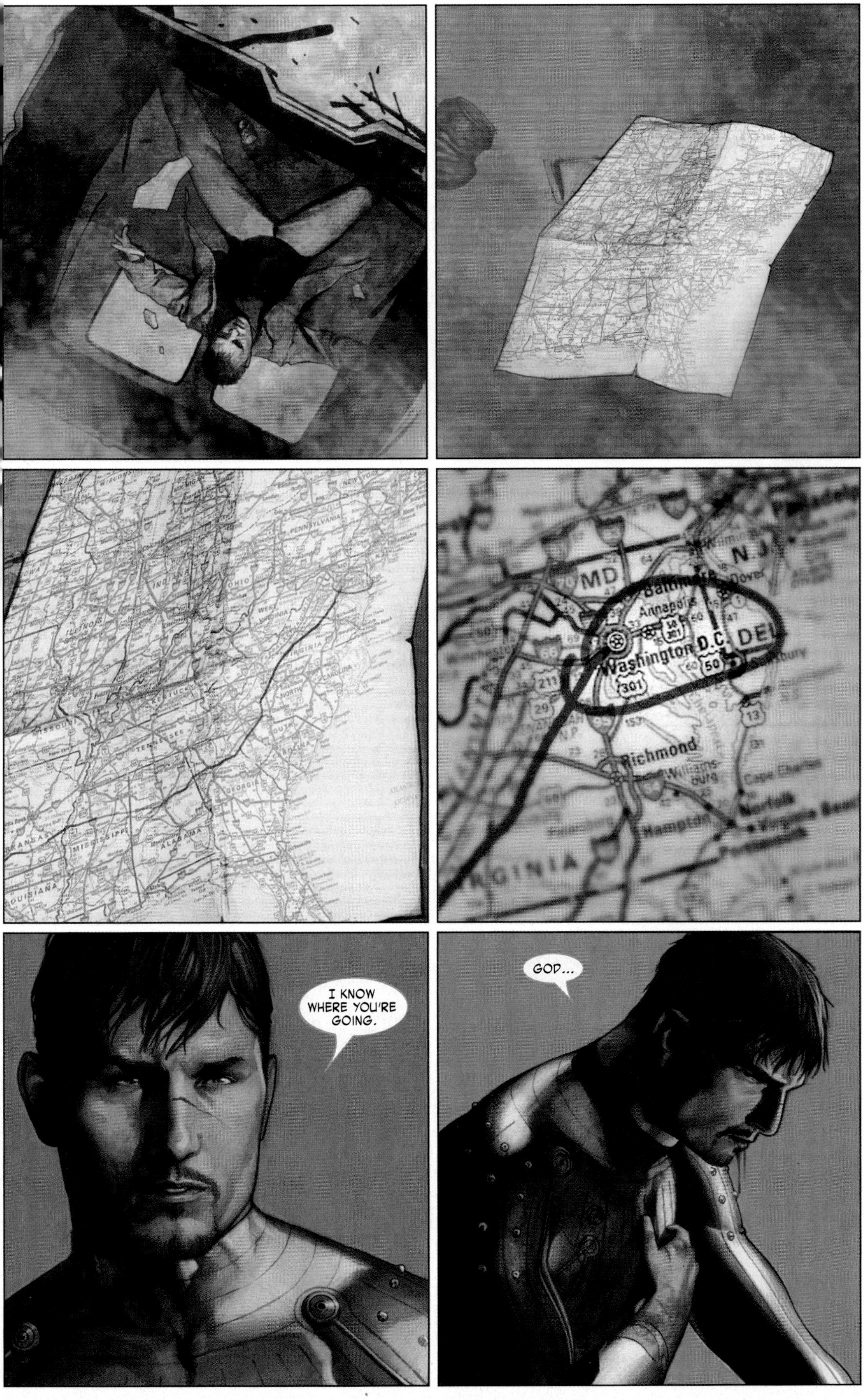
MD
N.J.
Dover
Annapolis
Washington
D.C.
DEL
Richmond
Cape Charles
Norfolk
Hampton
I KNOW WHERE YOU'RE GOING.
GOD...

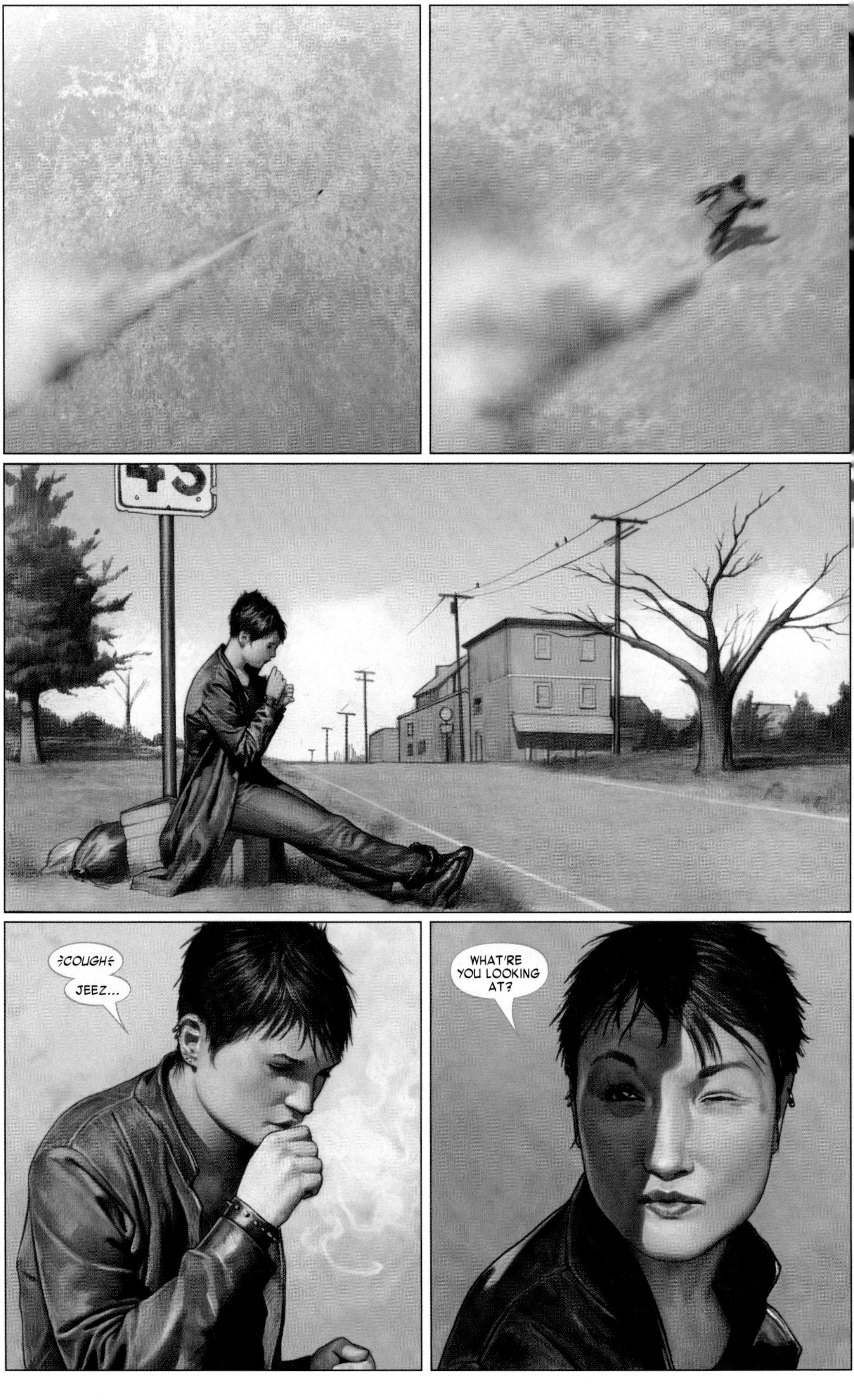

43
COUGH
JEEZ...
WHAT'RE YOU LOOKING AT?

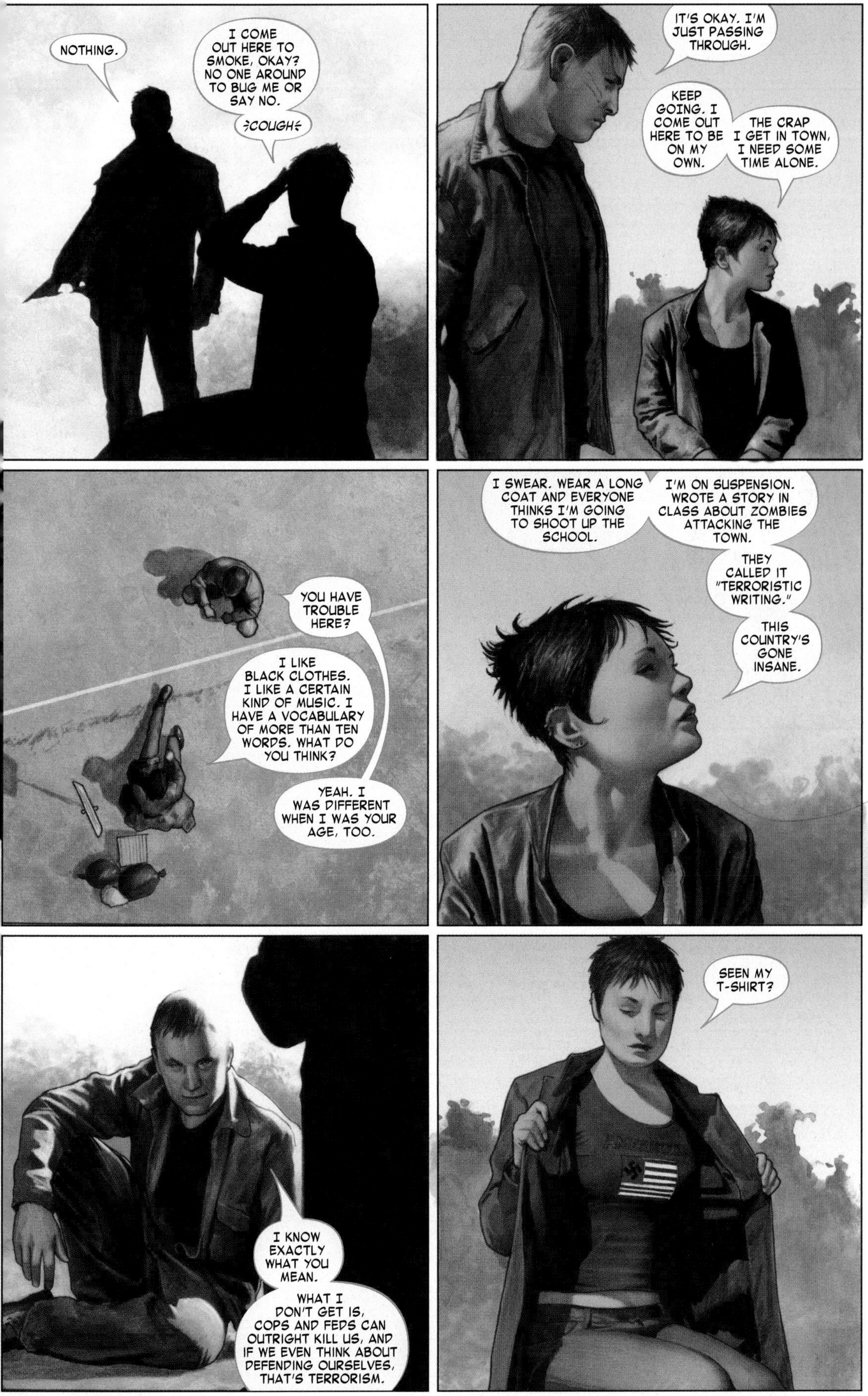

NOTHING.
I COME OUT HERE TO SMOKE, OKAY? NO ONE AROUND TO BUG ME OR SAY NO.
COUGH
IT'S OKAY. I'M JUST PASSING THROUGH.
KEEP GOING. I COME OUT HERE TO BE ON MY OWN.
THE CRAP I GET IN TOWN, I NEED SOME TIME ALONE.
YOU HAVE TROUBLE HERE?
I LIKE BLACK CLOTHES. I LIKE A CERTAIN KIND OF MUSIC. I HAVE A VOCABULARY OF MORE THAN TEN WORDS. WHAT DO YOU THINK?
YEAH. I WAS DIFFERENT WHEN I WAS YOUR AGE, TOO.
I SWEAR. WEAR A LONG COAT AND EVERYONE THINKS I'M GOING TO SHOOT UP THE SCHOOL.
I'M ON SUSPENSION. WROTE A STORY IN CLASS ABOUT ZOMBIES ATTACKING THE TOWN.
THEY CALLED IT "TERRORISTIC WRITING."
THIS COUNTRY'S GONE INSANE.
I KNOW EXACTLY WHAT YOU MEAN.
WHAT I DON'T GET IS, COPS AND FEDS CAN OUTRIGHT KILL US, AND IF WE EVEN THINK ABOUT DEFENDING OURSELVES, THAT'S TERRORISM.
SEEN MY T-SHIRT?

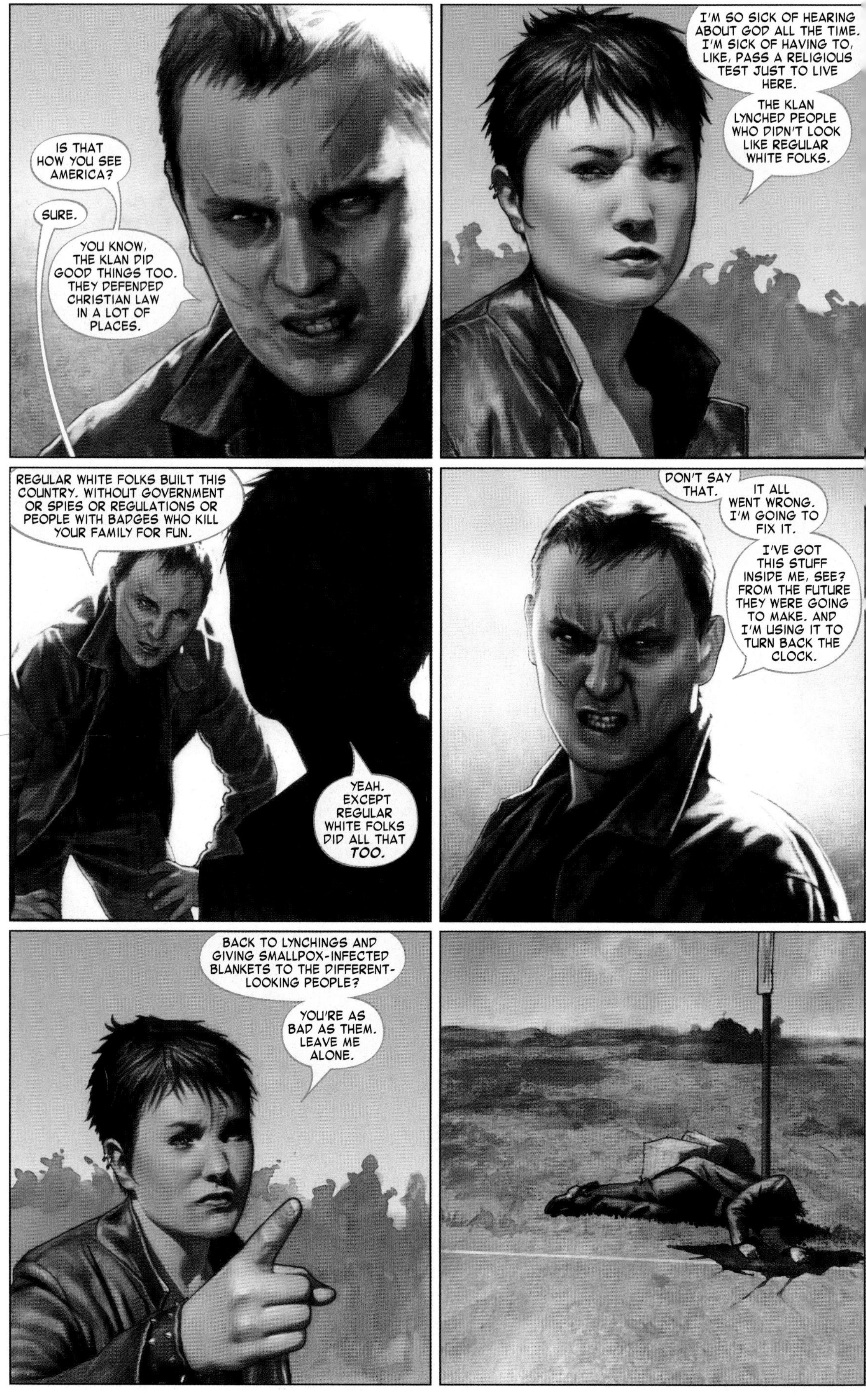
IS THAT HOW YOU SEE AMERICA?
SURE.
YOU KNOW, THE KLAN DID GOOD THINGS TOO. THEY DEFENDED CHRISTIAN LAW IN A LOT OF PLACES.
I'M SO SICK OF HEARING ABOUT GOD ALL THE TIME. I'M SICK OF HAVING TO, LIKE, PASS A RELIGIOUS TEST JUST TO LIVE HERE.
THE KLAN LYNCHED PEOPLE WHO DIDN'T LOOK LIKE REGULAR WHITE FOLKS.
REGULAR WHITE FOLKS BUILT THIS COUNTRY. WITHOUT GOVERNMENT OR SPIES OR REGULATIONS OR PEOPLE WITH BADGES WHO KILL YOUR FAMILY FOR FUN.
YEAH. EXCEPT REGULAR WHITE FOLKS DID ALL THAT TOO.
DON'T SAY THAT.
IT ALL WENT WRONG. I'M GOING TO FIX IT.
I'VE GOT THIS STUFF INSIDE ME, SEE? FROM THE FUTURE THEY WERE GOING TO MAKE. AND I'M USING IT TO TURN BACK THE CLOCK.
BACK TO LYNCHINGS AND GIVING SMALLPOX-INFECTED BLANKETS TO THE DIFFERENT-LOOKING PEOPLE?
YOU'RE AS BAD AS THEM. LEAVE ME ALONE.

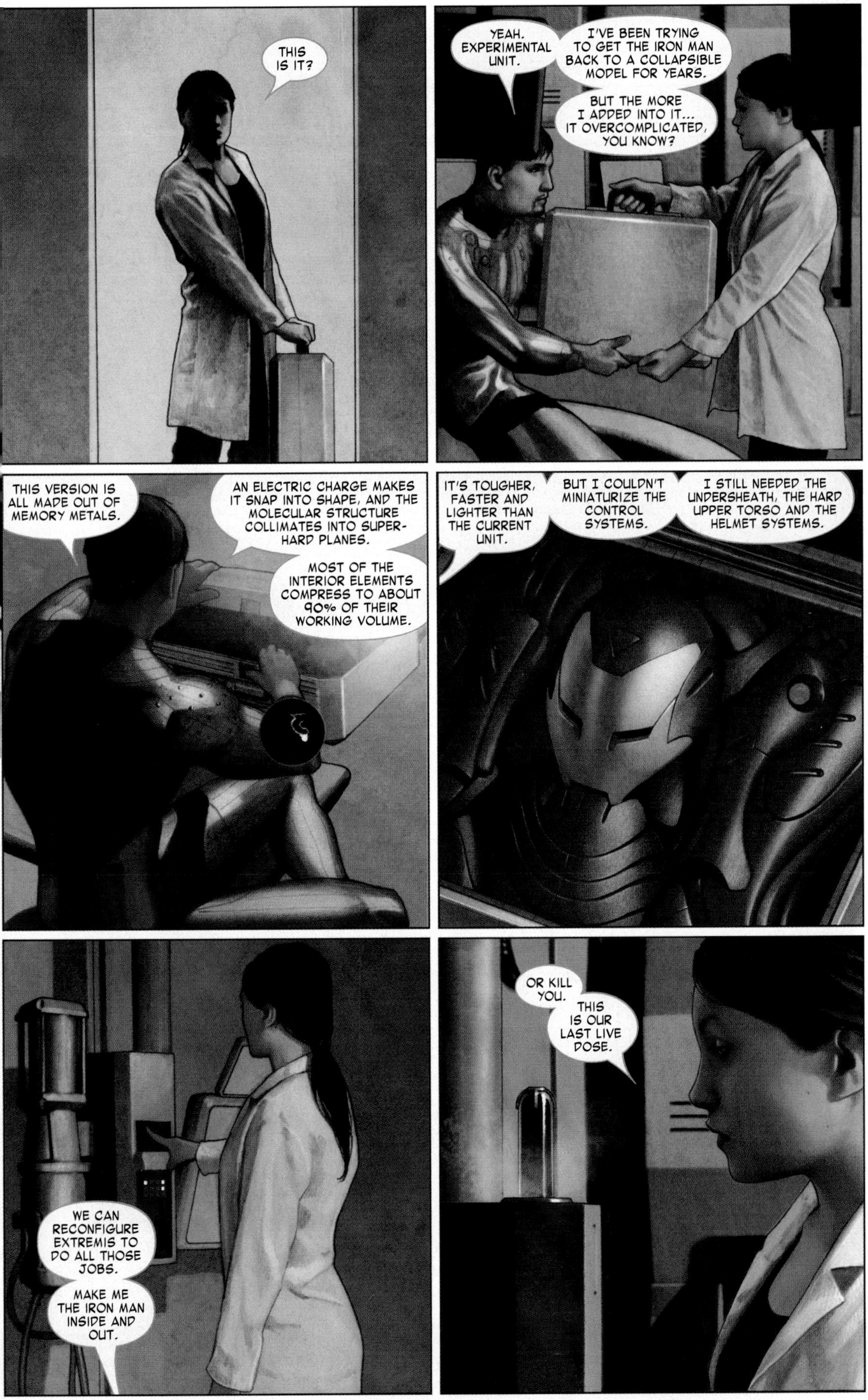
THIS IS IT?
YEAH. EXPERIMENTAL UNIT.
I'VE BEEN TRYING TO GET THE IRON MAN BACK TO A COLLAPSIBLE MODEL FOR YEARS.
BUT THE MORE I ADDED INTO IT... IT OVERCOMPLICATED, YOU KNOW?
THIS VERSION IS ALL MADE OUT OF MEMORY METALS.
AN ELECTRIC CHARGE MAKES IT SNAP INTO SHAPE, AND THE MOLECULAR STRUCTURE COLLIMATES INTO SUPER-HARD PLANES.
MOST OF THE INTERIOR ELEMENTS COMPRESS TO ABOUT 90% OF THEIR WORKING VOLUME.
IT'S TOUGHER, FASTER AND LIGHTER THAN THE CURRENT UNIT.
BUT I COULDN'T MINIATURIZE THE CONTROL SYSTEMS.
I STILL NEEDED THE UNDERSHEATH, THE HARD UPPER TORSO AND THE HELMET SYSTEMS.
WE CAN RECONFIGURE EXTREMIS TO DO ALL THOSE JOBS.
MAKE ME THE IRON MAN INSIDE AND OUT.
OR KILL YOU.
THIS IS OUR LAST LIVE DOSE.

AND THIS IS THE EXTREMIS COMPILER.

WE HAVE TO INSTRUCT IT WHAT TO DO TO YOU. THE COMPUTER WILL RECOMPILE THE DOSE-- REPROGRAM WHAT IT DOES.

ONE MISTAKE AND IT *WILL* KILL YOU.

WELL, LET'S NOT MAKE ANY MISTAKES.

YOU BETTER TYPE. I'M DOWN TO ONE HAND--

TONY

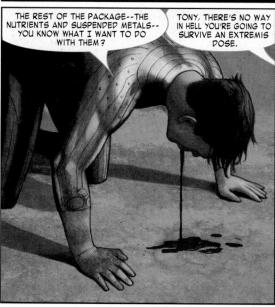

THE REST OF THE PACKAGE--THE NUTRIENTS AND SUSPENDED METALS-- YOU KNOW WHAT I WANT TO DO WITH THEM?

TONY, THERE'S NO WAY IN HELL YOU'RE GOING TO SURVIVE AN EXTREMIS DOSE.

I HAVE TO.

OR MY INTERNAL INJURIES ARE GOING TO KILL ME.

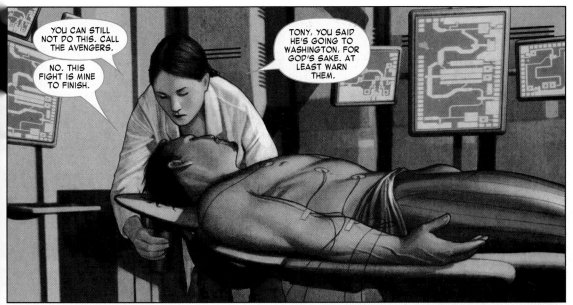

YOU CAN STILL NOT DO THIS. CALL THE AVENGERS.

NO. THIS FIGHT IS MINE TO FINISH.

TONY, YOU SAID HE'S GOING TO WASHINGTON, FOR GOD'S SAKE. AT LEAST WARN THEM.

IF I DIE ON THE TABLE, YOU WARN THEM.

OTHERWISE: THIS IS WHAT I DO. THIS IS ALL I HAVE.

ALL I HAVE IS MAKING THE FUTURE, AND STOPPING THE ANIMALS WHO WANT TO TAKE THE FUTURE AWAY FROM PEOPLE.

THIS MUCK OF YOURS IS THE FUTURE.

IT SHOULDN'T BE WASTED ON KILLERS.

THEY ALL NEED TO SEE THAT.

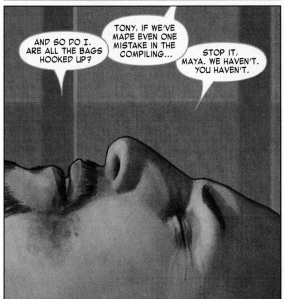

AND SO DO I. ARE ALL THE BAGS HOOKED UP?

TONY, IF WE'VE MADE EVEN ONE MISTAKE IN THE COMPILING...

STOP IT, MAYA. WE HAVEN'T. YOU HAVEN'T.

YOU'VE ALWAYS BEEN READY FOR THIS TO BE USED.

YOU'RE SMARTER THAN I AM. ALWAYS HAVE BEEN.

ME, I'M JUST A GUY IN AN IRON SUIT.

BUT I ALWAYS WANTED TO BE MORE. SAL SAID SOMETHING ABOUT BENCH-TESTING THE FUTURE?

TEST PILOT FOR THE FUTURE.

FUNNY: THIS IS THE SECOND TIME I'VE HAD TO WORK AGAINST THE CLOCK FOR THE IRON MAN TO SAVE MY LIFE.

KK
KKKAHHKK

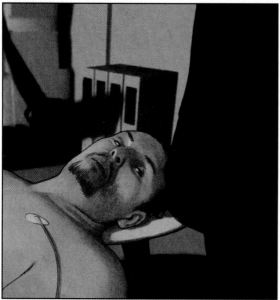

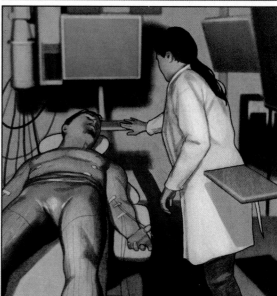

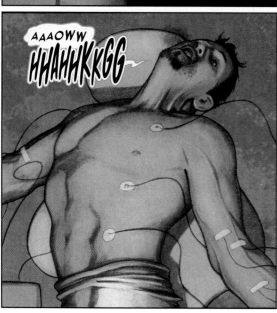

AAAOWW
HHAHHKKGG

HRUP

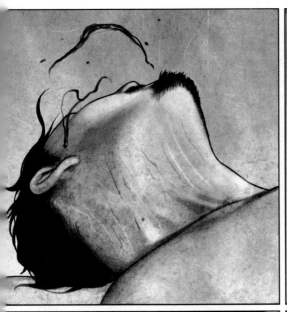

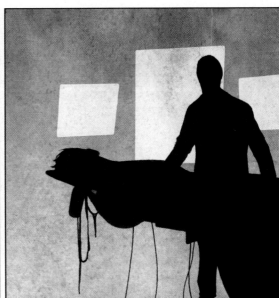

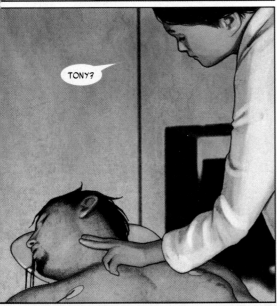

TONY?

TONY?

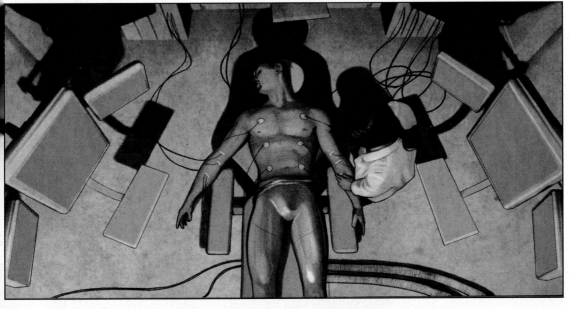

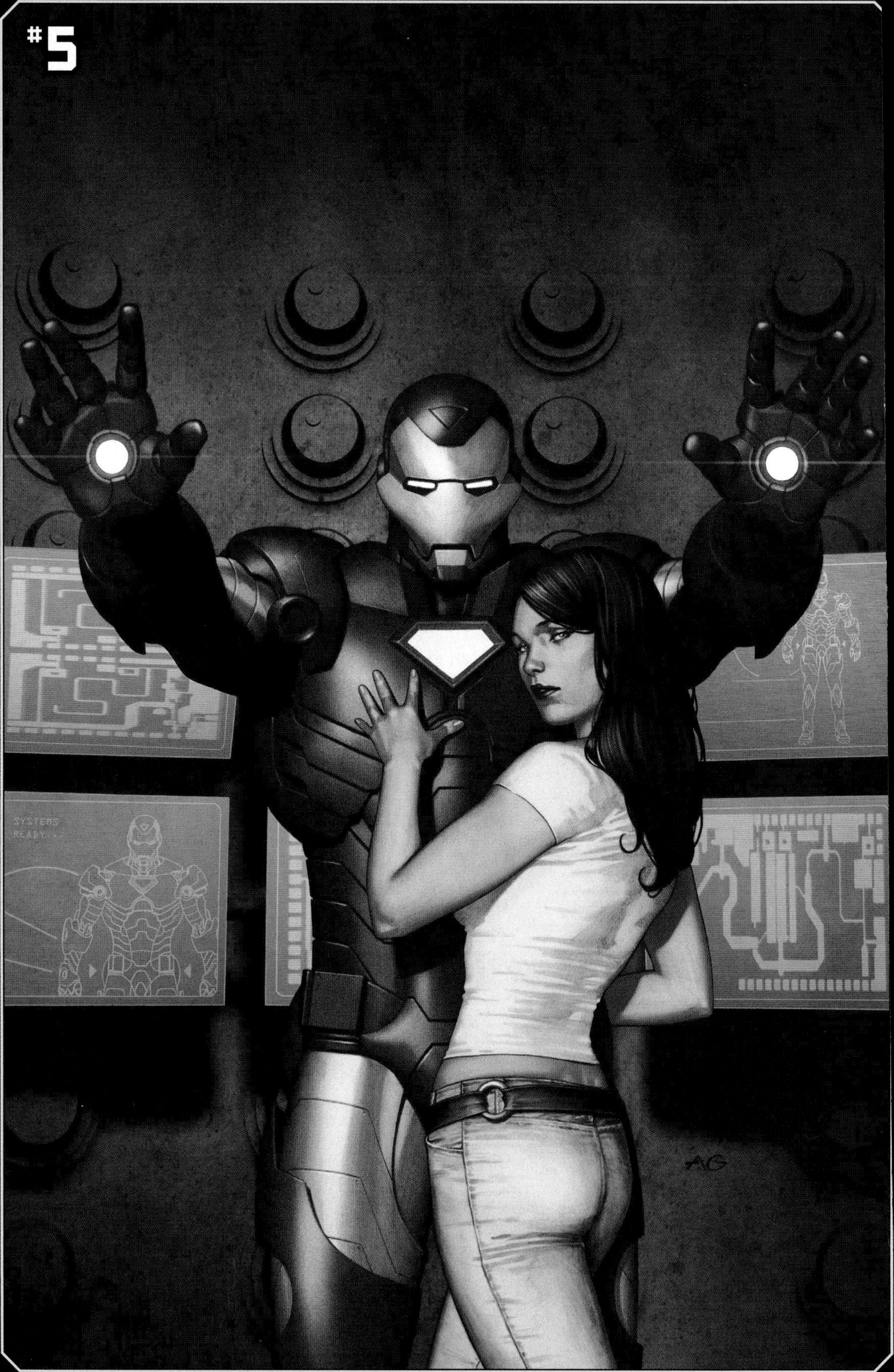
#5
SYSTEMS READY...

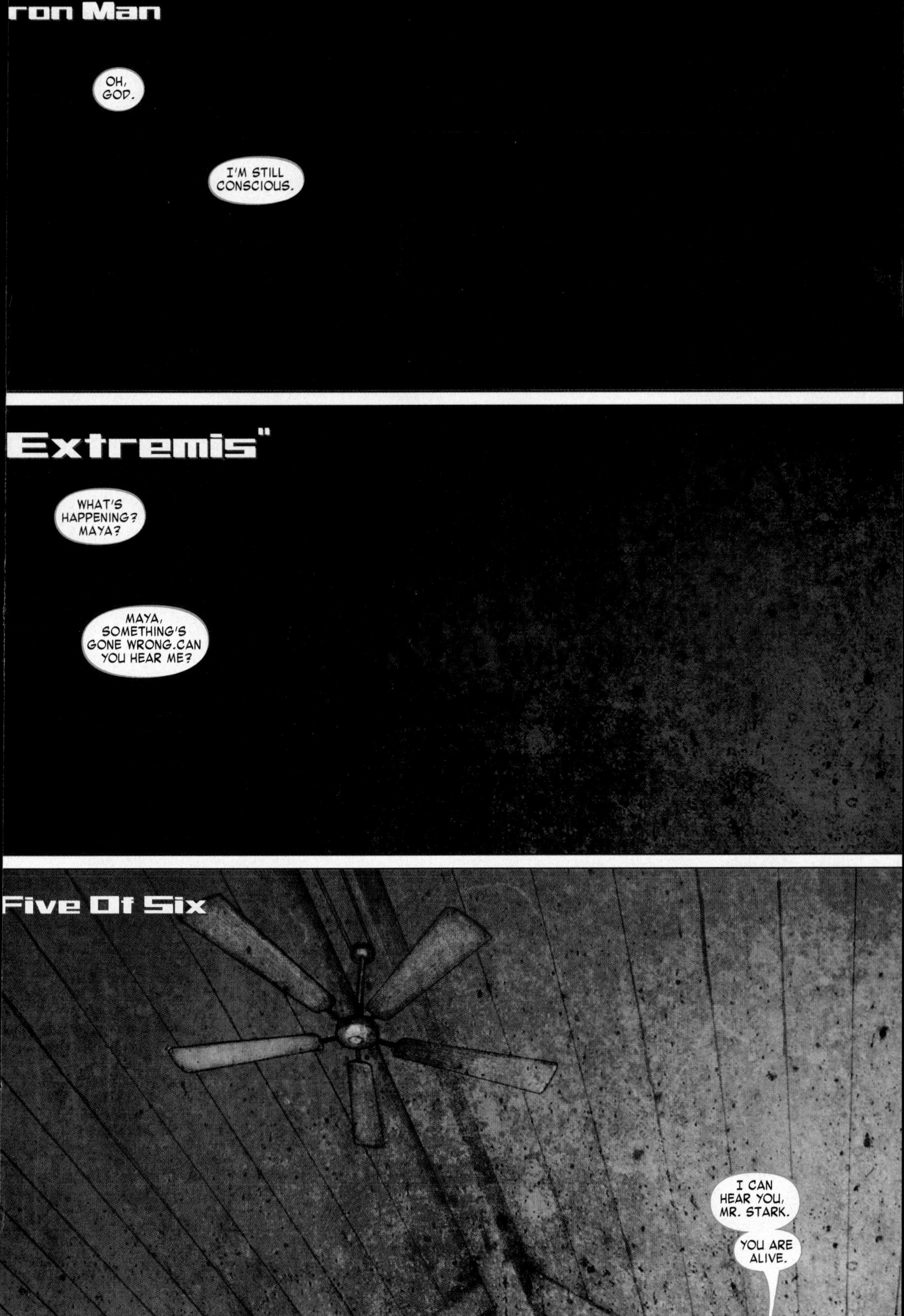
ron Man
OH, GOD.
I'M STILL CONSCIOUS.
Extremis"
WHAT'S HAPPENING? MAYA?
MAYA, SOMETHING'S GONE WRONG.CAN YOU HEAR ME?
Five Of Six
I CAN HEAR YOU, MR. STARK.
YOU ARE ALIVE.

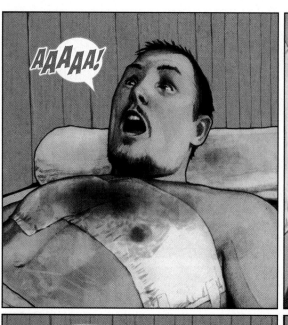

AAAAA!

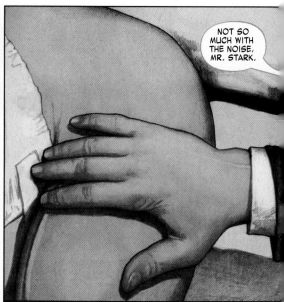

NOT SO MUCH WITH THE NOISE, MR. STARK.

AND NOT SO MUCH WITH THE MOVING.

THERE IS A PIECE OF SHRAPNEL LODGED NEXT TO YOUR HEART. I COULD NOT REMOVE IT.

I KNOW YOU. WE MET AT A CONFERENCE...

HO YINSEN. THE MEDICAL FUTURIST.

GOOD MEMORY FOR ONE WHO WAS SO BLISTERINGLY DRUNK.

I GOT TOO USED TO THE EASY LIVING OF THE CONFERENCE-TOURING SCIENTIST.

YOU TAKE ONE WRONG CORNER IN A FOREIGN CITY, AND...HERE I AM.

AND WHERE'S HERE?

A REMOTE CAMP OF THE... WELL, WHAT DO WE CALL THEM?

INSURGENTS? GUNMEN? TERRORISTS? GUERRILLAS? IT IS ALL THE SAME.

THEY HAVE YINSEN, THE GREAT MEDICAL INNOVATOR, FOR COMBAT MEDICINE.

AND NOW THEY HAVE ANTHONY STARK, THE GREAT WEAPONEER.

YOU SEE THIS? THIS IS YOUR FUTURE NOW.

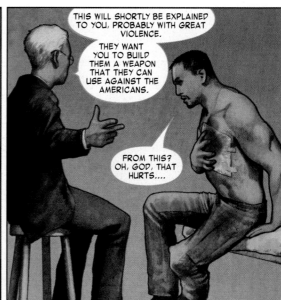

THIS WILL SHORTLY BE EXPLAINED TO YOU, PROBABLY WITH GREAT VIOLENCE.

THEY WANT YOU TO BUILD THEM A WEAPON THAT THEY CAN USE AGAINST THE AMERICANS.

FROM THIS? OH, GOD, THAT HURTS....

LUCKILY FOR YOU, YOUR WOUND IS FATAL. YOU WILL BE DEAD IN A WEEK.

THE SHRAPNEL IS MOVING. YOU WILL BE SLOWLY STABBED TO DEATH BY A CHUNK OF YOUR OWN MUNITION.

YINSEN IS NOT SO LUCKY, FOR HE IS TOUGHER THAN JOHN WAYNE'S OLD BOOTS AND WILL LIVE FOREVER.

I CAN'T GIVE THESE PEOPLE A WEAPON.

IF YOU TRY HARD, YOU COULD PERHAPS MAKE YOURSELF DIE FIRST.

YOU'RE NOT HELPING, YINSEN.

YOU ARE LUCKY TO HAVE ME AS YOUR FRIEND, WHITEY.

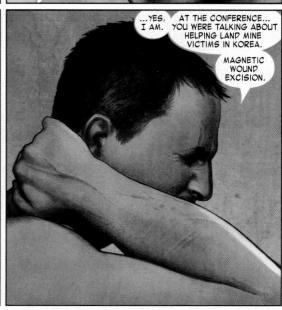

...YES, I AM.

AT THE CONFERENCE... YOU WERE TALKING ABOUT HELPING LAND MINE VICTIMS IN KOREA.

MAGNETIC WOUND EXCISION.

I CANNOT REMOVE THE SHRAPNEL. IT PRESSES ON YOUR HEART. THERE COULD BE A RUPTURE.

NOT REMOVE IT-- HOLD IT.

HOLD IT IN PLACE, STOP IT WORKING ITSELF DEEPER.

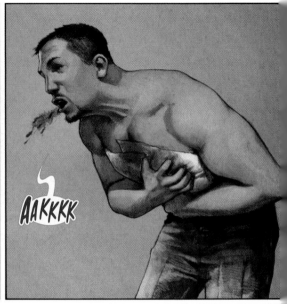

AAKKKK

BACK TO BED. DIE IN RELATIVE COMFORT AT LEAST.

I AM AFRAID I WALKED OUT. SOMETHING ABOUT EXO-SKELETONS FOR SOLDIERS. WAR STUFF.

DID...DID YOU SEE MY PRESENTATION AT THE CONFERENCE?

IT WASN'T FOR WAR. THAT WAS JUST TO GET THE FUNDING.

YOU CAN'T JUST...WISH THE FUTURE INTO BEING. IT HAS TO BE PAID FOR.

EVEN THE MUNITIONS... WERE JUST STEALING MONEY FROM THE ARMY FOR THE REAL WORK.

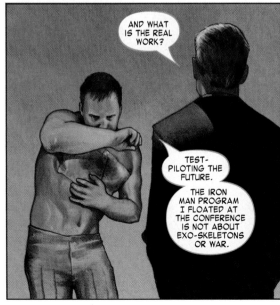

AND WHAT IS THE REAL WORK?

TEST-PILOTING THE FUTURE.

THE IRON MAN PROGRAM I FLOATED AT THE CONFERENCE IS NOT ABOUT EXO-SKELETONS OR WAR.

IT'S ABOUT BECOMING BETTER.

IT'S ABOUT BRINGING ON THE FUTURE.

THE EARLIEST STAGES OF ADAPTING MACHINE TO MAN AND MAKING US GREAT.

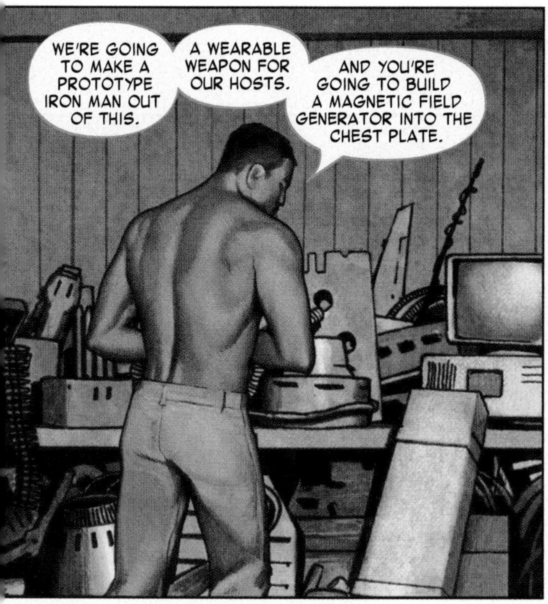
WE'RE GOING TO MAKE A PROTOTYPE IRON MAN OUT OF THIS.
A WEARABLE WEAPON FOR OUR HOSTS.
AND YOU'RE GOING TO BUILD A MAGNETIC FIELD GENERATOR INTO THE CHEST PLATE.

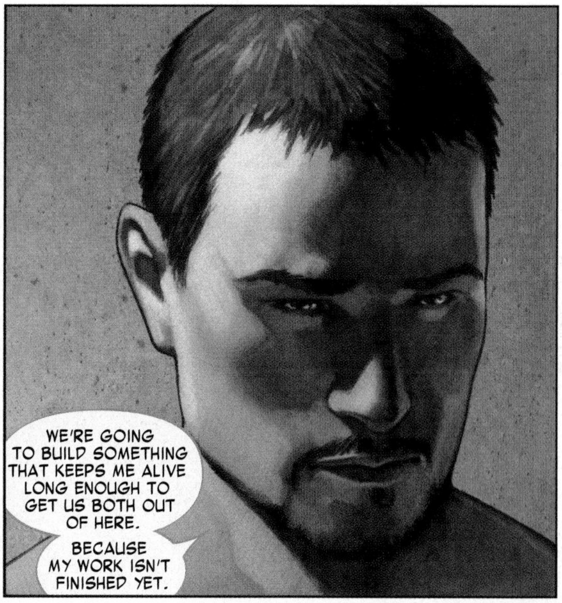
WE'RE GOING TO BUILD SOMETHING THAT KEEPS ME ALIVE LONG ENOUGH TO GET US BOTH OUT OF HERE.
BECAUSE MY WORK ISN'T FINISHED YET.

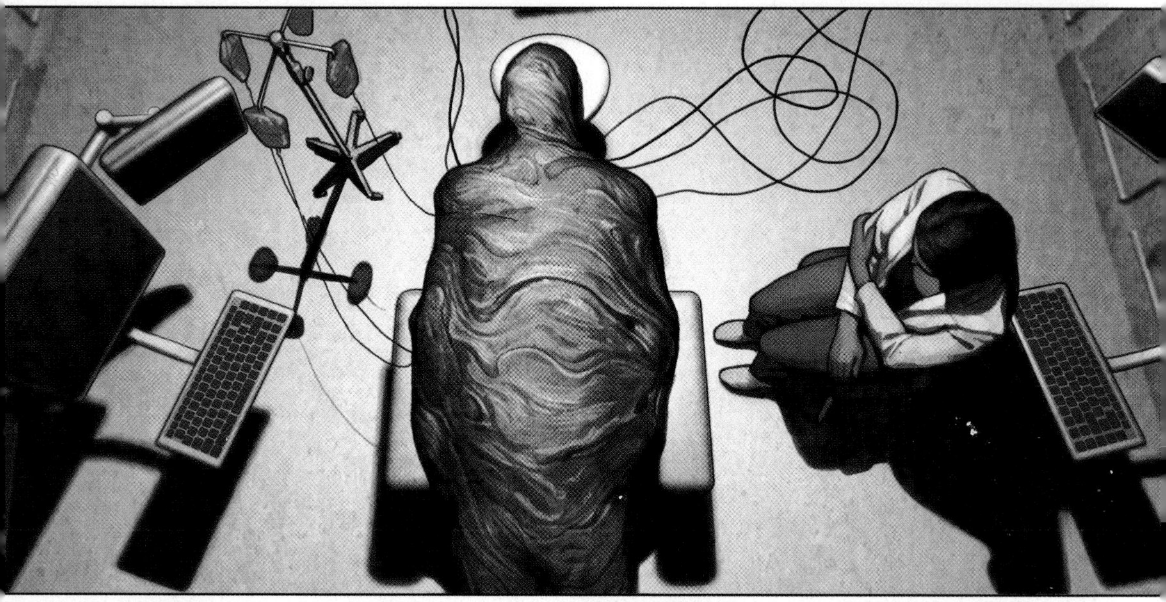

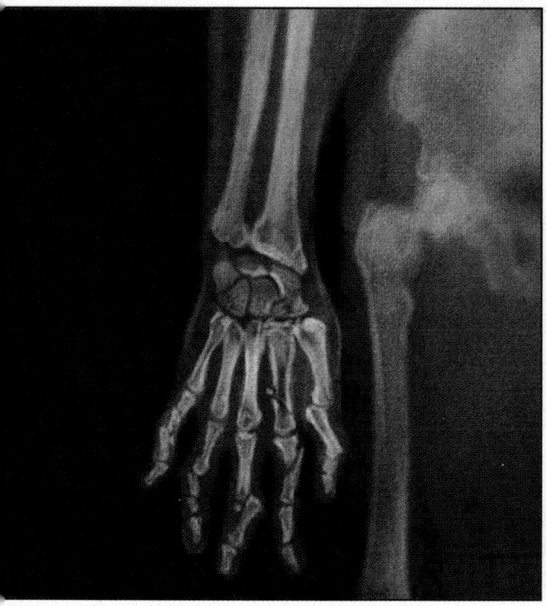

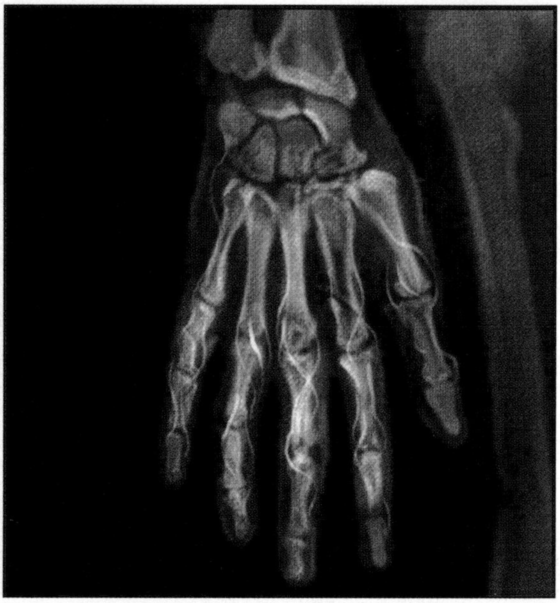

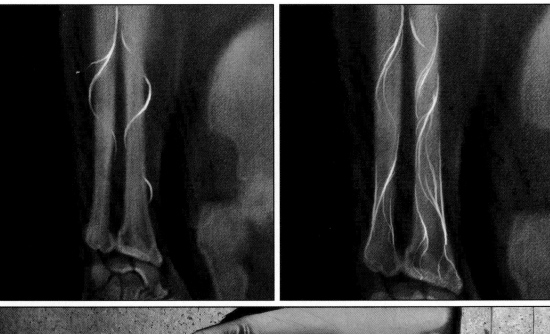

I TELL YOU...EITHER IT'S FINISHED, OR I AM.

IT IS DONE. AND PROBABLY SO ARE YOU.

QUICKLY, NOW.

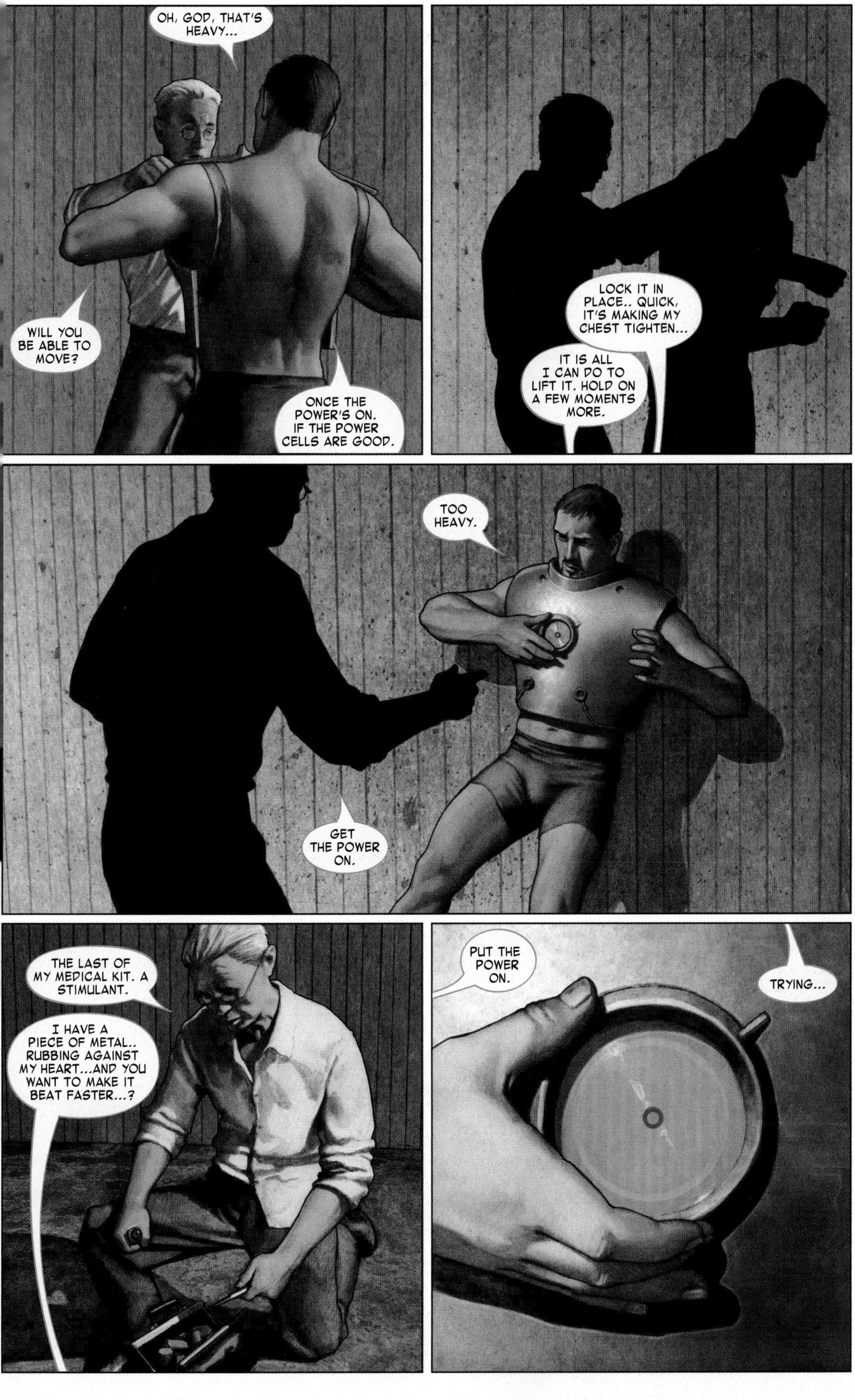
OH, GOD, THAT'S HEAVY...
WILL YOU BE ABLE TO MOVE?
ONCE THE POWER'S ON. IF THE POWER CELLS ARE GOOD.
LOCK IT IN PLACE.. QUICK, IT'S MAKING MY CHEST TIGHTEN...
IT IS ALL I CAN DO TO LIFT IT. HOLD ON A FEW MOMENTS MORE.
TOO HEAVY.
GET THE POWER ON.
THE LAST OF MY MEDICAL KIT. A STIMULANT.
I HAVE A PIECE OF METAL.. RUBBING AGAINST MY HEART...AND YOU WANT TO MAKE IT BEAT FASTER...?
PUT THE POWER ON.
TRYING...

UUUHHHH

TONY? TONY, ARE YOU WELL?

TONY, CAN YOU HEAR ME?

TONY, CAN YOU HEAR ME?

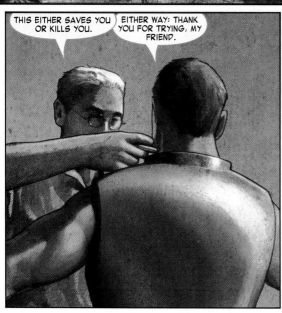

THIS EITHER SAVES YOU OR KILLS YOU.

EITHER WAY: THANK YOU FOR TRYING, MY FRIEND.

DAMN YOU FOR TRYING THIS, TONY.

THIS ISN'T HOW IT WAS SUPPOSED TO BE.

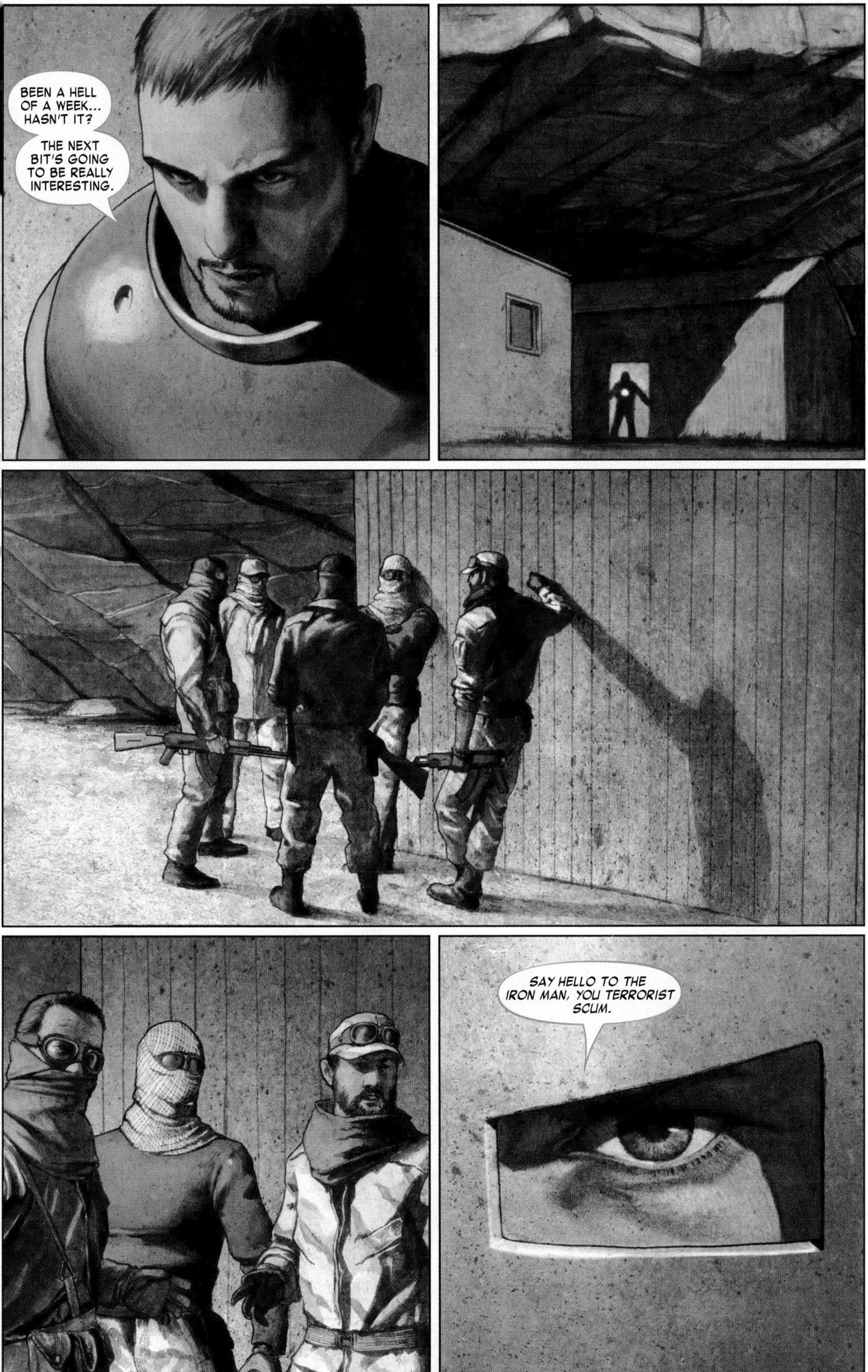
BEEN A HELL OF A WEEK... HASN'T IT?
THE NEXT BIT'S GOING TO BE REALLY INTERESTING.
SAY HELLO TO THE IRON MAN, YOU TERRORIST SCUM.

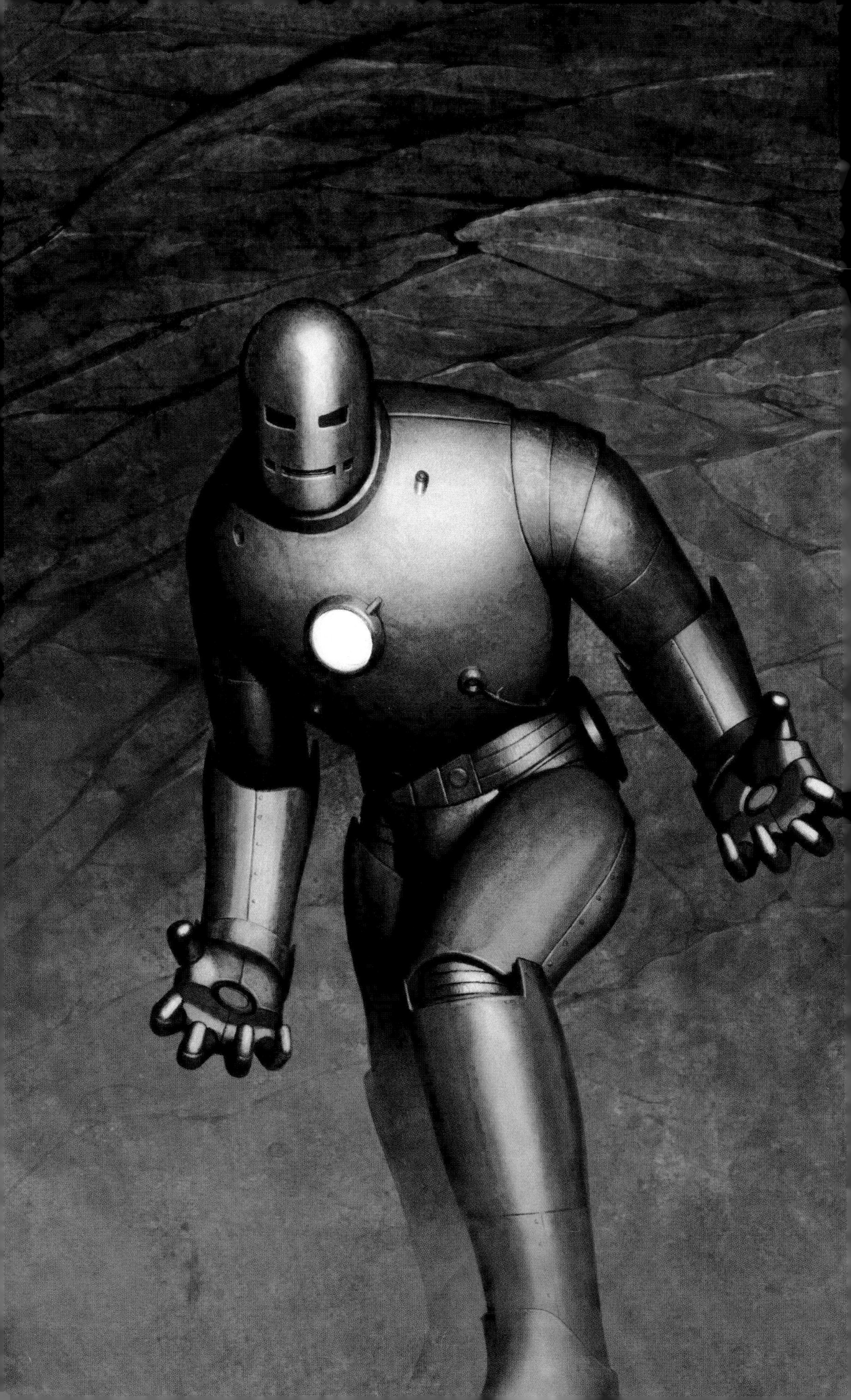

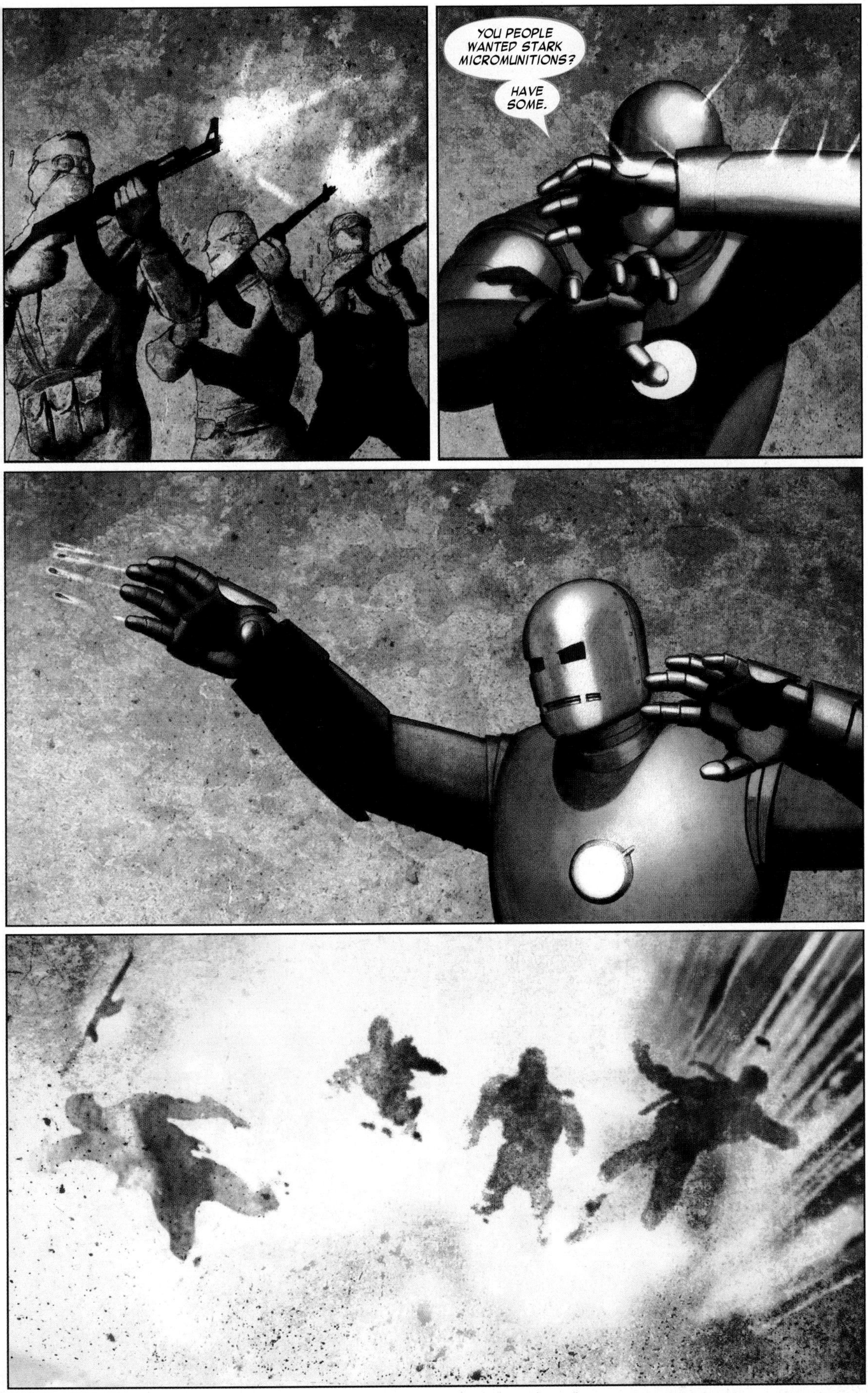
YOU PEOPLE WANTED STARK MICROMUNITIONS?
HAVE SOME.

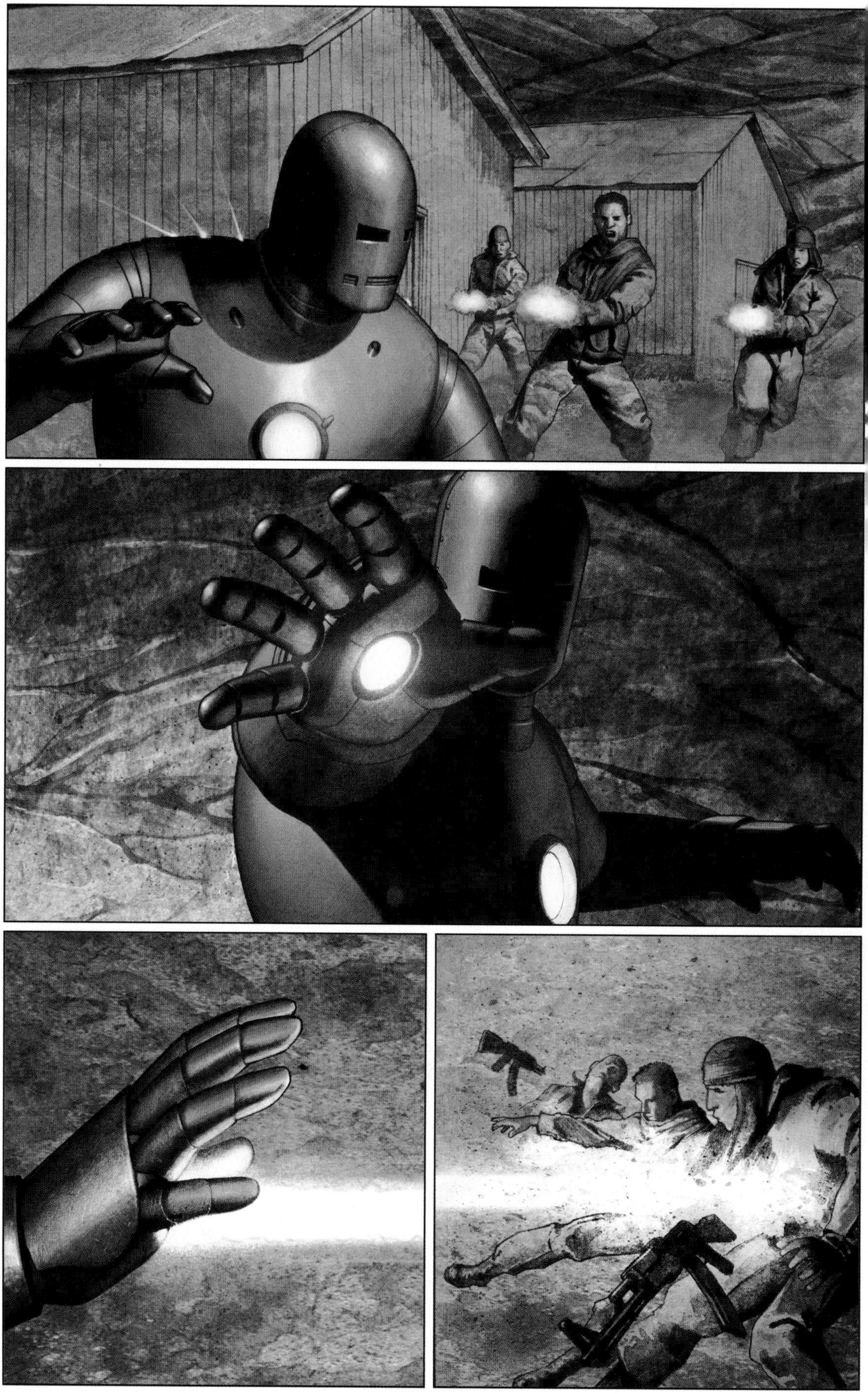

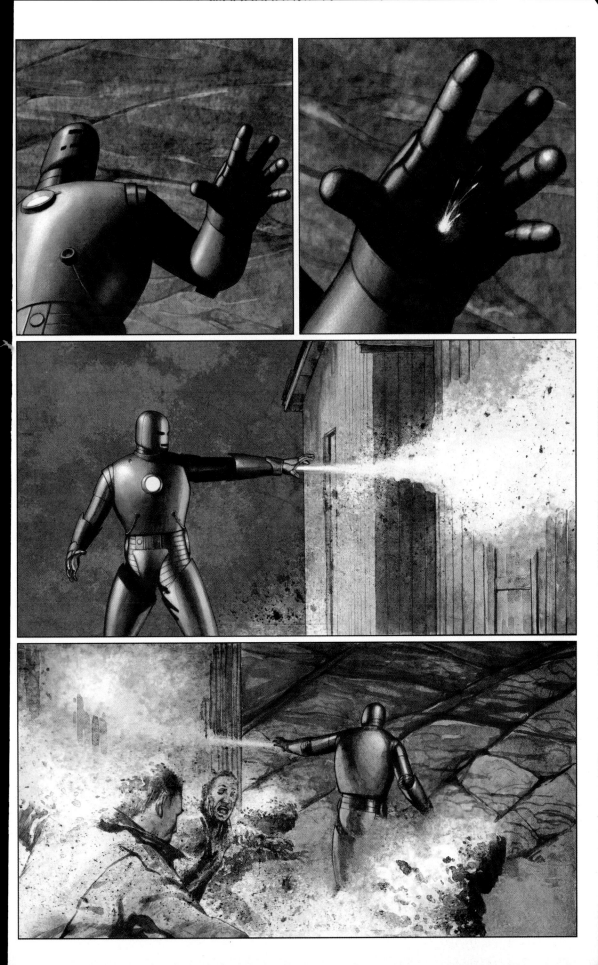

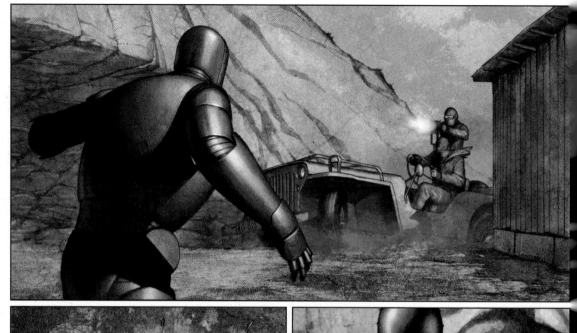

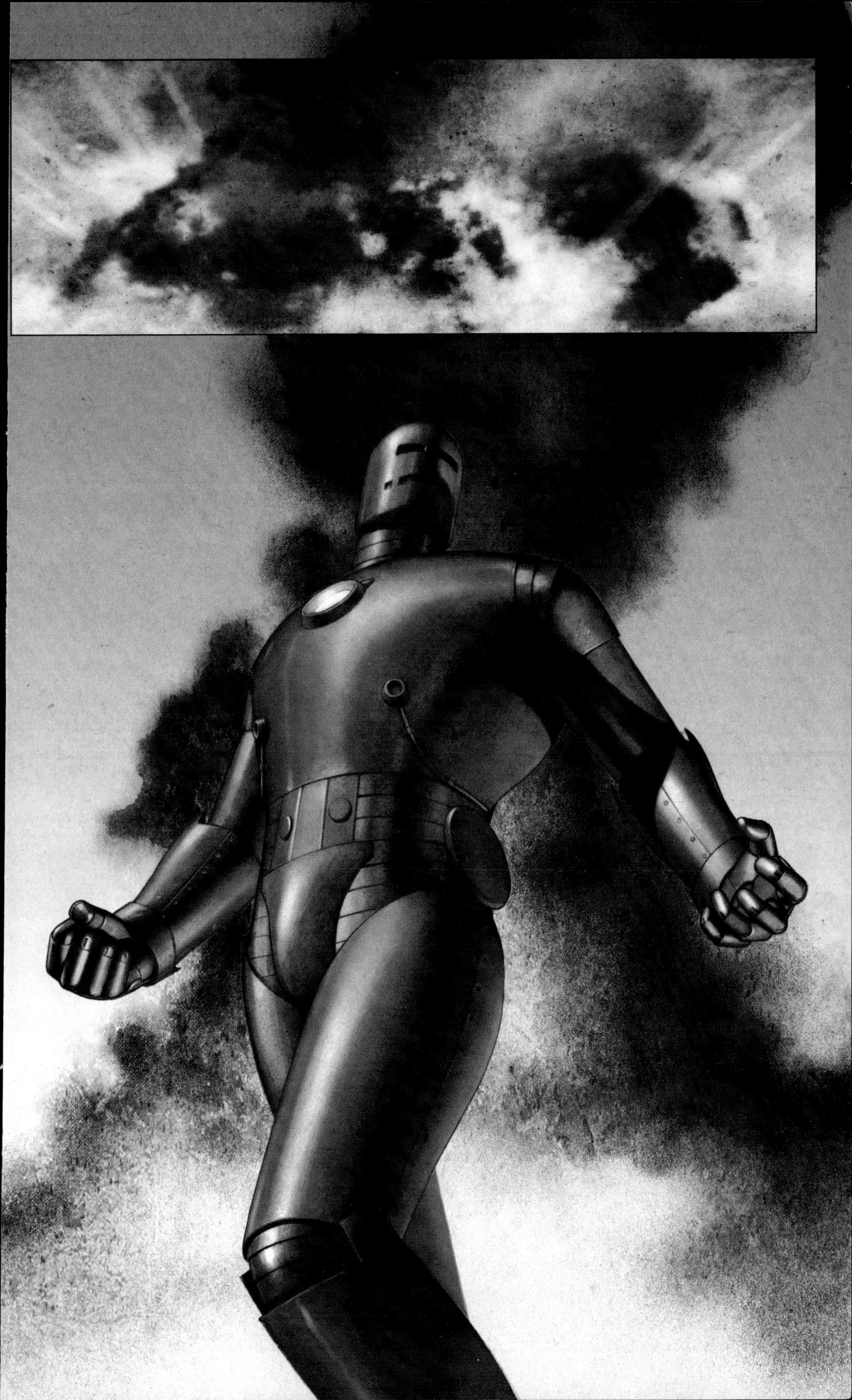

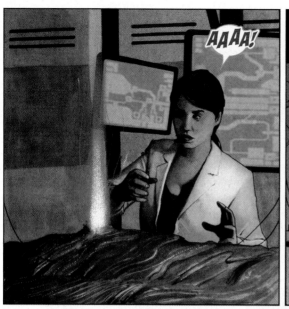

AAAA!

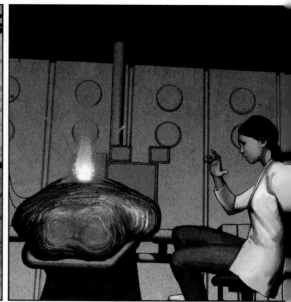

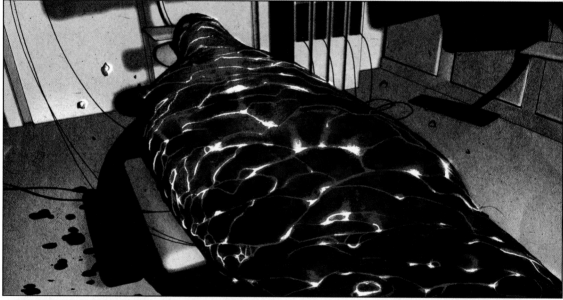

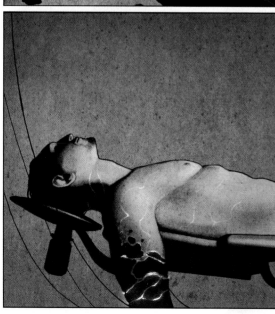

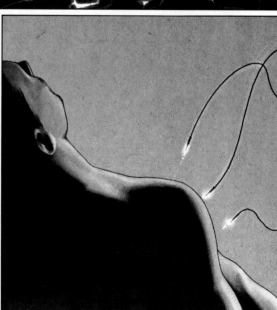

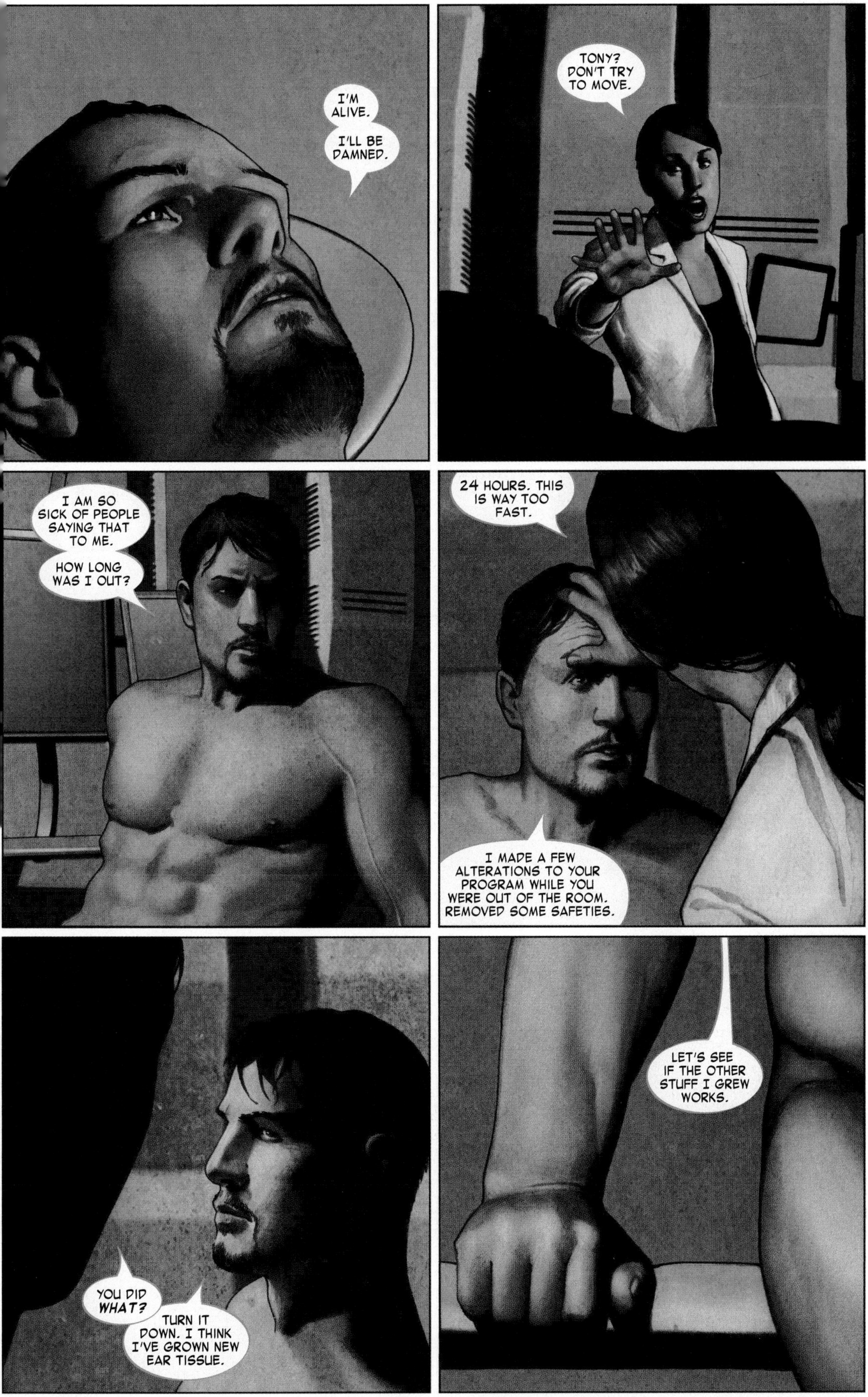
I'M ALIVE.
I'LL BE DAMNED.
TONY? DON'T TRY TO MOVE.
I AM SO SICK OF PEOPLE SAYING THAT TO ME.
HOW LONG WAS I OUT?
24 HOURS. THIS IS WAY TOO FAST.
I MADE A FEW ALTERATIONS TO YOUR PROGRAM WHILE YOU WERE OUT OF THE ROOM. REMOVED SOME SAFETIES.
YOU DID WHAT?
TURN IT DOWN. I THINK I'VE GROWN NEW EAR TISSUE.
LET'S SEE IF THE OTHER STUFF I GREW WORKS.

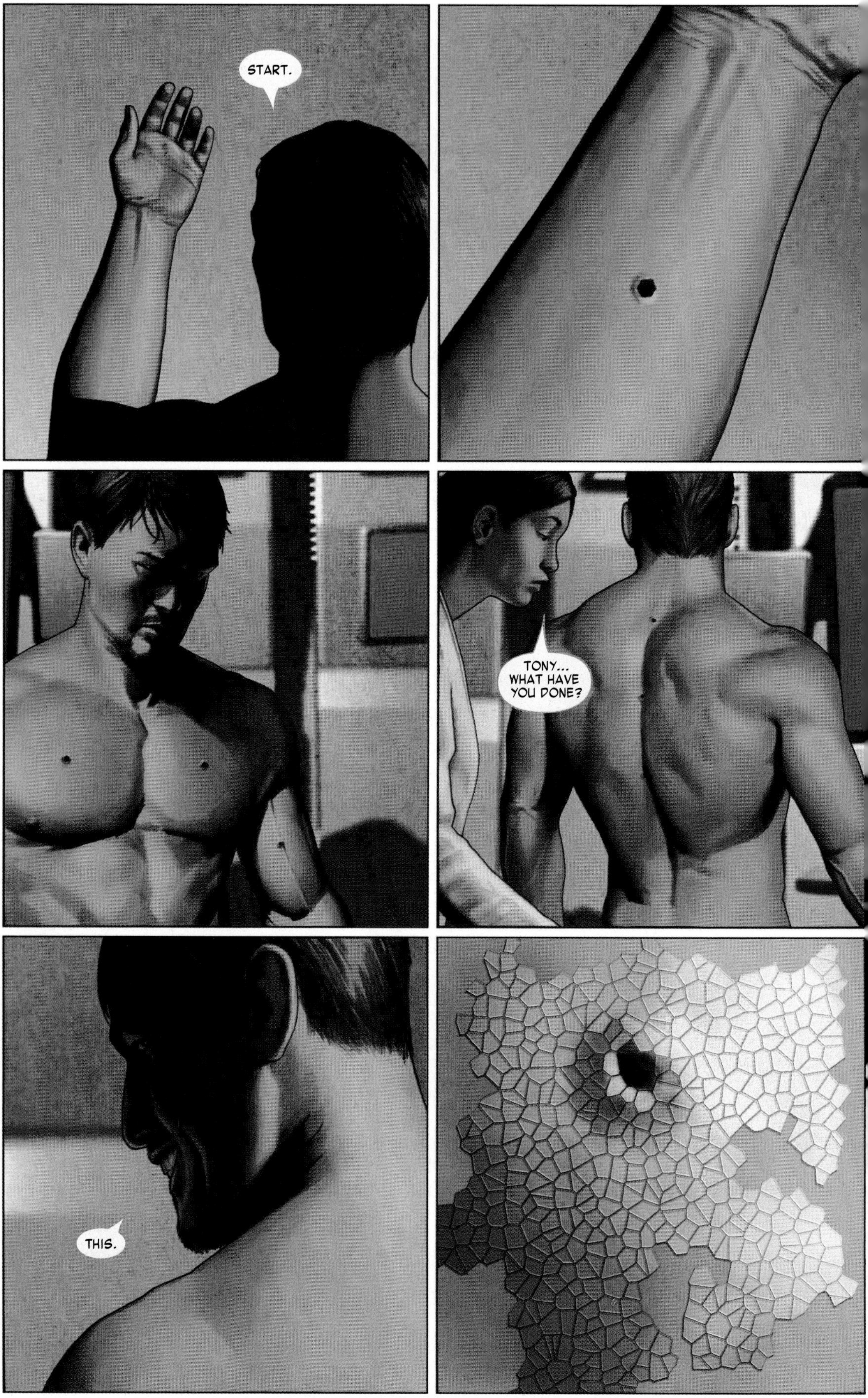
START.
TONY... WHAT HAVE YOU DONE?
THIS.

SUPERCOMPRESSED AND STORED IN THE HOLLOWS OF MY BONES, MAYA. I CARRY THE CRUCIAL UNDERSHEATH OF THE IRON MAN SUIT INSIDE MY BODY NOW.

WIRED DIRECTLY INTO MY BRAIN.

I CONTROL THE IRON MAN WITH THOUGHT, LIKE IT WAS ANOTHER LIMB.

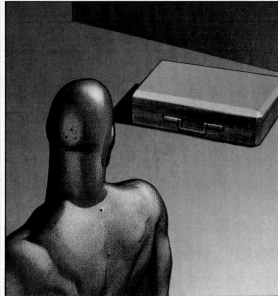

TKK!

HOW DID YOU DO THAT?

I SENT IT THE SIGNAL FROM THE LOCKCHIP IN MY ARM.

BRRR BRRR

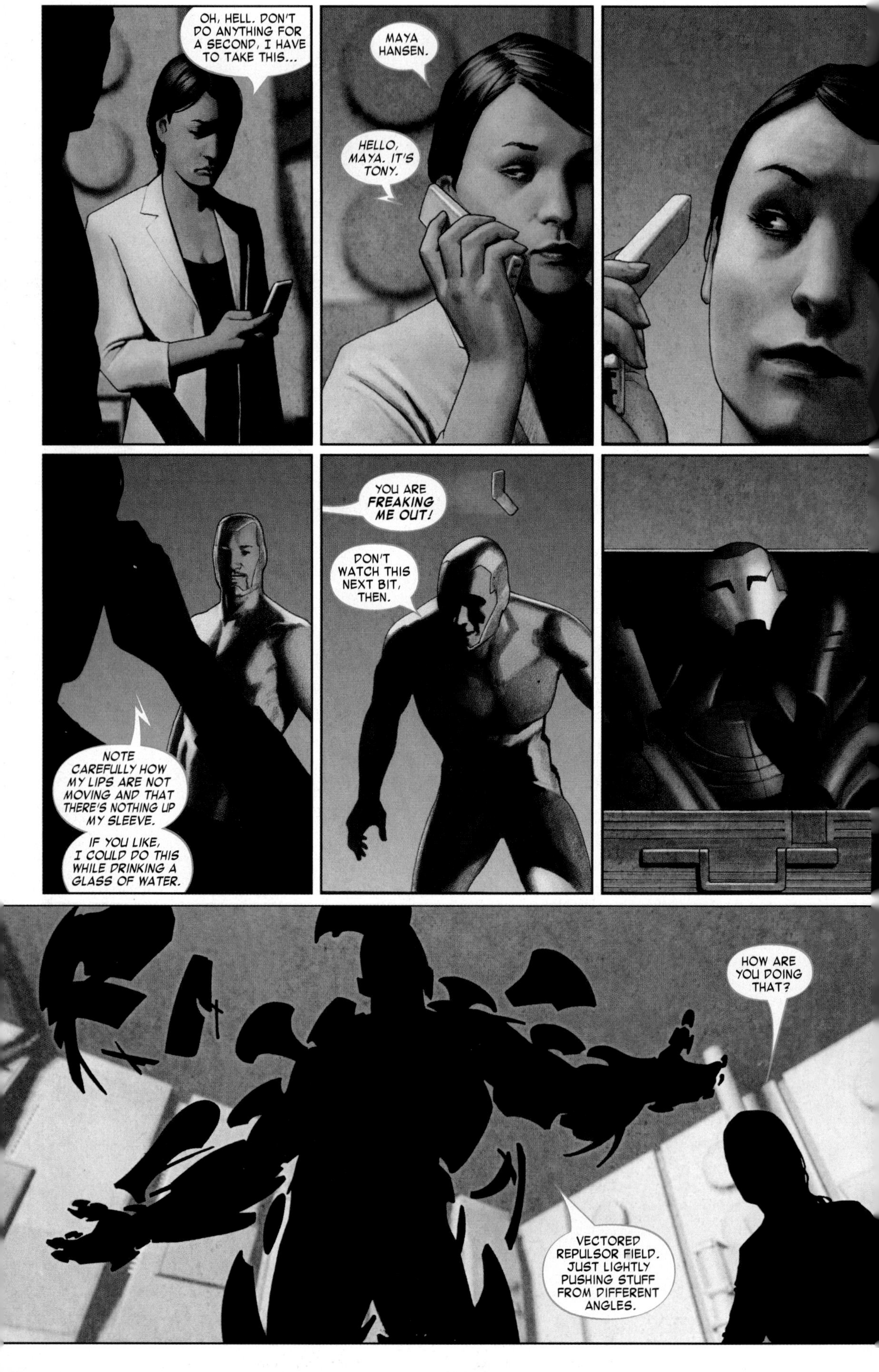
OH, HELL. DON'T DO ANYTHING FOR A SECOND, I HAVE TO TAKE THIS...
MAYA HANSEN.
HELLO, MAYA. IT'S TONY.
NOTE CAREFULLY HOW MY LIPS ARE NOT MOVING AND THAT THERE'S NOTHING UP MY SLEEVE.
IF YOU LIKE, I COULD DO THIS WHILE DRINKING A GLASS OF WATER.
YOU ARE FREAKING ME OUT!
DON'T WATCH THIS NEXT BIT, THEN.
HOW ARE YOU DOING THAT?
VECTORED REPULSOR FIELD. JUST LIGHTLY PUSHING STUFF FROM DIFFERENT ANGLES.

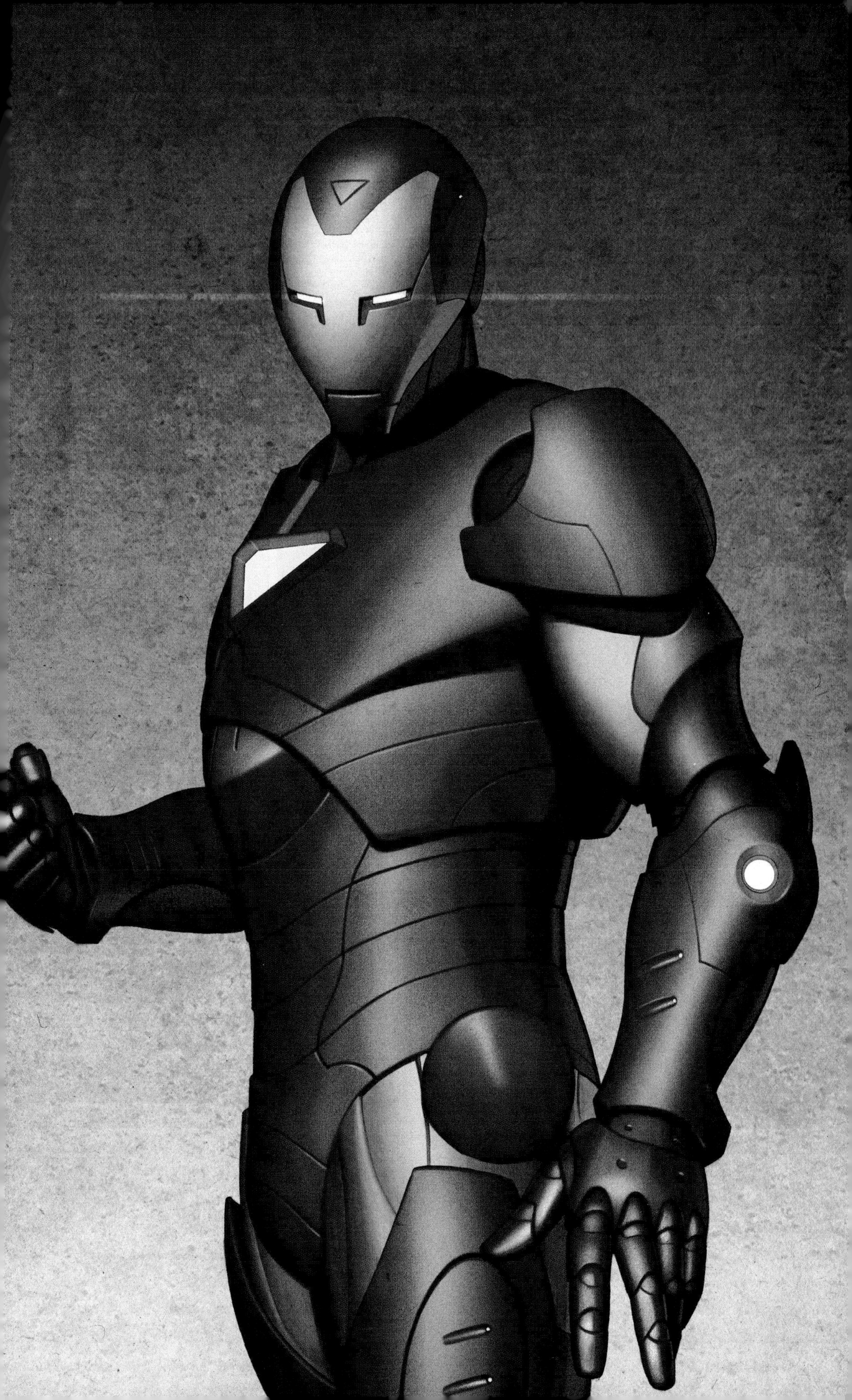

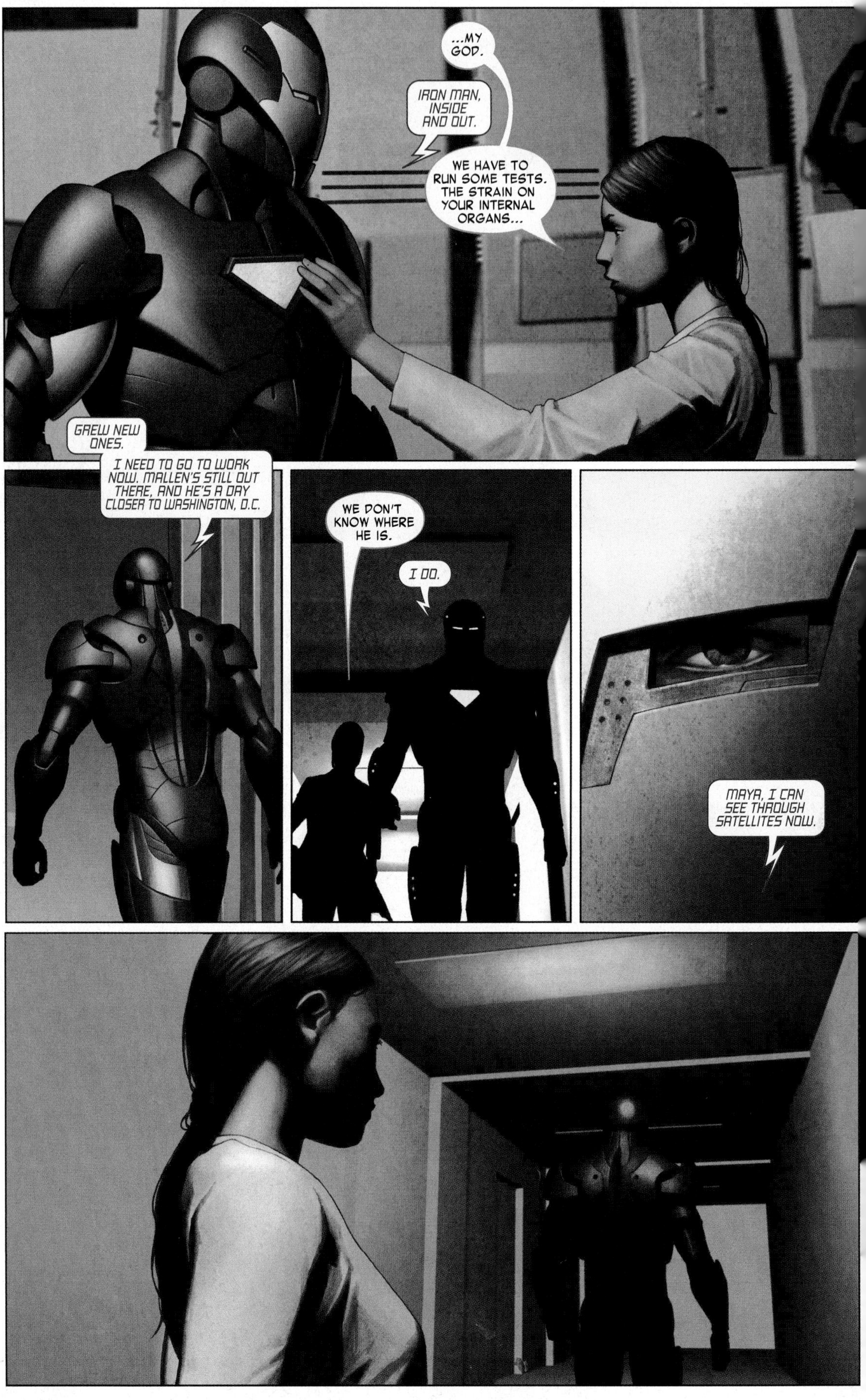
...MY GOD.
IRON MAN, INSIDE AND OUT.
WE HAVE TO RUN SOME TESTS. THE STRAIN ON YOUR INTERNAL ORGANS...
GREW NEW ONES.
I NEED TO GO TO WORK NOW. MALLEN'S STILL OUT THERE, AND HE'S A DAY CLOSER TO WASHINGTON, D.C.
WE DON'T KNOW WHERE HE IS.
I DO.
MAYA, I CAN SEE THROUGH SATELLITES NOW.

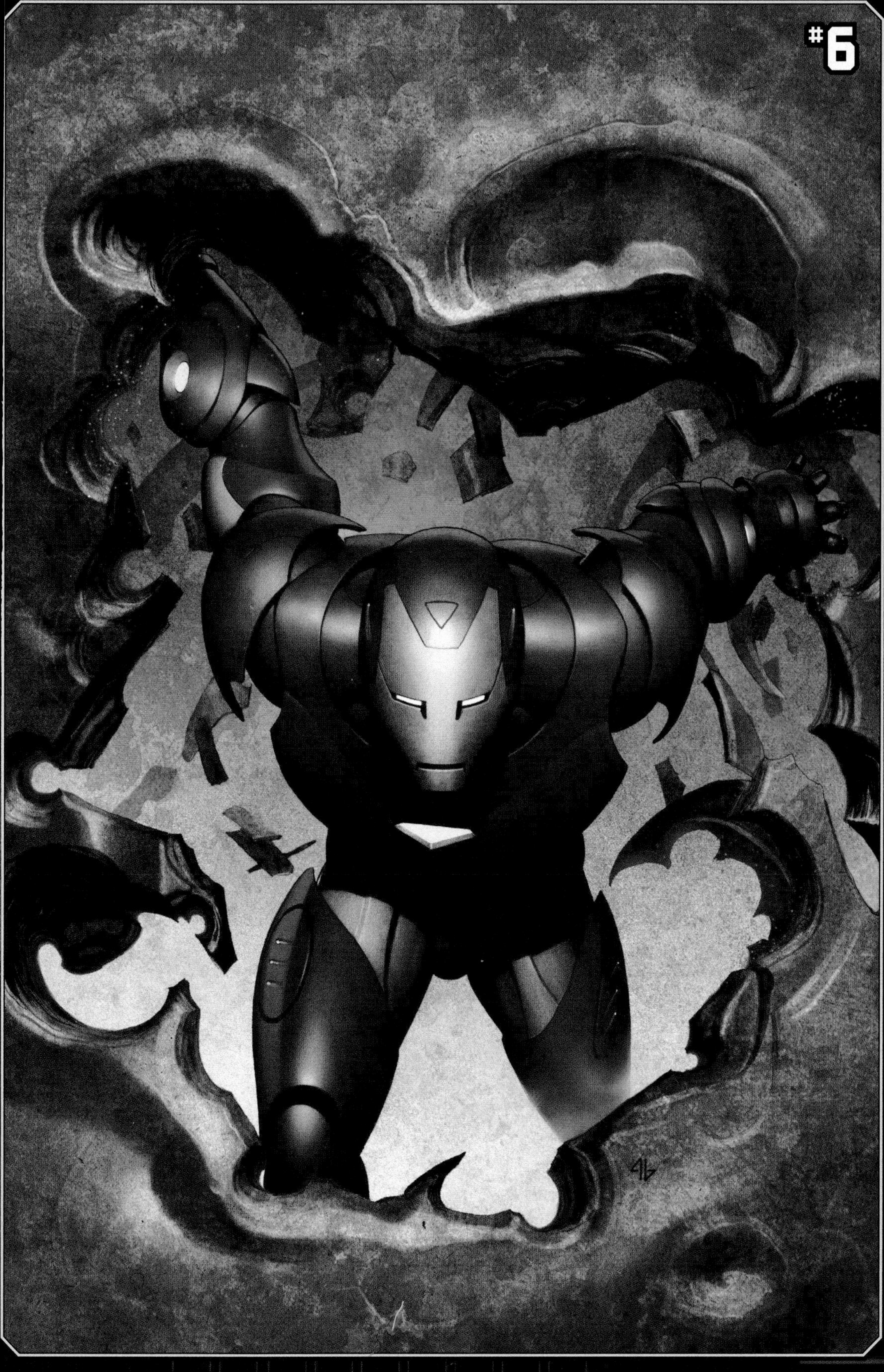

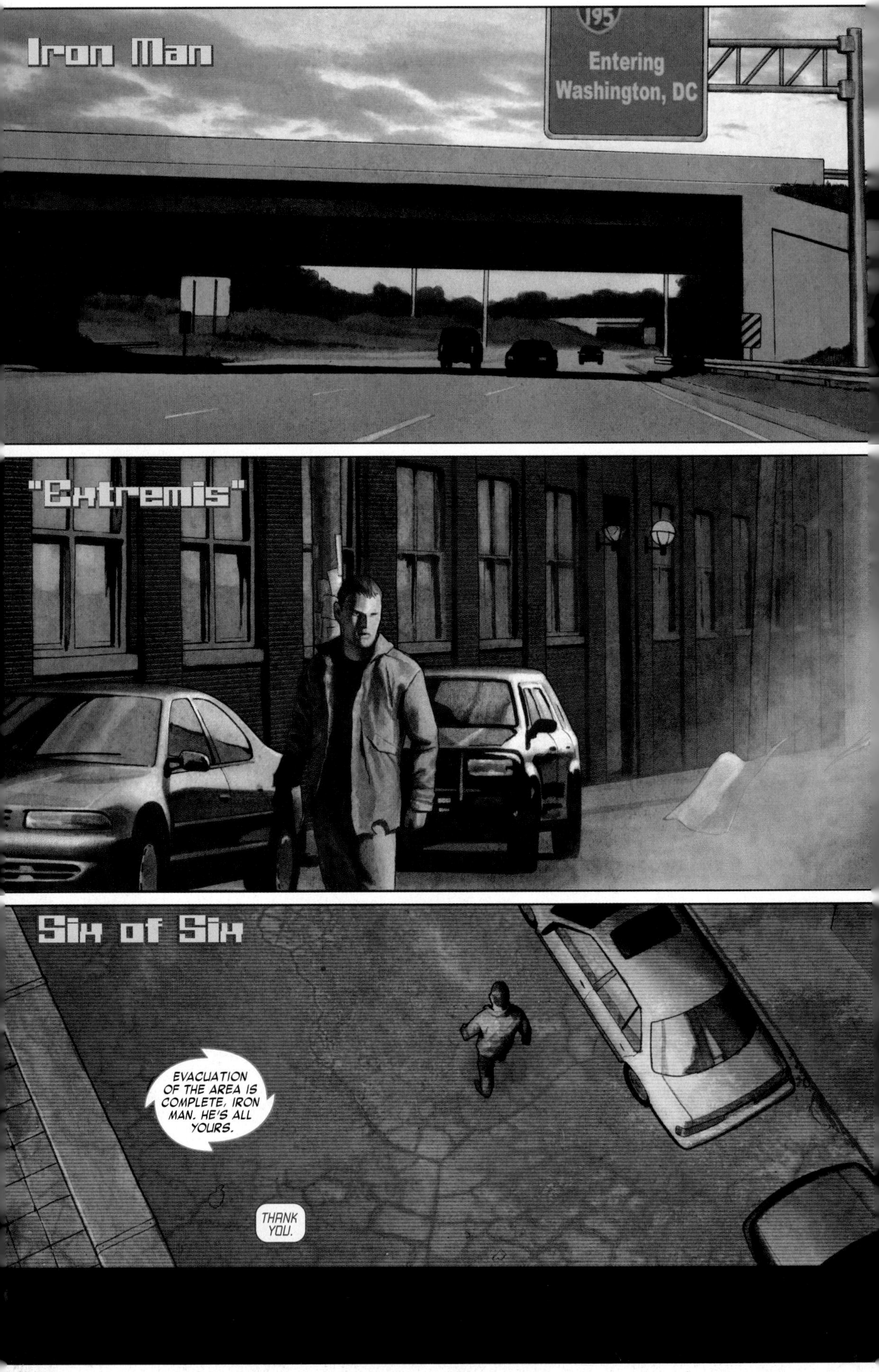
Iron Man
195
Entering
Washington, DC
"Extremis"
Six of Six
EVACUATION OF THE AREA IS COMPLETE, IRON MAN. HE'S ALL YOURS.
THANK YOU.

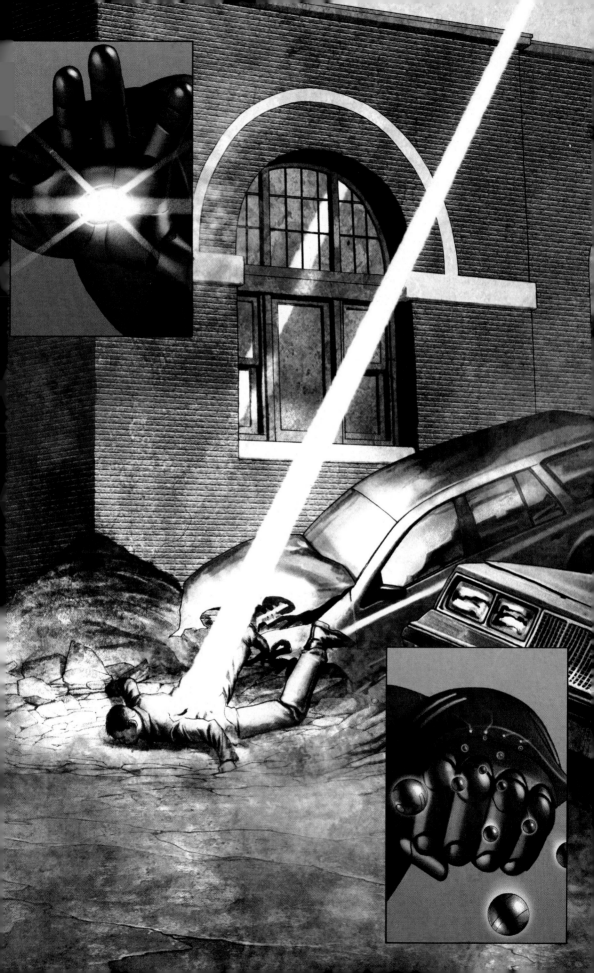

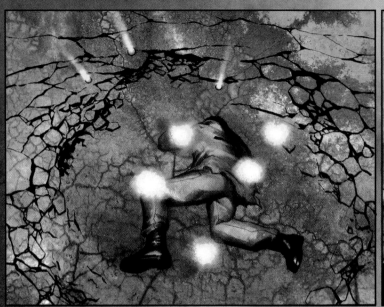

MR. MALLEN.

LAY ON THE GROUND, HANDS BEHIND YOUR HEAD, ANKLES CROSSED.

OR I'M GOING TO HAVE TO KILL YOU.

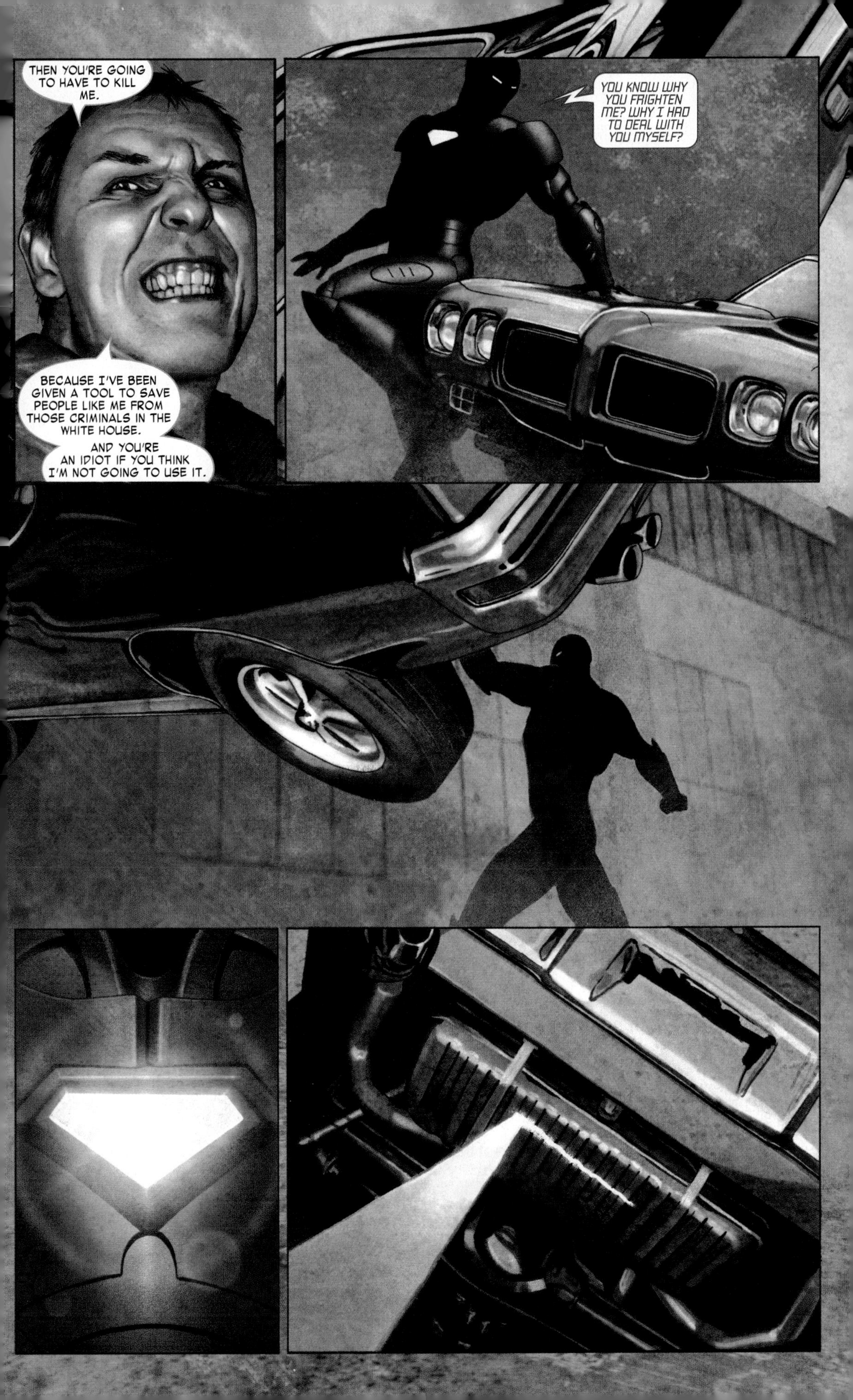
THEN YOU'RE GOING TO HAVE TO KILL ME.
YOU KNOW WHY YOU FRIGHTEN ME? WHY I HAD TO DEAL WITH YOU MYSELF?
BECAUSE I'VE BEEN GIVEN A TOOL TO SAVE PEOPLE LIKE ME FROM THOSE CRIMINALS IN THE WHITE HOUSE.
AND YOU'RE AN IDIOT IF YOU THINK I'M NOT GOING TO USE IT.

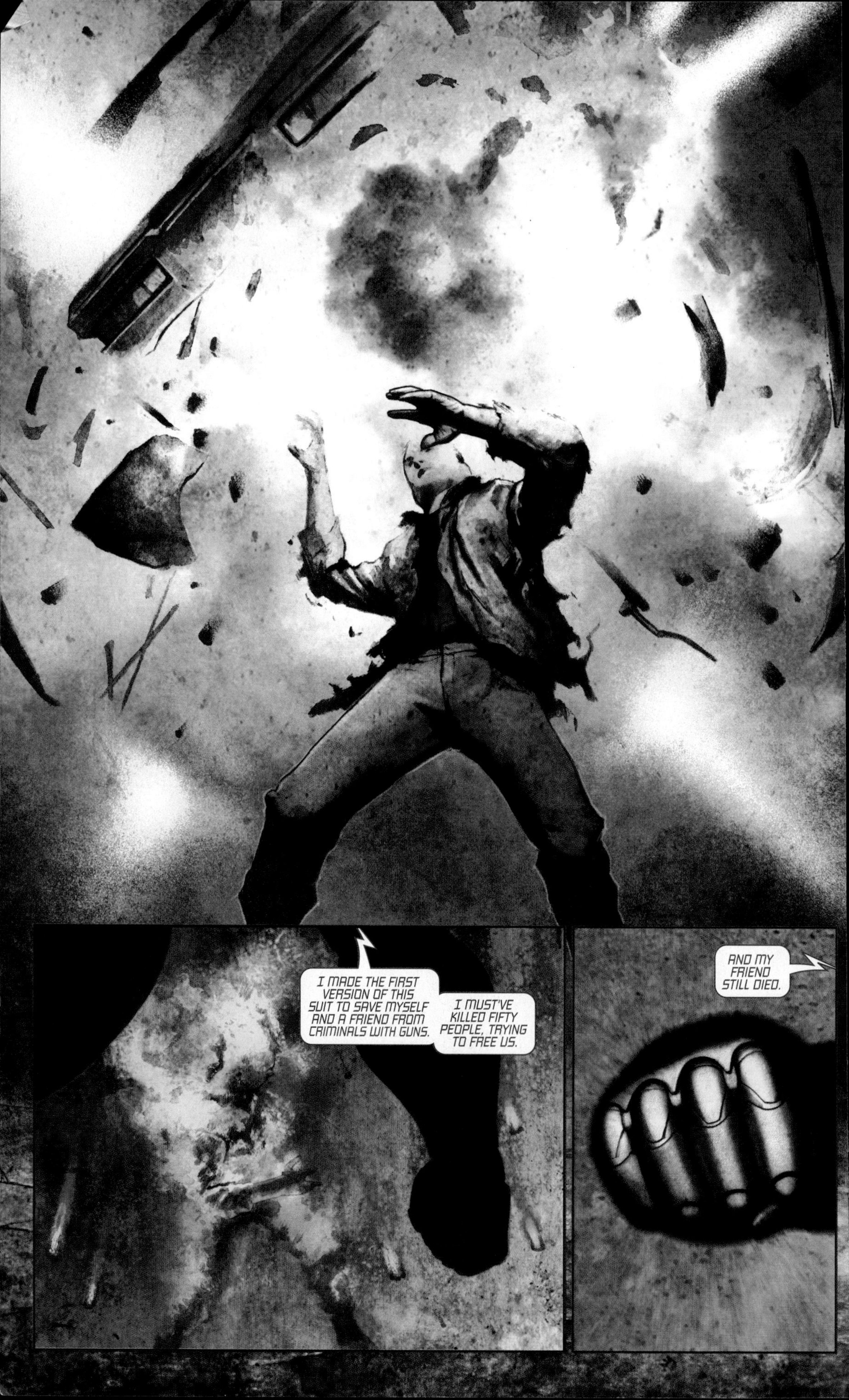
I MADE THE FIRST VERSION OF THIS SUIT TO SAVE MYSELF AND A FRIEND FROM CRIMINALS WITH GUNS.
I MUST'VE KILLED FIFTY PEOPLE, TRYING TO FREE US.
AND MY FRIEND STILL DIED.

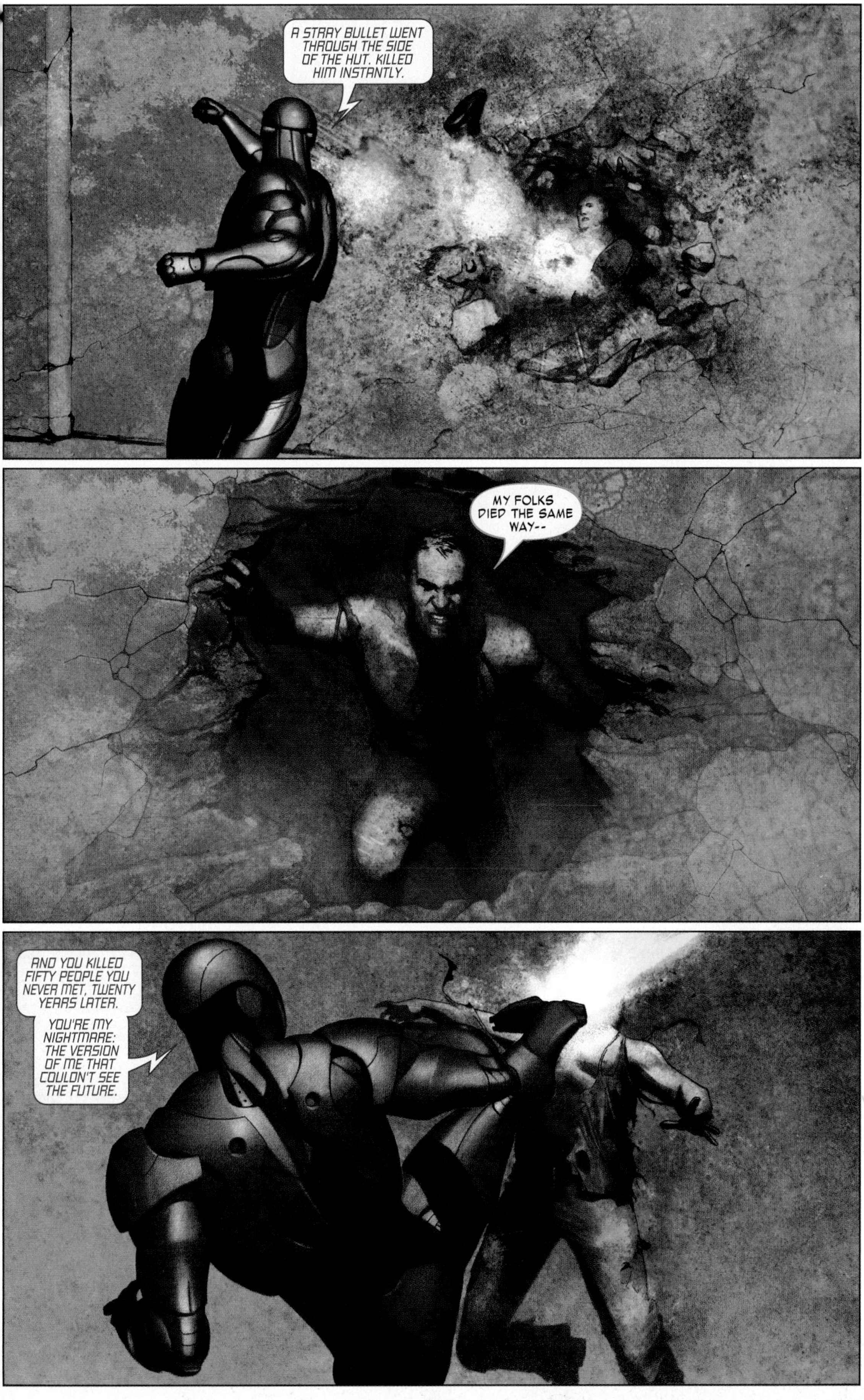
A STRAY BULLET WENT THROUGH THE SIDE OF THE HUT. KILLED HIM INSTANTLY.
MY FOLKS DIED THE SAME WAY--
AND YOU KILLED FIFTY PEOPLE YOU NEVER MET, TWENTY YEARS LATER.
YOU'RE MY NIGHTMARE: THE VERSION OF ME THAT COULDN'T SEE THE FUTURE.

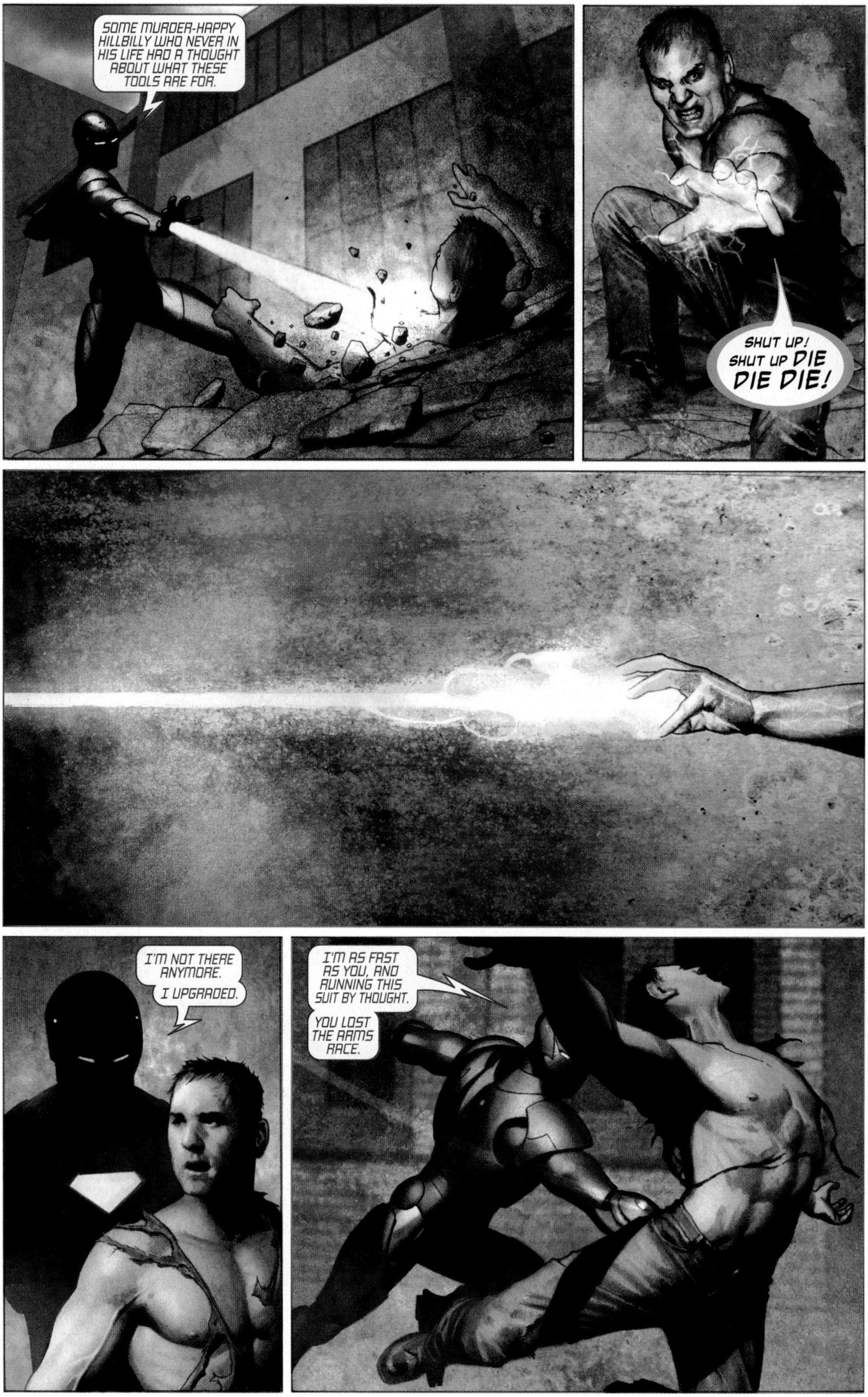
SOME MURDER-HAPPY HILLBILLY WHO NEVER IN HIS LIFE HAD A THOUGHT ABOUT WHAT THESE TOOLS ARE FOR.
SHUT UP! SHUT UP DIE DIE DIE!
I'M NOT THERE ANYMORE.
I UPGRADED.
I'M AS FAST AS YOU, AND RUNNING THIS SUIT BY THOUGHT.
YOU LOST THE ARMS RACE.

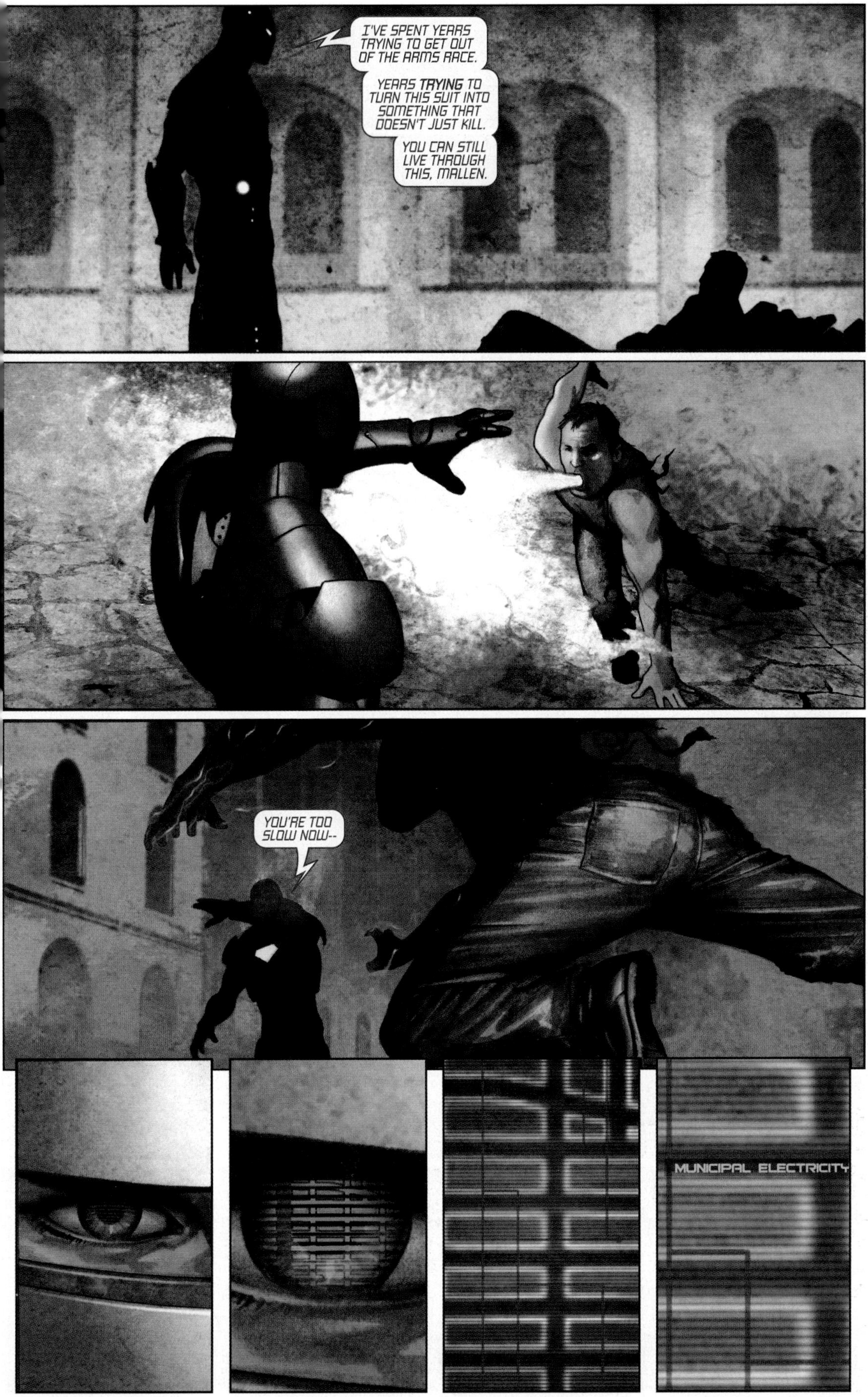
I'VE SPENT YEARS TRYING TO GET OUT OF THE ARMS RACE.
YEARS TRYING TO TURN THIS SUIT INTO SOMETHING THAT DOESN'T JUST KILL.
YOU CAN STILL LIVE THROUGH THIS, MALLEN.
YOU'RE TOO SLOW NOW--
MUNICIPAL ELECTRICITY

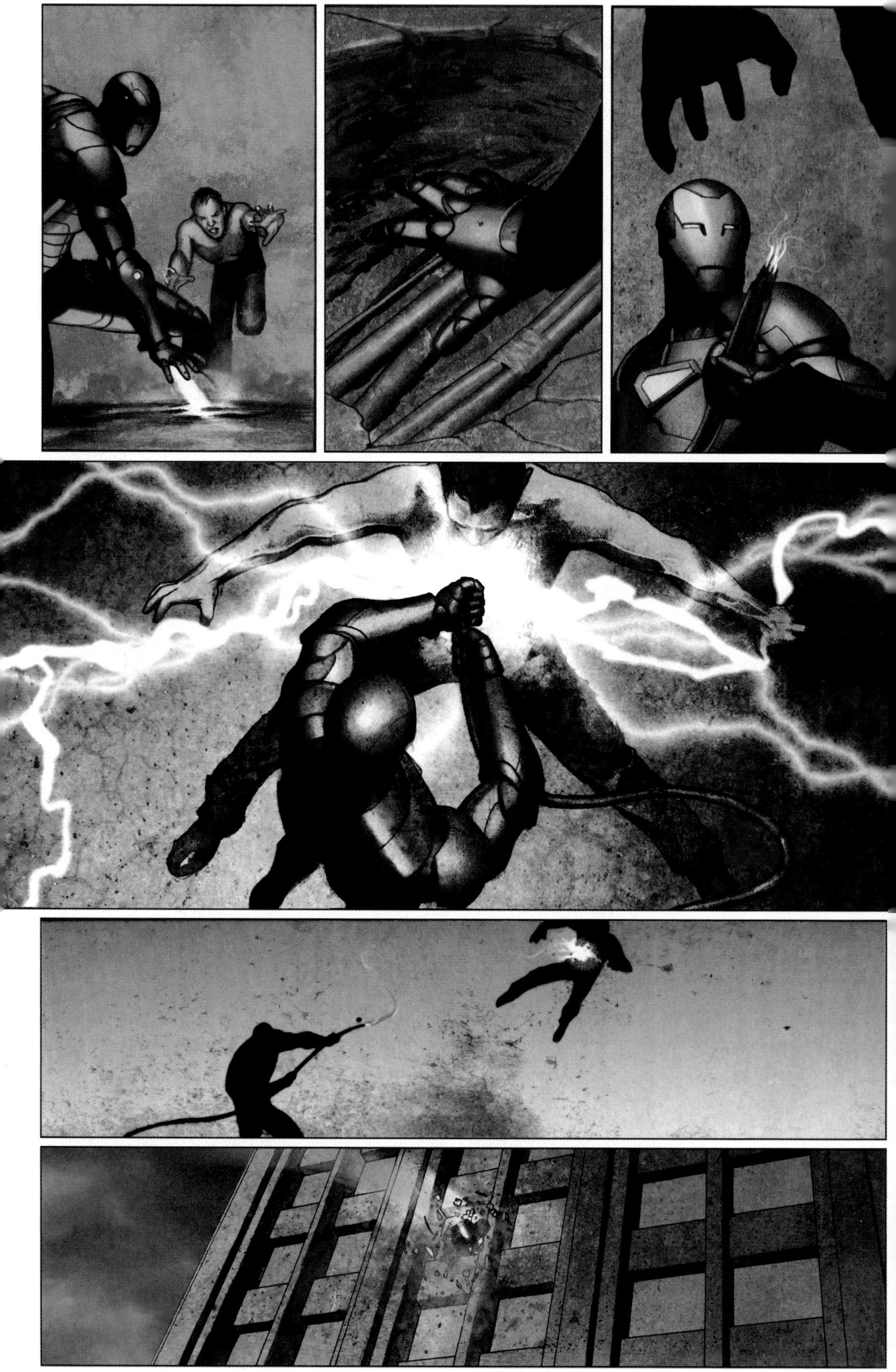

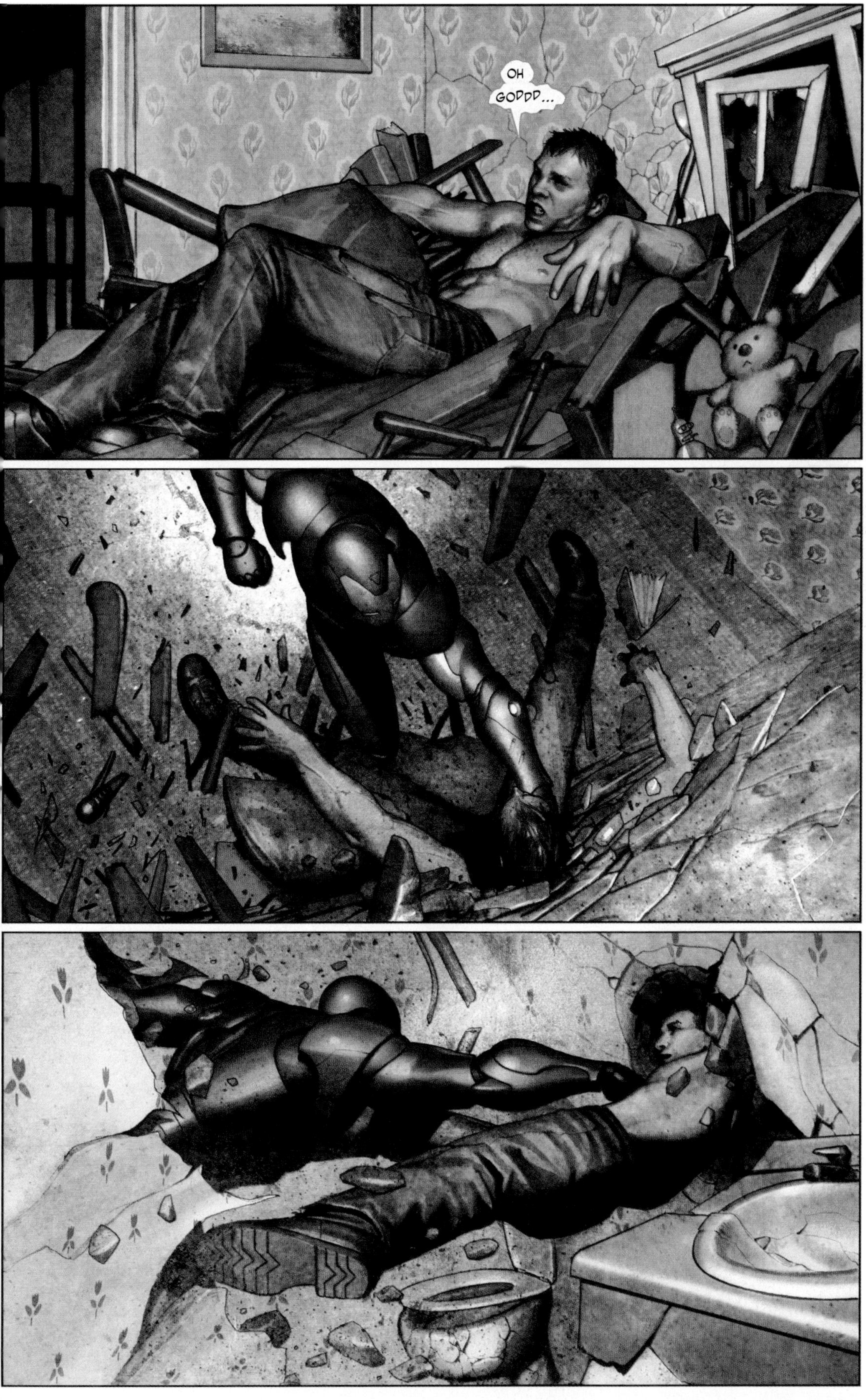
OH GODDD...

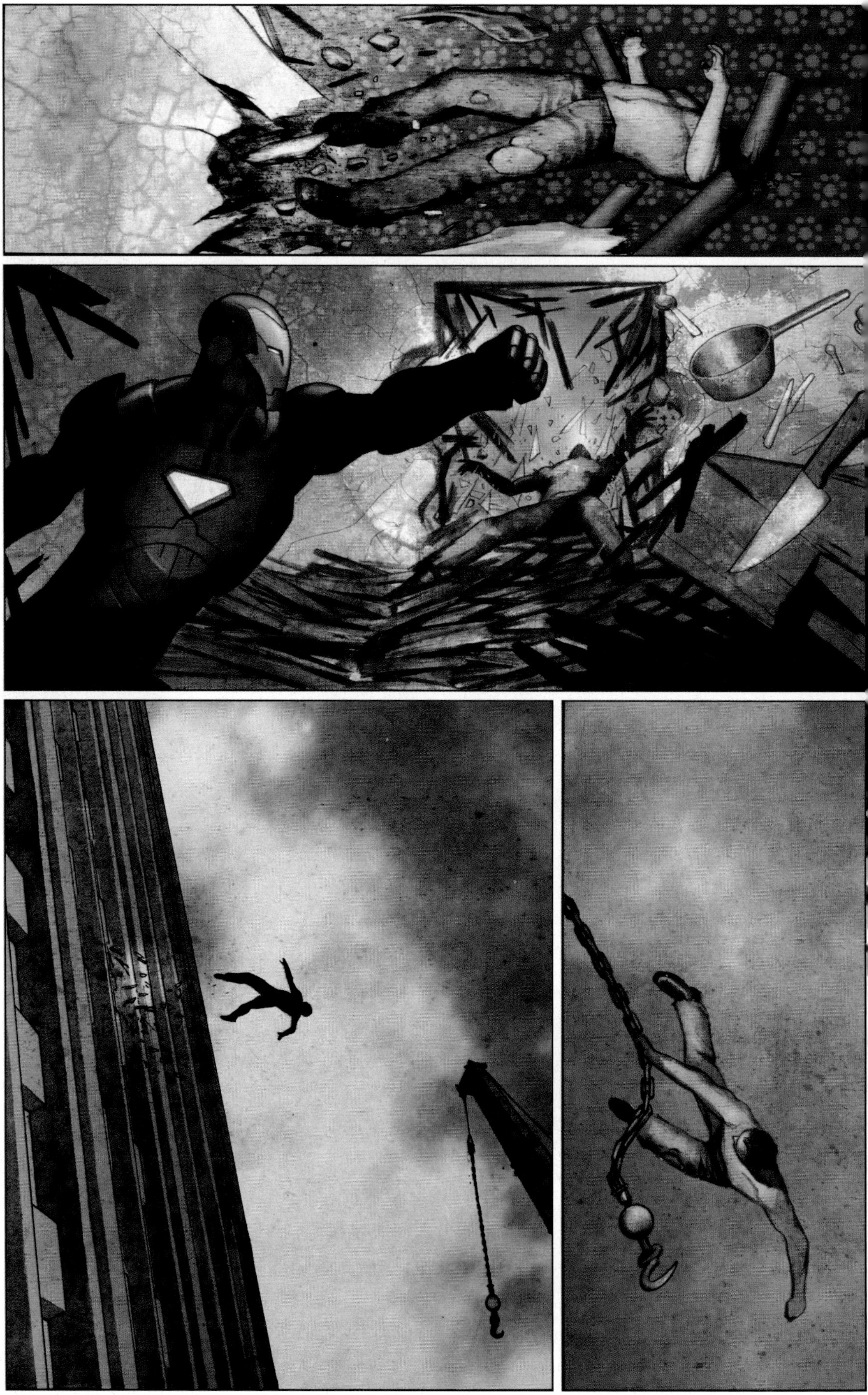

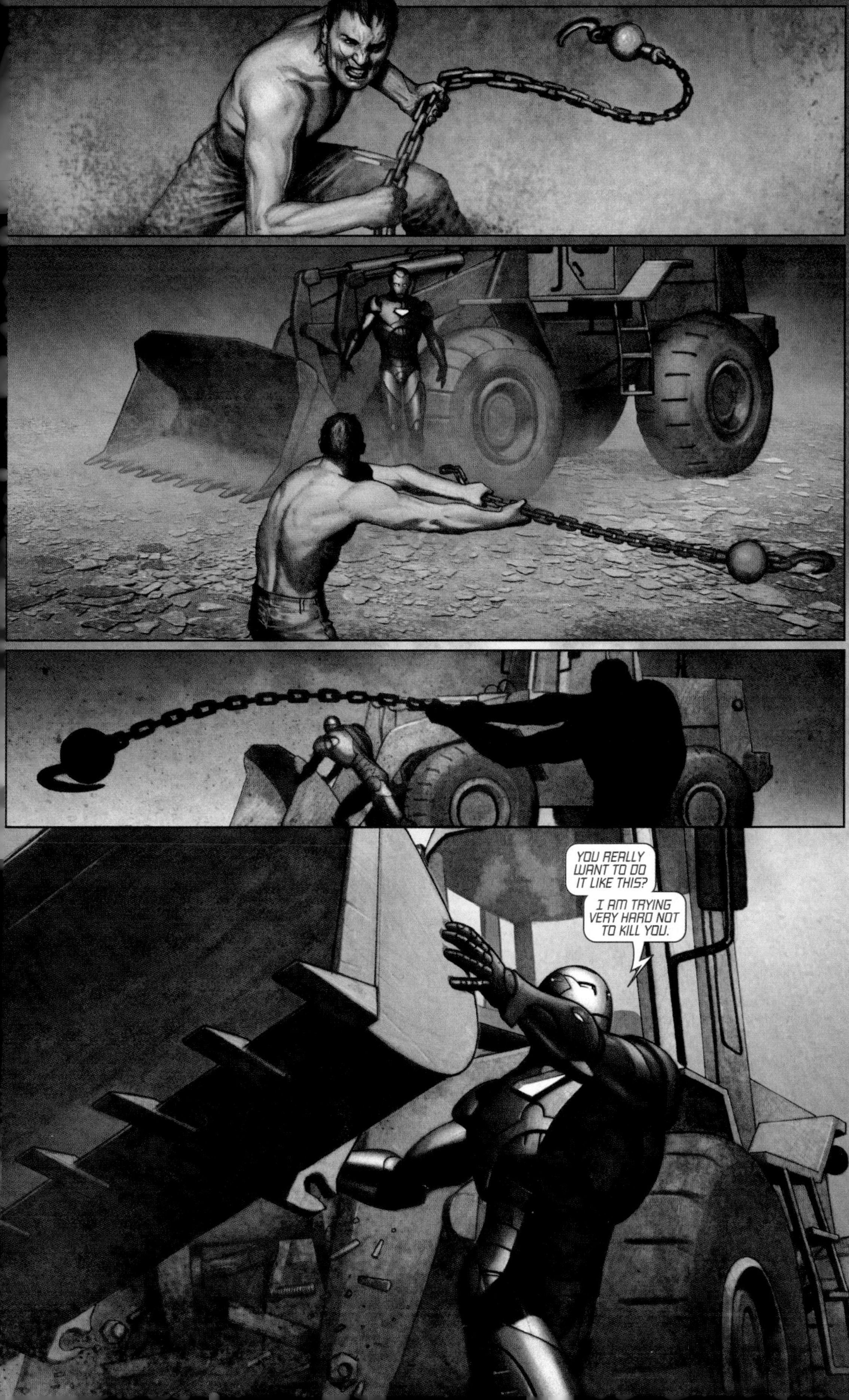
YOU REALLY WANT TO DO IT LIKE THIS?
I AM TRYING VERY HARD NOT TO KILL YOU.

I ONLY LEFT YOU ALIVE IN TEXAS BECAUSE I WAS BUSY--

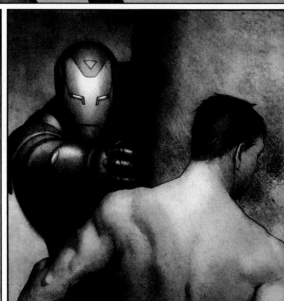

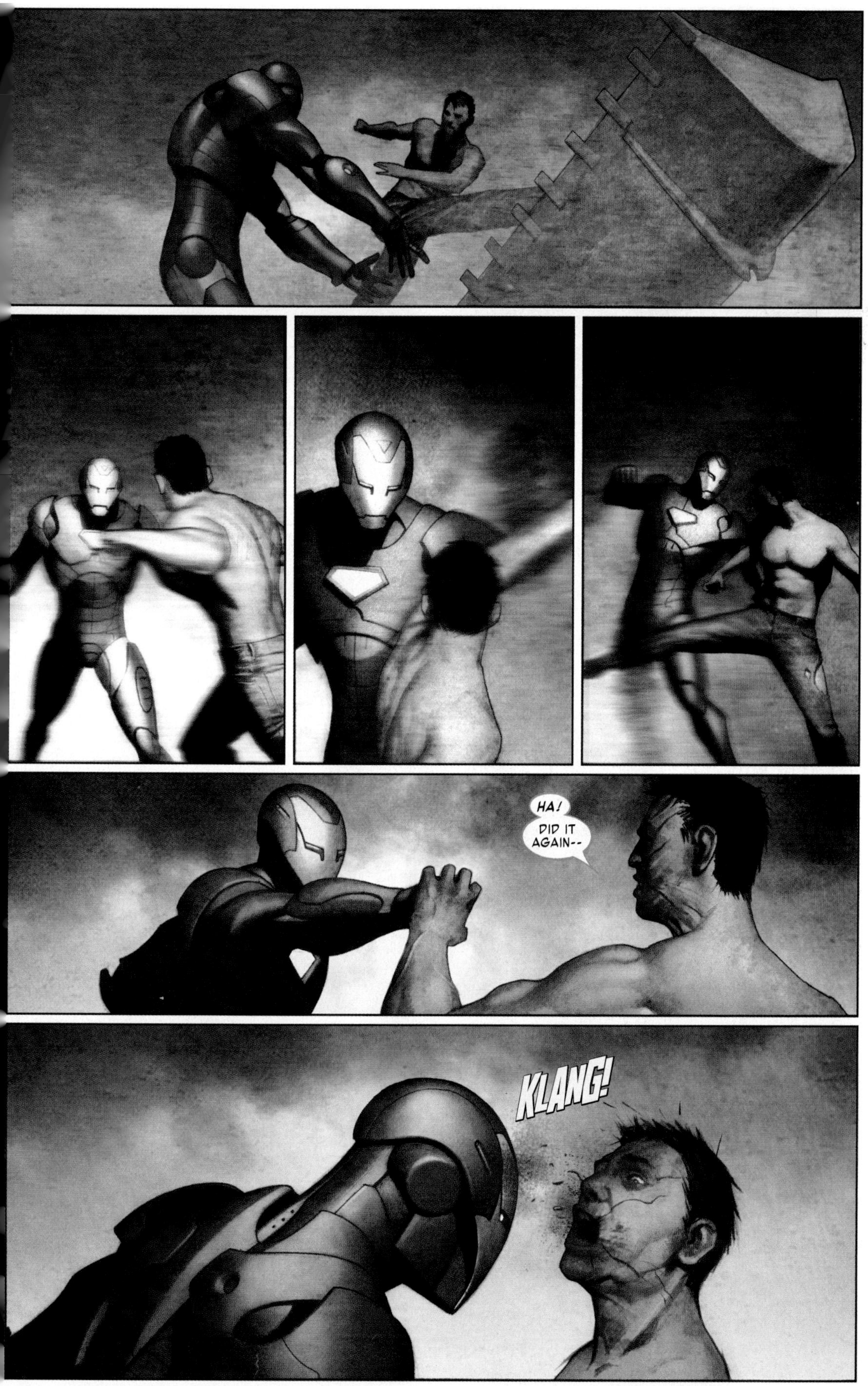
HA! DID IT AGAIN--
KLANG!

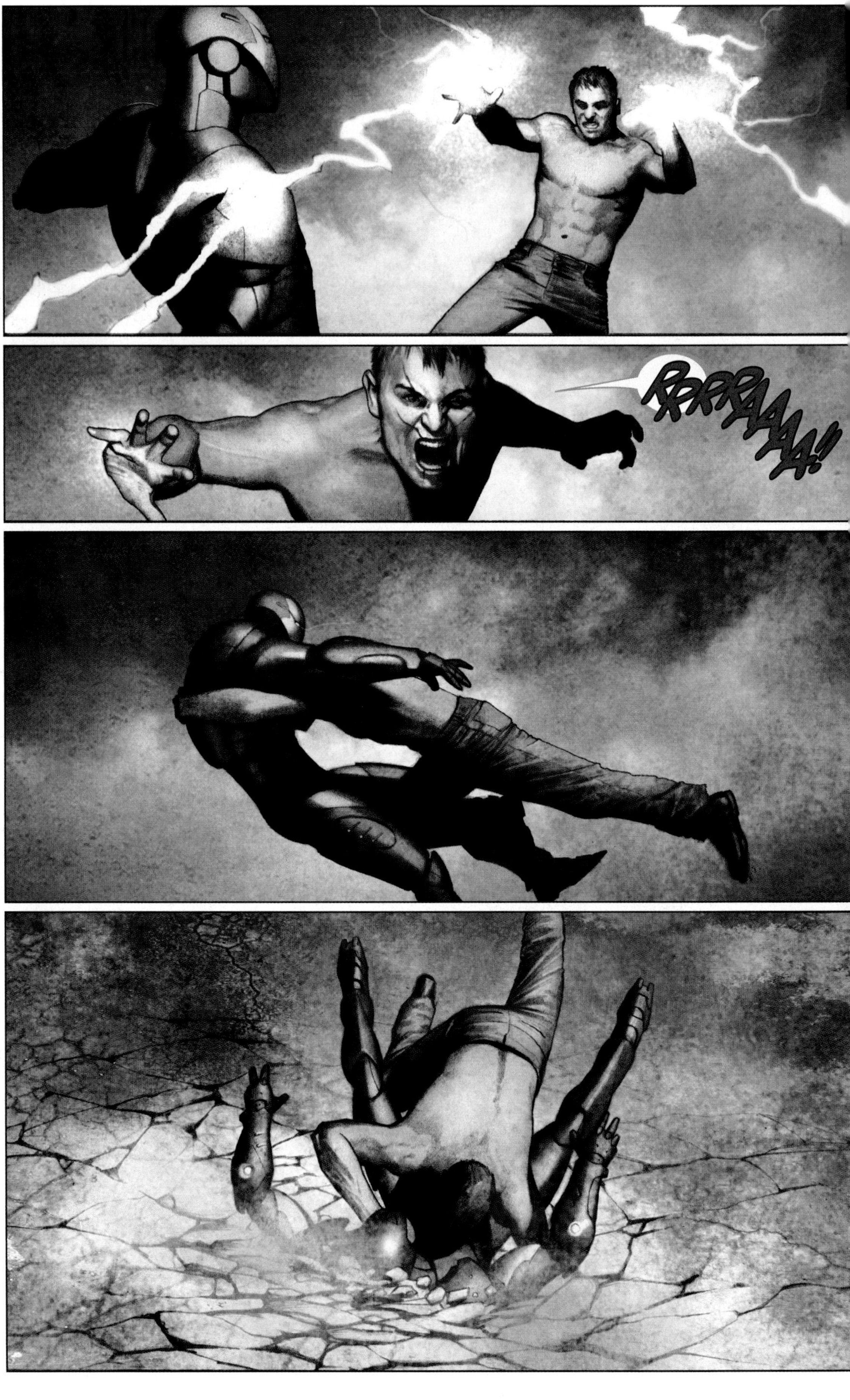
RRRRAAAA!!

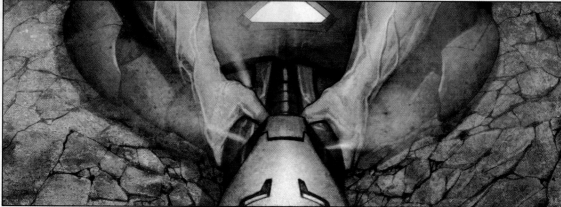

MALLEN... FOR GOD'S SAKE... DON'T MAKE ME...

THERE ISN'T ANY FUTURE!

I'M GOING TO KILL IT!

AAHKK!

UK
HRRR

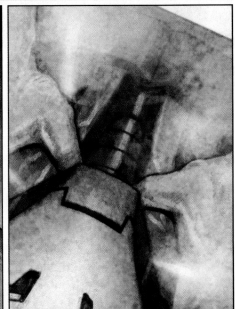

GKK
MALLEN
YOU
STUPID--

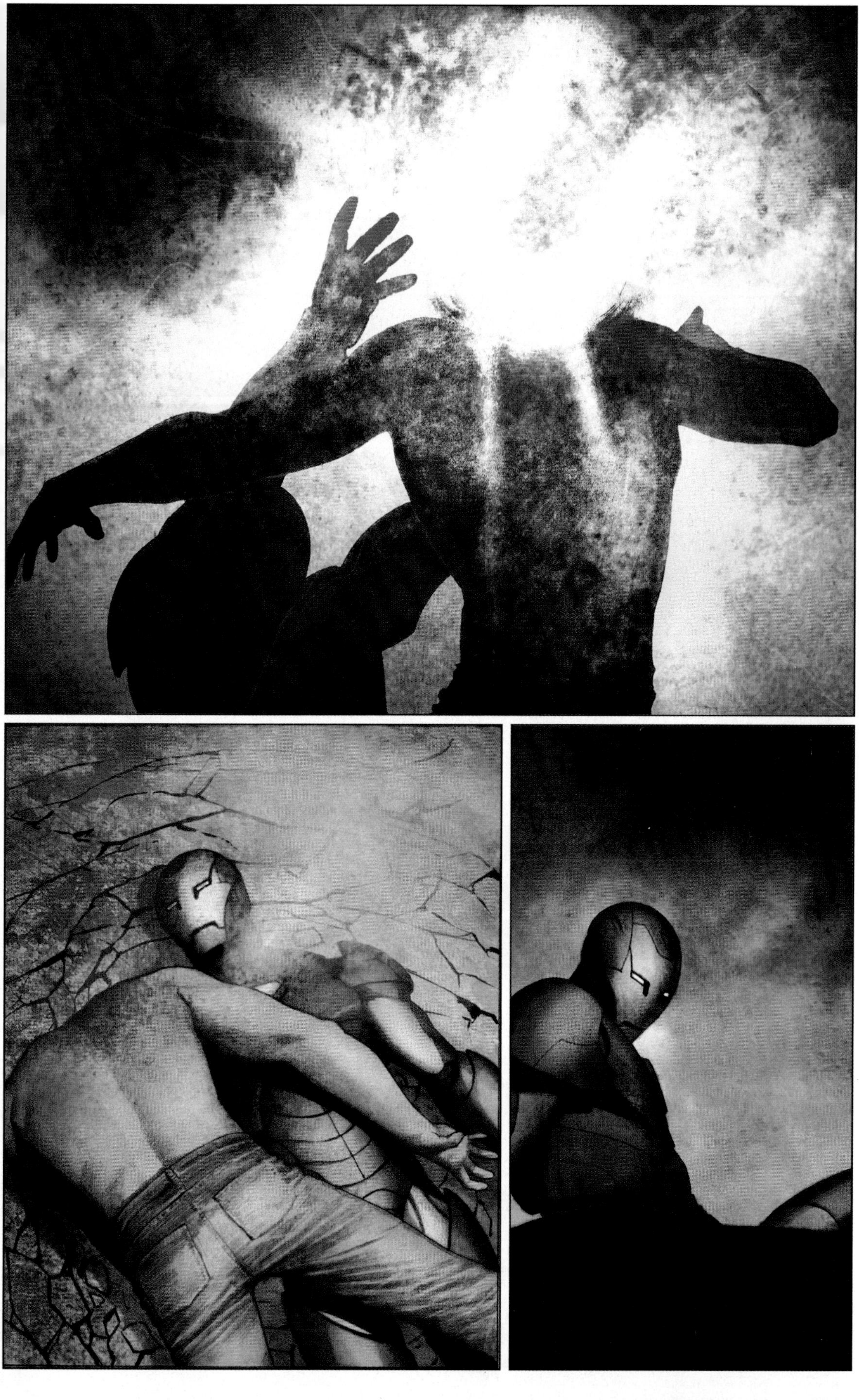

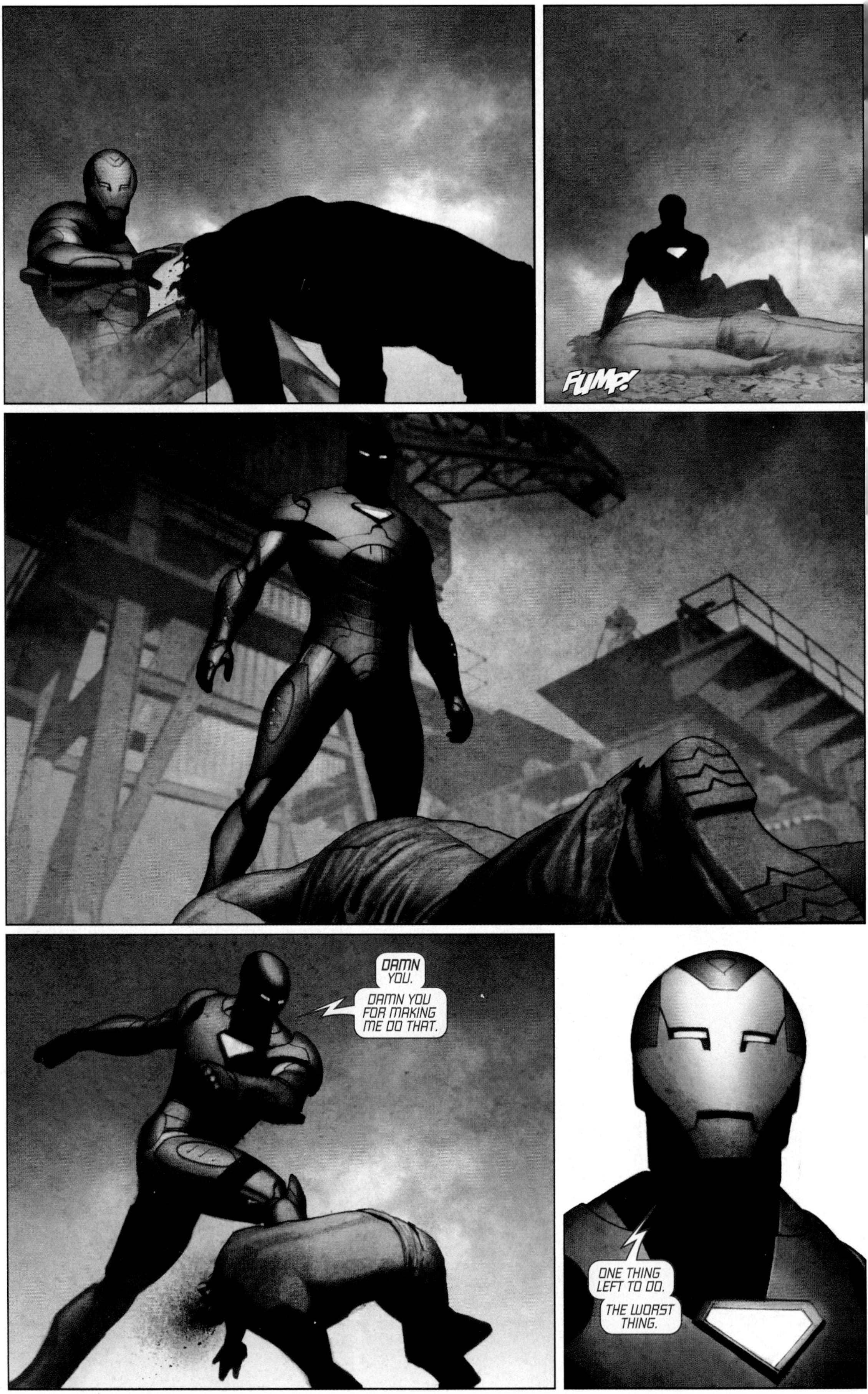
FUMP!
DAMN YOU.
DAMN YOU FOR MAKING ME DO THAT.
ONE THING LEFT TO DO.
THE WORST THING.

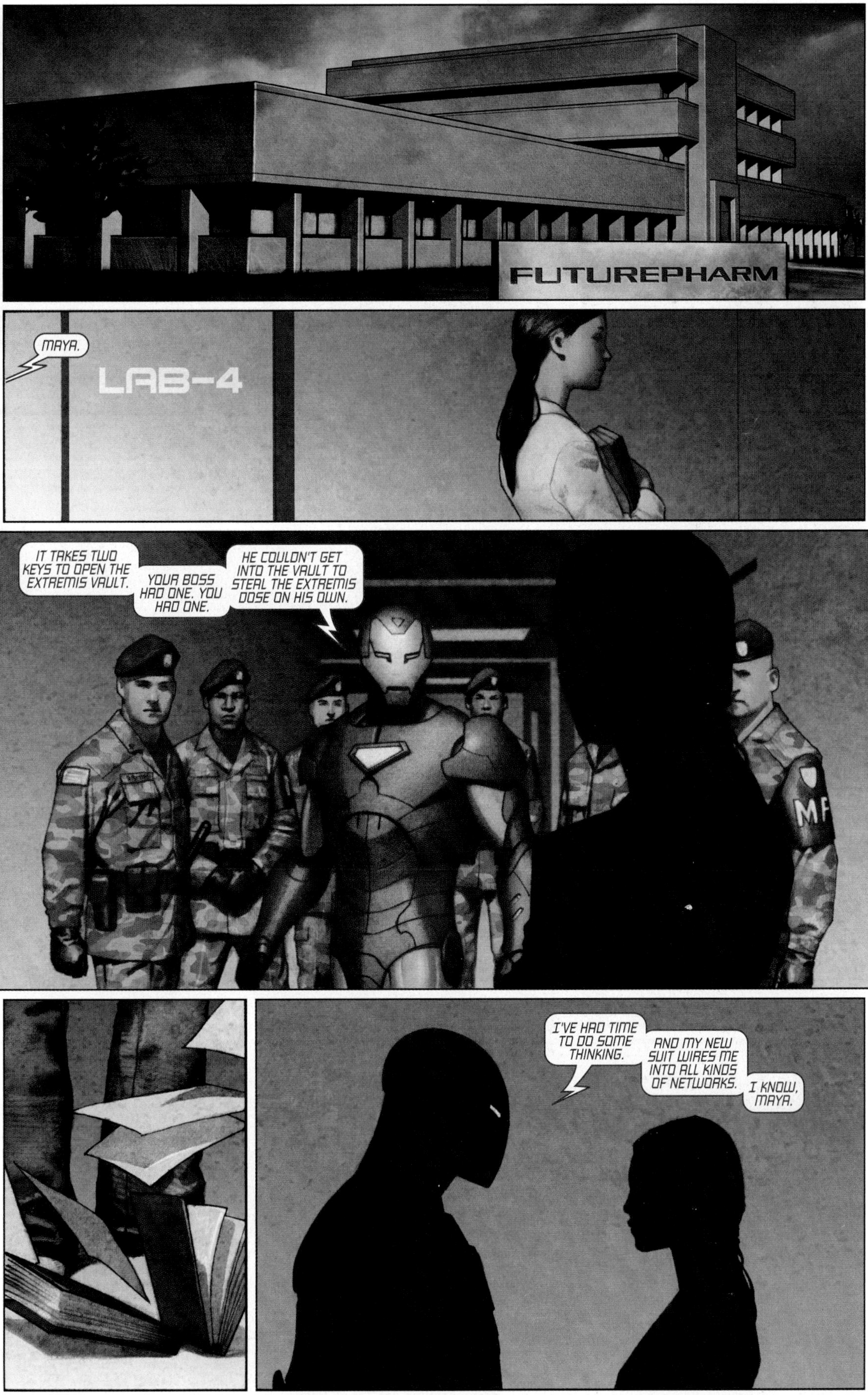
FUTUREPHARM
MAYA.
LAB-4
IT TAKES TWO KEYS TO OPEN THE EXTREMIS VAULT.
YOUR BOSS HAD ONE. YOU HAD ONE.
HE COULDN'T GET INTO THE VAULT TO STEAL THE EXTREMIS DOSE ON HIS OWN.
MP
I'VE HAD TIME TO DO SOME THINKING.
AND MY NEW SUIT WIRES ME INTO ALL KINDS OF NETWORKS.
I KNOW, MAYA.

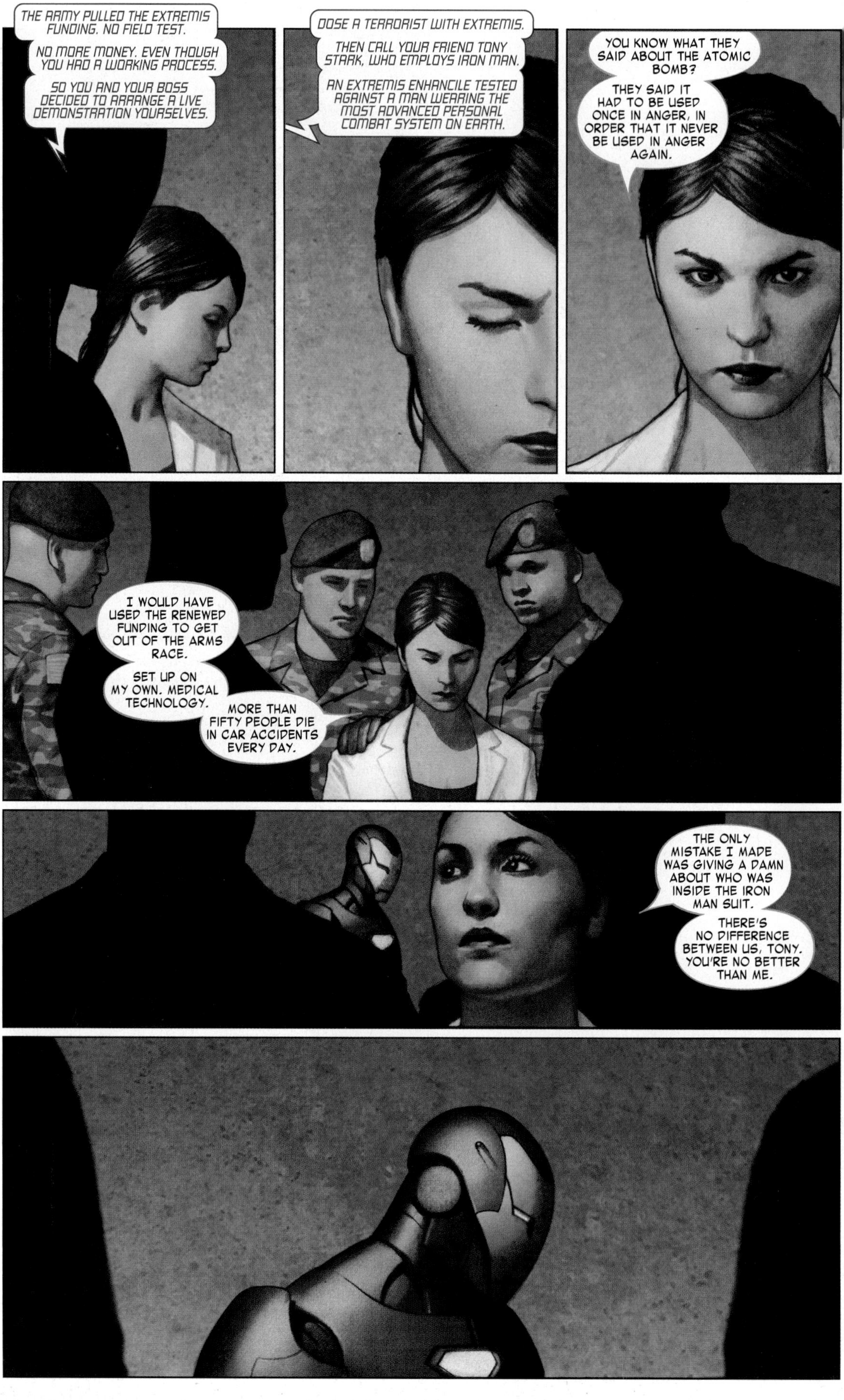
THE ARMY PULLED THE EXTREMIS FUNDING. NO FIELD TEST.
NO MORE MONEY. EVEN THOUGH YOU HAD A WORKING PROCESS.
SO YOU AND YOUR BOSS DECIDED TO ARRANGE A LIVE DEMONSTRATION YOURSELVES.
DOSE A TERRORIST WITH EXTREMIS.
THEN CALL YOUR FRIEND TONY STARK, WHO EMPLOYS IRON MAN.
AN EXTREMIS ENHANCILE TESTED AGAINST A MAN WEARING THE MOST ADVANCED PERSONAL COMBAT SYSTEM ON EARTH.
YOU KNOW WHAT THEY SAID ABOUT THE ATOMIC BOMB?
THEY SAID IT HAD TO BE USED ONCE IN ANGER, IN ORDER THAT IT NEVER BE USED IN ANGER AGAIN.
I WOULD HAVE USED THE RENEWED FUNDING TO GET OUT OF THE ARMS RACE.
SET UP ON MY OWN. MEDICAL TECHNOLOGY.
MORE THAN FIFTY PEOPLE DIE IN CAR ACCIDENTS EVERY DAY.
THE ONLY MISTAKE I MADE WAS GIVING A DAMN ABOUT WHO WAS INSIDE THE IRON MAN SUIT.
THERE'S NO DIFFERENCE BETWEEN US, TONY. YOU'RE NO BETTER THAN ME.

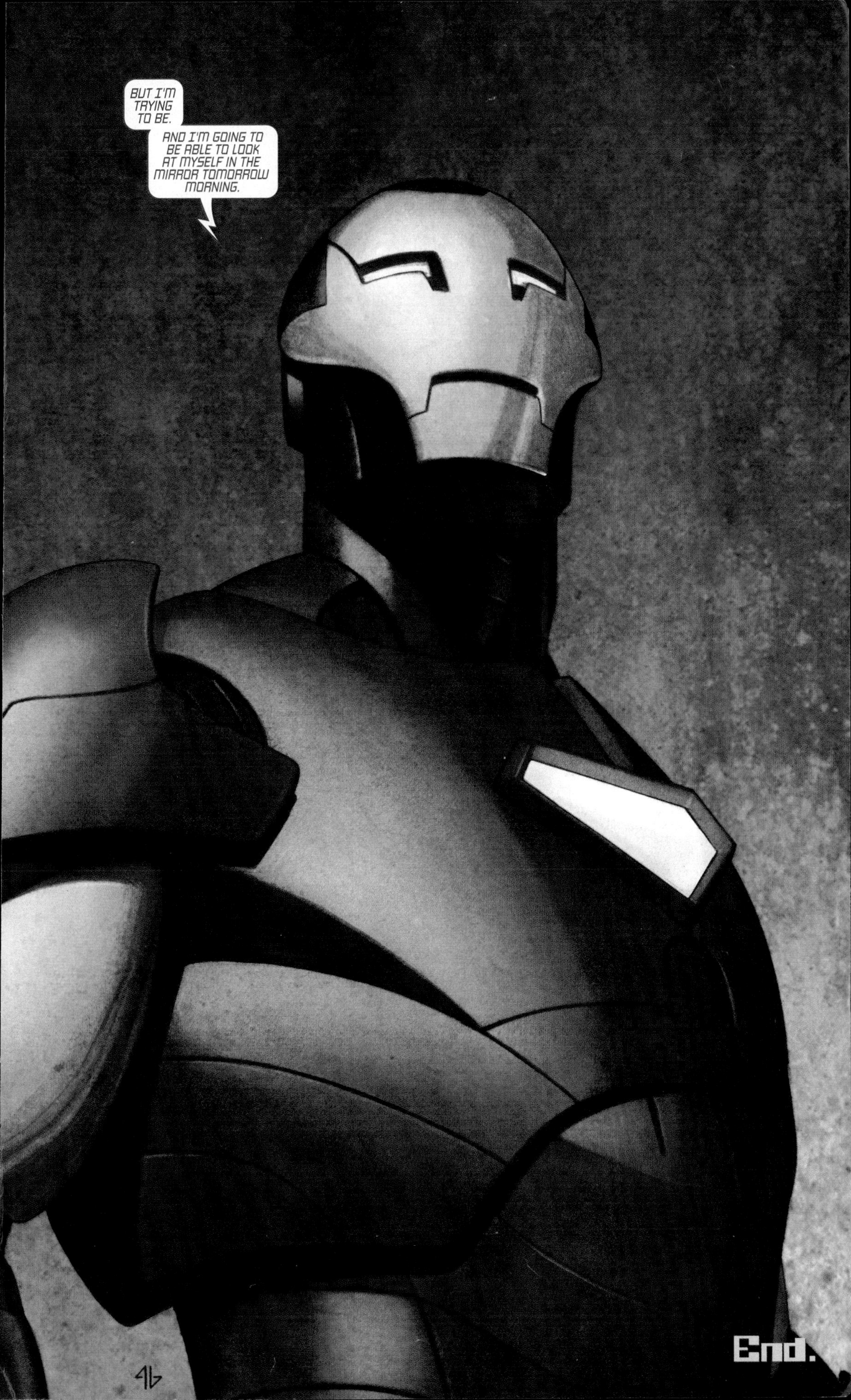
BUT I'M TRYING TO BE.
AND I'M GOING TO BE ABLE TO LOOK AT MYSELF IN THE MIRROR TOMORROW MORNING.
End.

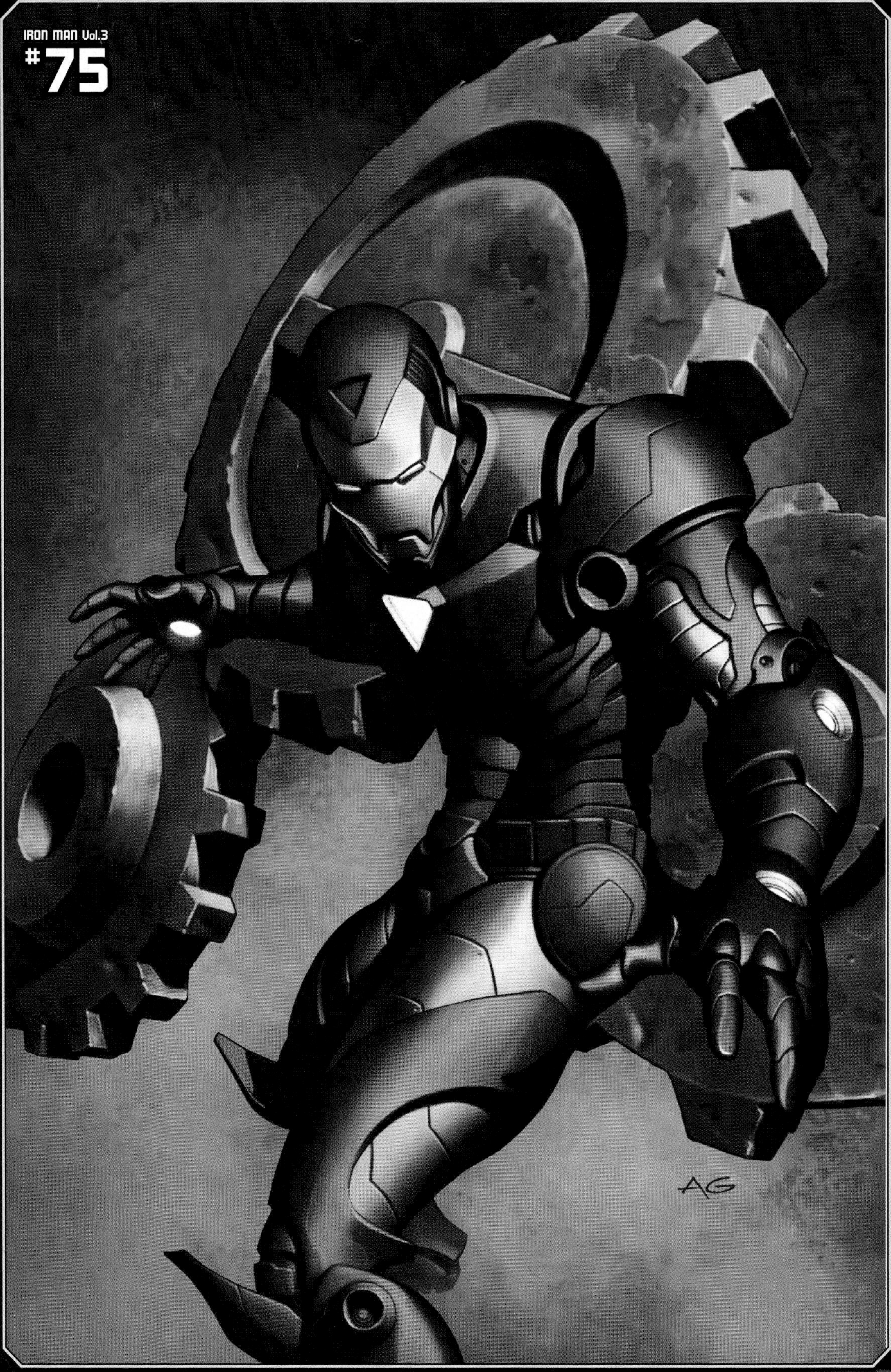
IRON MAN Vol.3
#75
AG

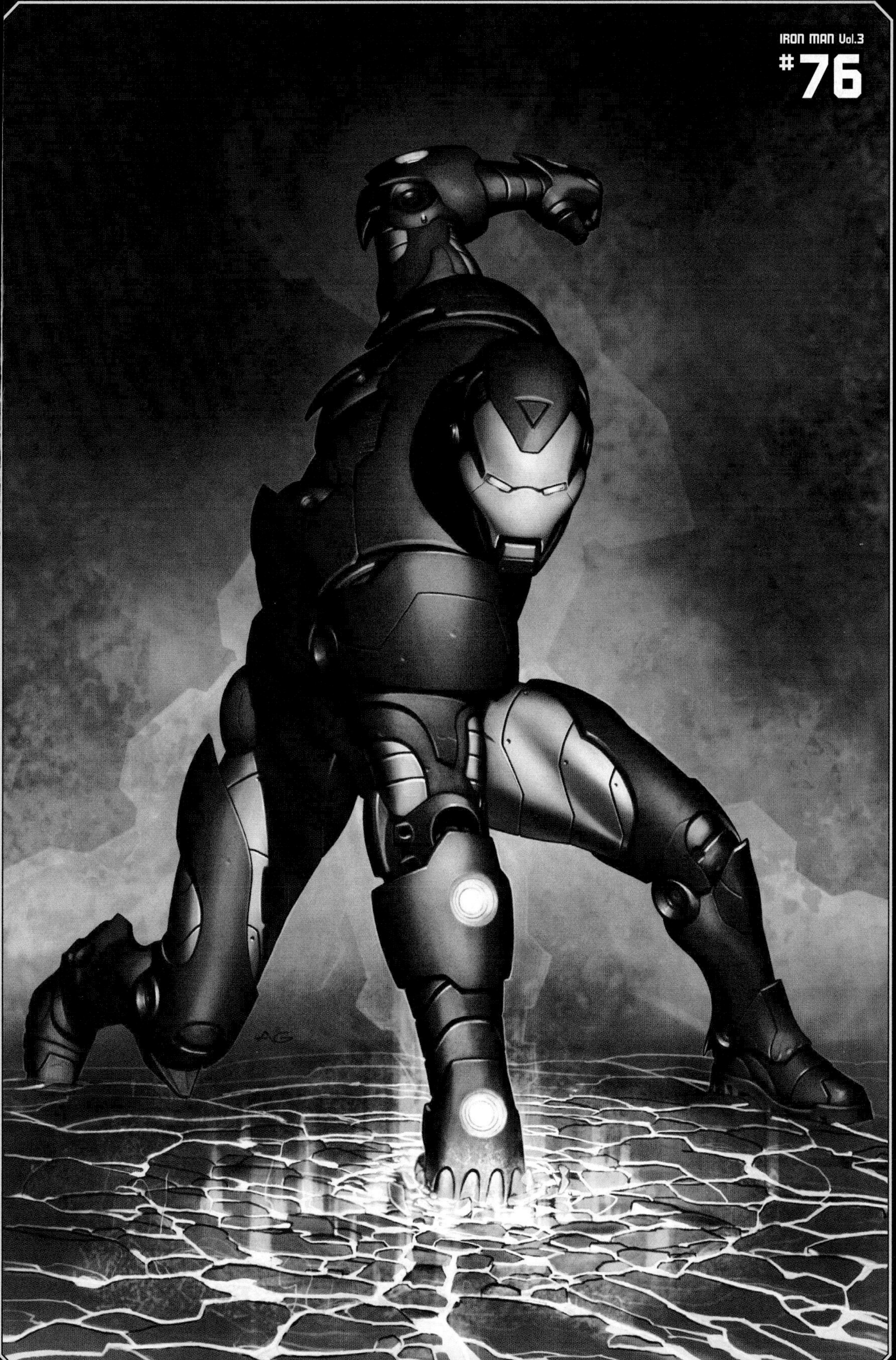
IRON MAN Vol.3
#76

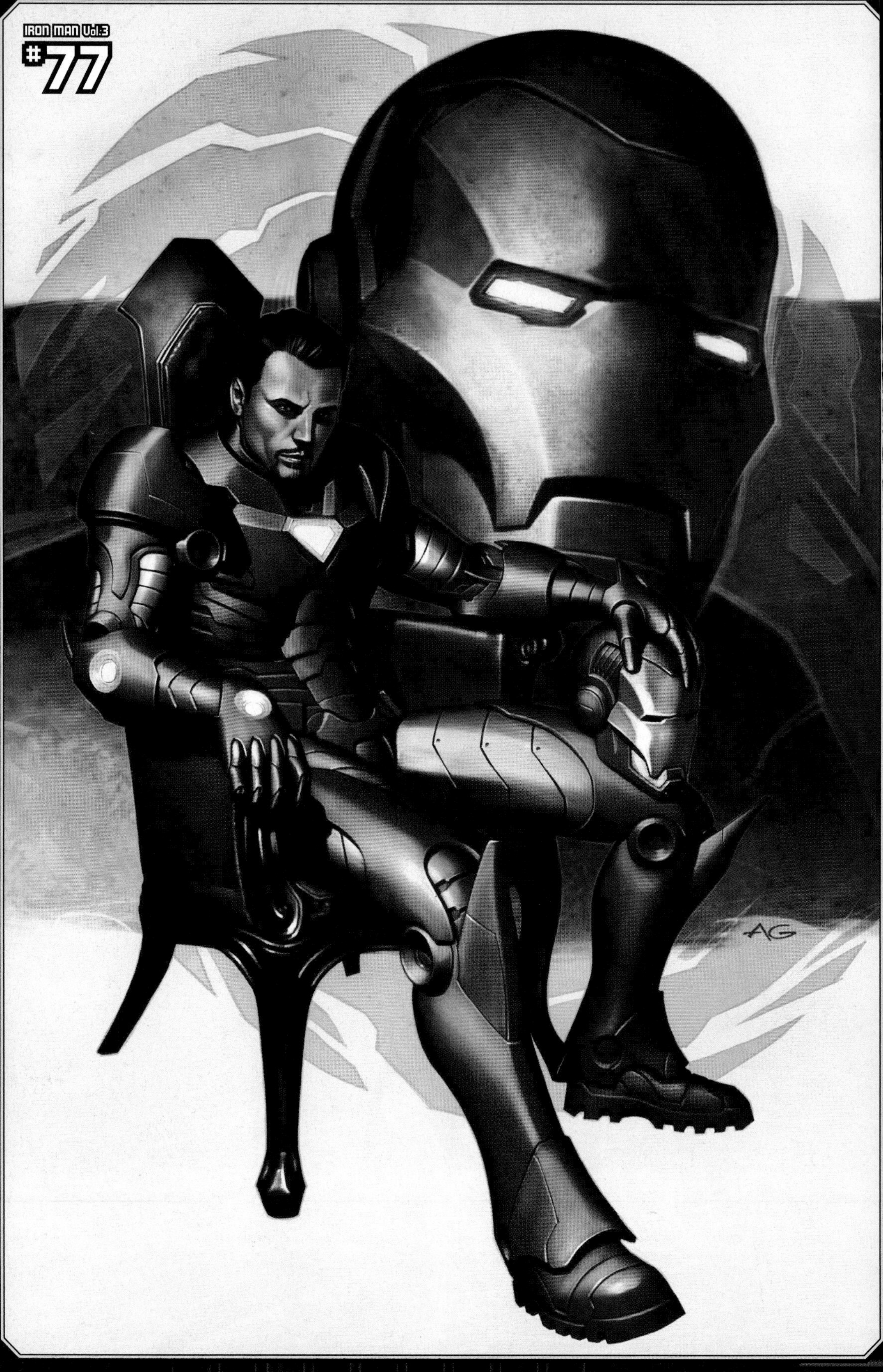
IRON MAN Vol.3
#77
AG

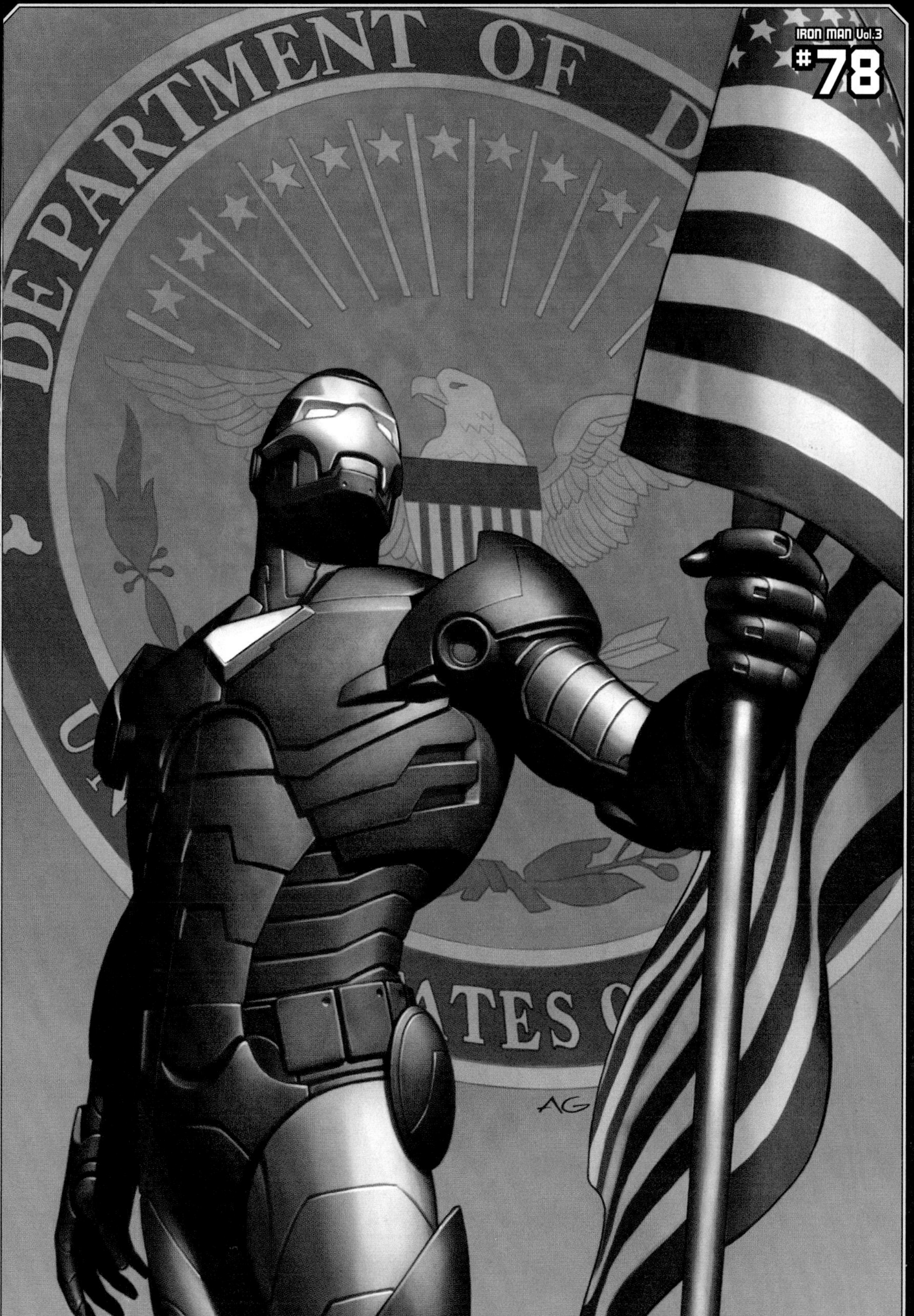
IRON MAN Vol.3
#78
DEPARTMENT OF D

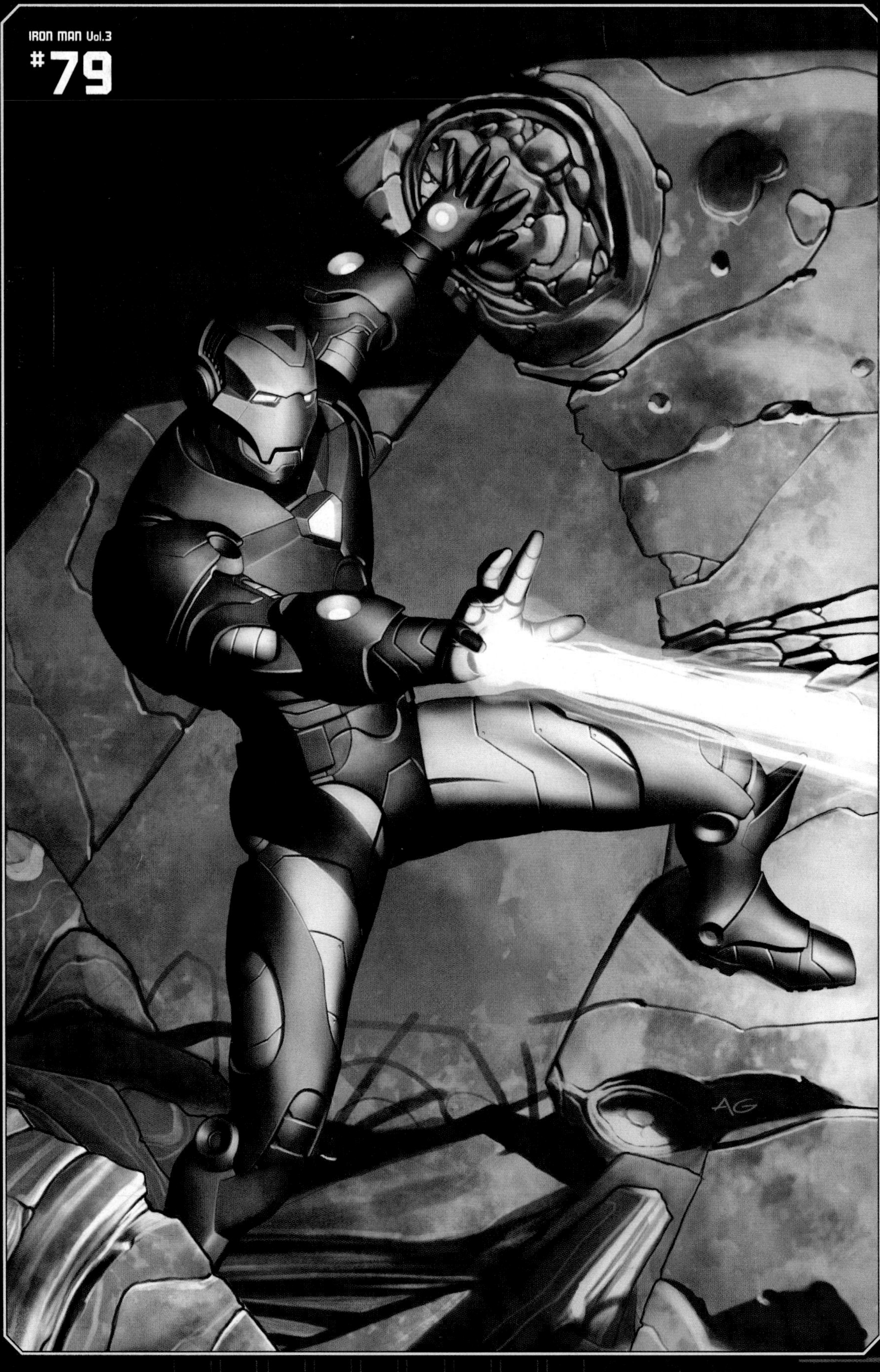
IRON MAN Vol.3
#79
AG

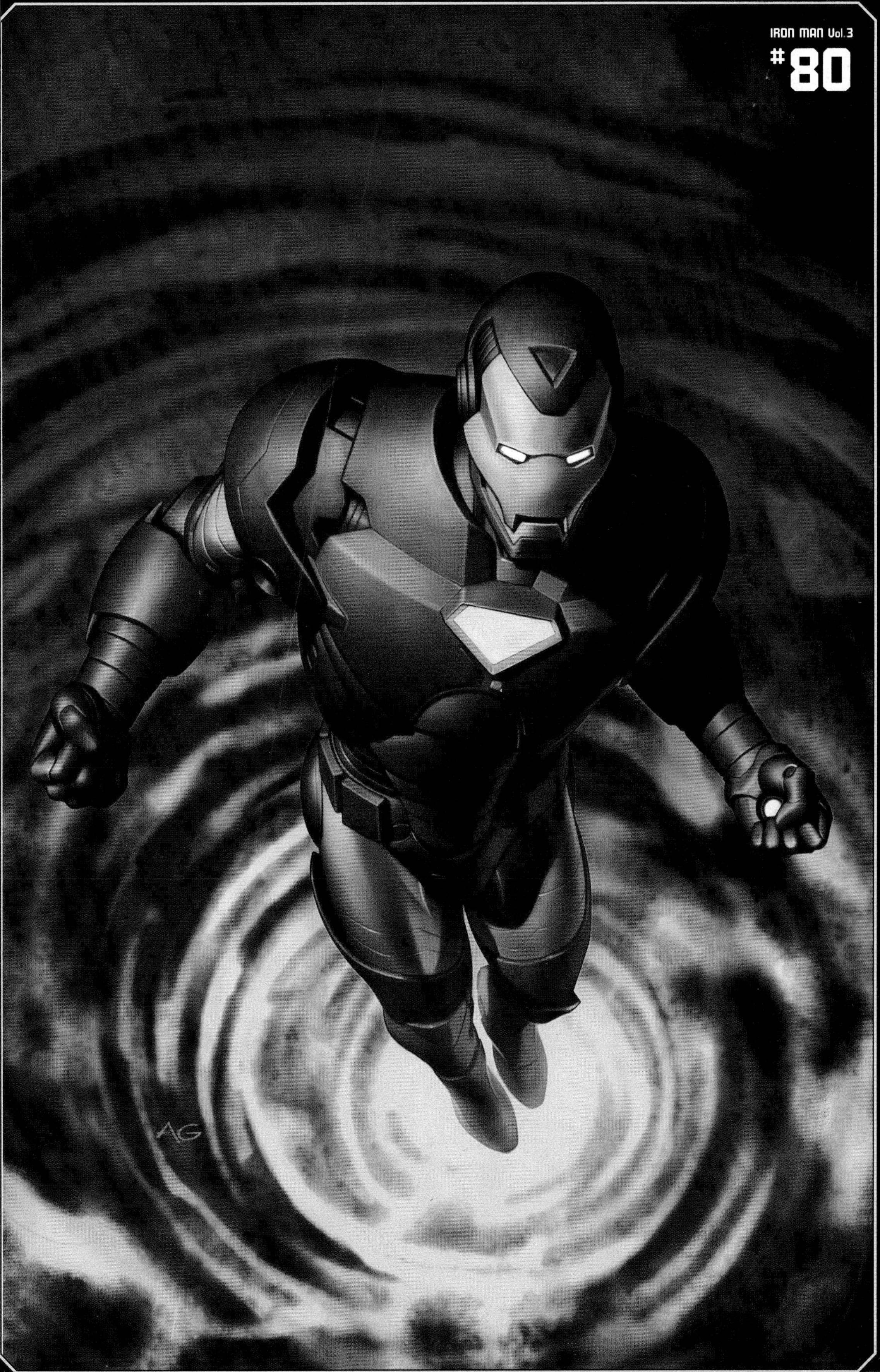
IRON MAN Vol.3
#80
AG

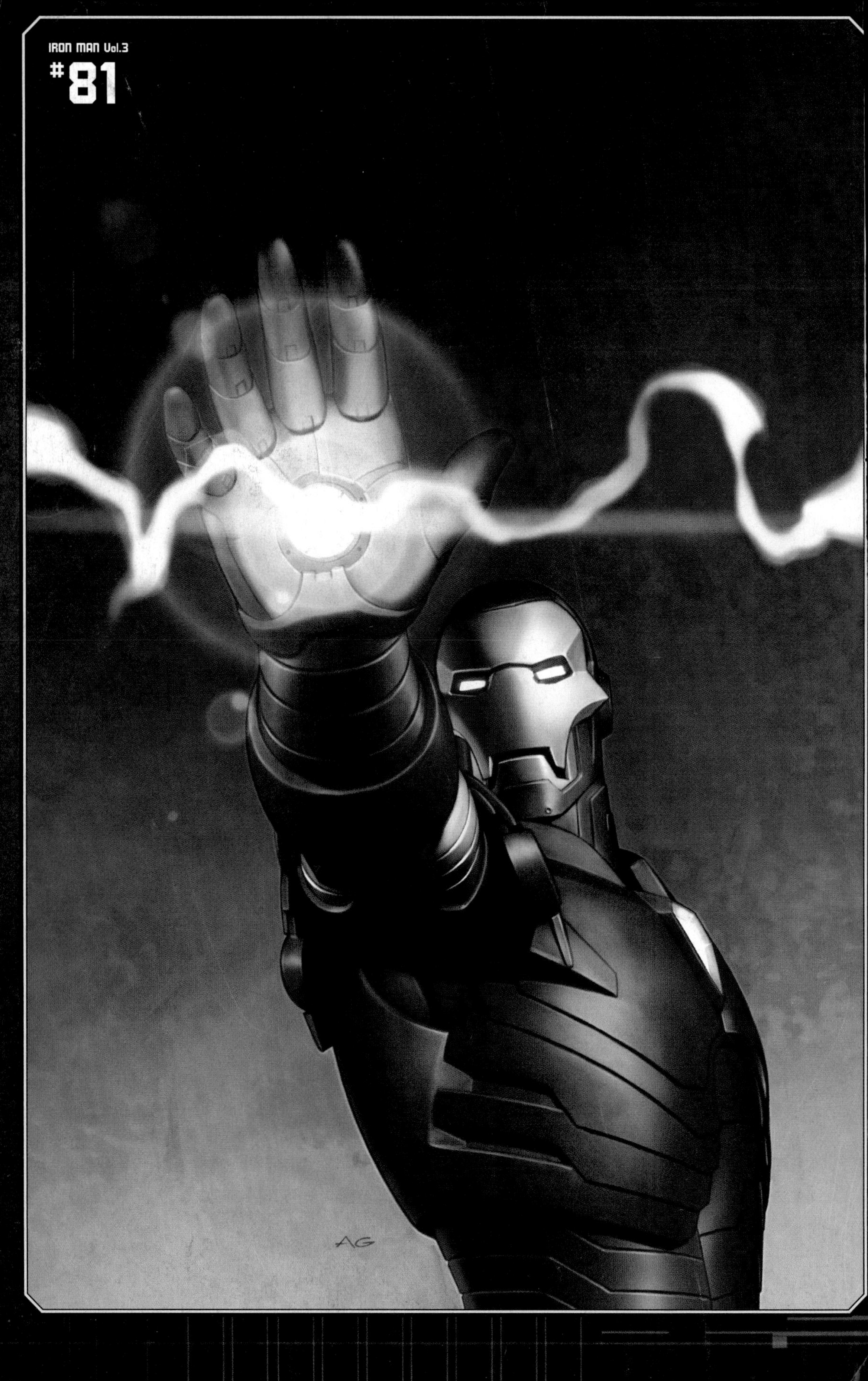
IRON MAN Vol.3
#81
AG

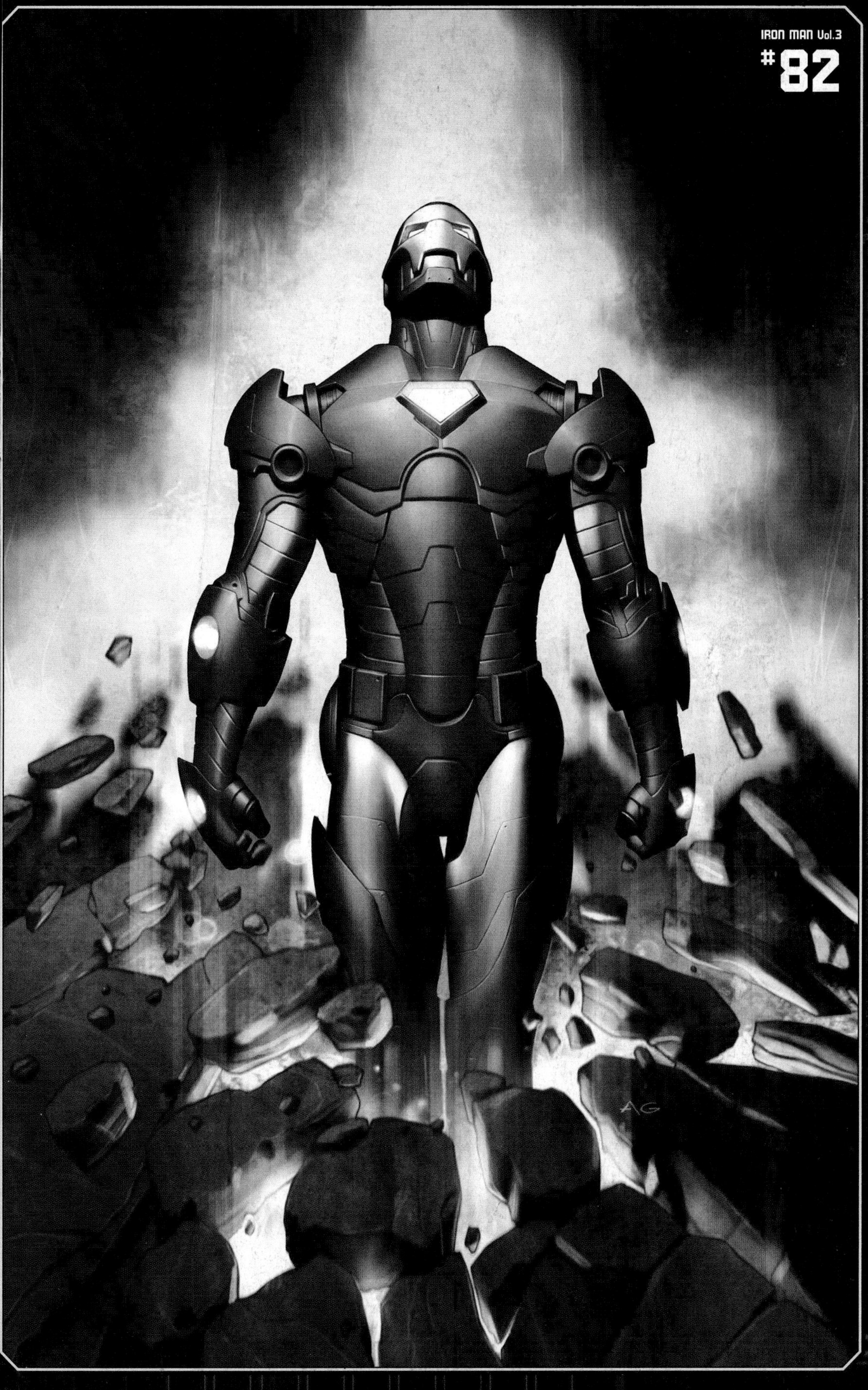
IRON MAN Vol.3
#82
AG

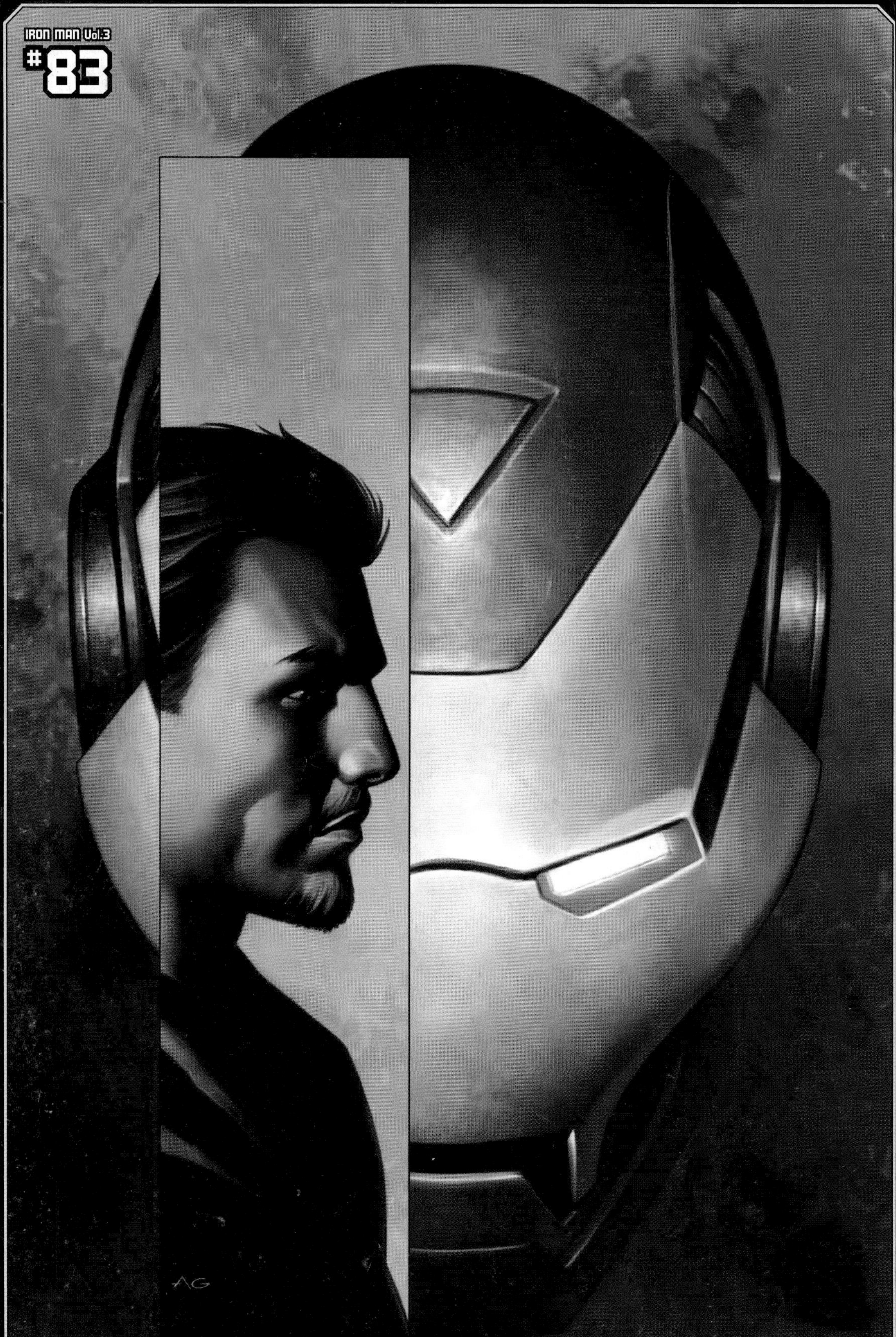
IRON MAN Vol.3
#83
AG